MARK H NEWHOUSE

The Devil's Bookkeepers

Book 1: The Noose

Newhouse Creative Group

Dear Reader

This is a novel of love, friendship, and courage that follows the timeline of the tightening of the Nazi noose on the Lodz Ghetto in Poland, 1941-44, as described in the *Chronicle of the Lodz Ghetto*, edited by Lucjan Dobroszycki, (Yale University Press, 1984). Some character names are real, while most attributes, conversations, and actions are fictitious. Little is known about the authors who wrote this largely anonymous record of the suffering, they, and those they loved, experienced. The dialogue incorporates some of their anonymous entries and is my attempt to imagine their reactions to the extraordinary occurrences they struggled to overcome. While the characters' behaviors and relationships are figments of my imagination, unfortunately, the historical facts are real. If only we had recordings of what was said as the nightmare unfolded.

Some chapters open with *Chronicle* excerpts. Thank you Yale University Press for permission to include these. I've retained their wording, tone, and even errors, to preserve the 'chill factor' as people vanished without explanation, and hope flared only to be extinguished by terrible uncertainty. Of approximately two hundred thousand human beings who suffered in the Lodz ghetto, less than five thousand survived despite the controversial efforts of the ghetto Chairman. Two of these survivors were my parents. I dedicate this work to them, the grandparents and relatives I never knew, and all victims of hate and genocide past, present, and future. The Holocaust is not only about Jews during World War 2, but a warning and call

1

for tolerance for all of us. I hope this story will inspire you to read the original *Chronicle,* written under the noses of the Nazis, so we may say, "Never again to anyone."

CHAPTER 1

L odz Ghetto, Poland – December 10, 1940

It was the Devil's signature on the note. Hands trembling, I hid it from Miriam, my young wife, in my coat pocket. We were relatively new to the ghetto, and I was afraid the summons meant we would be driven out of the barbed wire enclosed slum, as we had been chased from the city that surrounded it. Miriam's parents had given their daughter to me to protect, but there wasn't any safety for Jews in Europe, only uncertainty under Nazi occupation.

The thin soles of my shoes were little protection from the cobblestone gutters as I walked to the headquarters of the Jewish ghetto administration. I thought back to any actions, any statements I might have made that could have gotten me this unwanted attention. The rumors were that Chairman Rumkowski's spies were everywhere. Had one informed on me? Had a neighbor turned me in to curry favor? What would Miriam do if I were imprisoned? How would she manage if I were sent away? People disappeared, and nobody ever heard from them again.

The headquarters of Chairman Rumkowski, the Eldest of the Jews, was as run-down as the rest of the ghetto's buildings. The double doors had yellow Stars of David crudely painted across their rough wood surface. The star, a symbol of what was once the famous Jewish kingdom, was now used to brand us as undesirables by the Nazi regime.

There was a small crowd outside. Everyone wore yellow stars on their right rear shoulders and on the chests of their tattered coats.

Some men were seeking work, any kind of work. A few were there to protest the stream of decrees issued by the Chairman to enforce the occupier's rules. I steered clear of politics. Miriam had to be my first concern, my only concern.

Two guards in black caps, wearing thick coats with wide armbands, stared balefully at the crowd. Members of Rumkowski's Order Service, his personal police force, they were armed with thick black rubber clubs. Like all Jews, the police were forbidden to have other weapons by the Germans. They did not hesitate to use the clubs and were almost as feared as the Gestapo that were observing nearby.

"Identification?" A guard demanded.

"I've been summoned to see the Eldest of the Jews." I held up my letter, hoping my hands weren't shaking.

The Jewish policeman took it, examined the document, returned it, and said, "Pass."

I pressed between the burly guards, eyeing the black clubs.

"Your business?" Another policeman ordered in the lobby, which had an odor of rotting fish. Ah, what I would have given for a piece of fish, even partly rotten.

I handed him my summons. I felt nauseous. Nerves.

"The Archives." He shoved my documents toward me and pointed down the hall.

"Thank you, sir," I said.

He didn't respond.

I walked past a long row of closed doors, searching for the Archives. None of the people rushing through the hall smiled. None said hello. Some appeared dazed. In a way, we all were.

At the end of the hall, I spotted a cardboard sign. I wanted to leave but couldn't ignore the Chairman's summons. I knocked lightly on the door.

A tall man, with a clean-shaven face, shiny black hair, and slender build, greeted me. "I'm Henryk Neftalin, Deputy to the Chairman, The Eldest of the Jews. Please come in."

The room didn't look as if it was set up for interrogations. There were three half-empty shelving units along the walls. I was surprised to see books stacked in short, uneven, piles on the floor, with more on a desk near the far wall. "You have books?"

Neftalin smiled. "You may look at them. Books are my passion."

"I thought all books were confiscated by the Germans," I remarked, afraid to touch any lest they crumble to dust.

"We preserve what we can while they allow."

I didn't know what to say. I didn't understand why I was here.

Neftalin settled in his chair. "Please sit. I organized the Archives, or more formally, The Department of the Archives a year ago." He shoved several folders aside and then flipped one open. "I've studied your work registration. We are looking for someone who is highly organized and discreet."

"A job, sir?" I hadn't worked since being forced into the ghetto six months earlier. Miriam would be ecstatic.

Neftalin peered at me. "You didn't answer my question."

"I'm sorry, sir. What was the question?"

"Are you discreet? Are you someone we can trust?"

Strange question, I thought, squirming on the hard seat of the chair. "Oh, yes sir. I'm very trustworthy."

Neftalin said, "Even if it means risking your life?"

Startled, I didn't reply. Being five-foot-nine-inches tall, slender, losing my hair, and wearing thick eyeglasses, I'd never considered myself the heroic type. Neftalin, on the other hand, appeared athletic and surprisingly well-fed. I admired his tailored black suit. I pulled my shabby coat tighter around me and attempted to sit up taller.

"Your file says you are thirty-five and married. No children?"

"With God's help, soon." I included God in case he was religious.

Neftalin jotted something on the page. "Bernard Ostrowski, you are an engineer by trade?"

"Yes, sir. I design buildings, bridges, and roadways."

"I know. It is why I selected you." He pointed to a stack of papers on

5

his desk. "There are others on my list who would kill for a position. An engineer struck me as someone with logic. Hopefully, you are as grounded as the edifices you design."

"Is that what I will be doing?"

Neftalin frowned. "No. The Germans won't allow us decent dwellings and roadways. No, our mission is different." He leaned over his desk. "The Chairman believes this work is vital for the future of the Jewish way of life."

I was about to ask what this task was, but there was a knock on the door, and a woman in a black skirt and jacket said, "The Chairman is ready for you."

Neftalin bolted from his seat. "I think you'll do. Now you must convince him."

The way he sprang from his seat and tightened his tie drove home to me that my future rested on the next few minutes and the man many called the Devil.

CHAPTER 2

I followed Deputy Neftalin to a door at the end of the hall. A plaque read Chairman M.C. Rumkowski.

The woman said, "You may go in."

Neftalin said. "I'll return shortly."

Was I to meet the Chairman alone? Nervous, I peered around me. This room, lit by a single bulb hanging from the ceiling, looked as if set up for interrogations. A desk, four by six feet, reddish wood, faced two wood chairs with uncomfortable looking backs that resembled iron prison bars. Faded squares and rectangles marked the sickly yellow walls. The only artwork was a greatly enlarged framed photograph on the wall behind the desk.

I walked closer. It was a portrait of the Chairman, also called The Eldest of the Jews, tall, broad-shouldered, in a tweed coat, unruly white hair pouring from beneath a wide-brimmed felt hat. His eyes, enlarged by thick lenses, were gray and appeared to be glaring down at the onlooker. The mouth, no mustache, no beard, was unsmiling. While, by tradition, he was supposed to be head of the Council of Jews, everyone knew that he had become the sole leader of the ghetto. This portrait was appearing in public areas throughout our walled-in quarter of the city of Lodz. I stared into the hard eyes of the Devil and thought of Miriam.

"They took that when I opened the orphanage in 1939," a gravelly voice erupted from the doorway. "That was scarcely a year ago. People forget that and much good I have done." He shrugged his shoulders. "That is human nature for you."

The Chairman, taller than me by a head, was a near-perfect match for the imposing figure in the photograph over his desk, but round-shouldered and with deep hollow cheeks. His eyes were gray and tired-looking, not as piercing as depicted in the portrait.

I summoned my courage. "Sir, it is an honor to meet the Eldest of the Jews." I bowed my head.

"Don't bow to me." Rumkowski barked, eyes examining me. "Mr. Ostrowski, Neftalin, my Deputy, says you are trustworthy."

"Yes, sir. You may ask my previous employers." I wondered if any could be found in the upheaval created by the Nazi invaders.

"I want people I can trust without reservation." Rumkowski peered at me from behind his high-back leather chair, a rarity in the ghetto. "The well-being of my people demands workers who are loyal."

"Yes, sir." I was standing before the supreme authority in the ghetto, what else could I say?

Rumkowski crushed a sheet of paper in his fist.

I felt as if he was crushing my body. The portrait was glaring down at me. It was as if two Chairmen were skewering me with their eyes at the same instant.

Rumkowski tossed the crumpled paper on his desk. "How old are you?"

"Thirty-five, your honor, but I have much experience."

"Half my age." He sighed. "If I approve, you will work directly under Neftalin. He will report solely to me. Your work must not be shared with anyone else."

I nodded again. What did he want me to do?

Rumkowski walked to the window and lifted the side of the shade. "Every day there are rabble-rousers in the square," he muttered, letting the shade drop. "My people depend on me. It is not an easy responsibility." He turned back to me. "I am proud to serve the populace even if they do not appreciate all I do for them. I must do what is best for the most."

"Everyone speaks of the good works of your honor." I glanced at the portrait again. Did it know I was flattering him for the chance of work?

"I'm afraid some of my fellow Jews do not understand how difficult my role is. I must appease the German authorities as well as meet the demands of my community. It is daunting, frustrating, exhausting, but I do so with the welfare of my people as my primary concern always." He sat down again. "What work did you do before the war?"

"He was an engineer, sir." Neftalin, who had entered behind the Chairman, said. "That is why I selected him."

"An engineer?" Rumkowski mulled this over. "An engineer. Yes, that may be a good fit."

"Is there something you want to be built, sir? I'm very good at design."

"No. There is something I want to be preserved."

"I apologize, sir, I don't understand."

"I will explain, but swear that what we discuss will remain confidential, solely between us."

"I swear."

"Good. Very good." He flicked his finger at the ball of paper on his desk, and it nearly fell off the edge before he caught it. "Let me begin by saying the Germans appreciate our unique status in Lodz."

I almost shouted, "The Germans appreciate nothing! They hate Jews," but kept my tongue. I couldn't afford to alienate our leader.

Rumkowski sat tall in his chair. "Lodz workers are recognized throughout Europe for our skill and productivity, a result of our good governance."

Neftalin nodded his head.

Rumkowski looked at me, his eyes penetrating. "Yes, the Germans realize they need our factories for their economy. Our industriousness is our salvation."

I realized he was waiting for a response. "Yes, sir. I can see that we may be important for their economy. But, sir, Hitler hates Jews."

Rumkowski picked up the ball of paper and stared at it as if wishing he could make it burst into flame with the power of his eyes.

I wondered if it was a mistake to say our oppressor's name. He was the most hated man in the world to us. Most Jews would spit on the floor if anyone mentioned the German dictator's name.

Rumkowski's jaw tightened and he said, "Hitler, like most leaders, is a practical man."

I glanced at Neftalin to see if he bought this, but the Deputy didn't show any reaction.

Rumkowski continued, "Yes, even Hitler knows the industrial strength of Lodz must be preserved, especially during war. Biebow, the current area commander, told me, in confidence of course, that our community is a vital part of the war effort."

He sounded proud. I'd heard rumors that some of the Chairman's factories were filling orders for the Germans. Some dissidents accused him, in secret, of course, of aiding the enemy. Others argued that the only thing that mattered was that the Nazis were leaving us alone. Looking up at the portrait, I thought Miriam and I would be safe here if I could land a job.

Rumkowski cast a quick glance at Neftalin. "The Commander assured me personally that all matters will be still in the 'able hands,' his exact words, of the Jewish Council of Elders. In other words, we will continue to be an autonomous government in the ghetto."

"That is good news, sir," Neftalin said.

Rumkowski nodded. "Yes. It shows what hard work and good leadership can achieve even in the most terrible of times. It must be our guide to the future. We must do everything we can to convince the authorities we are maintaining a smooth-running machine. Everything."

I thought of the police with their clubs and realized I had not seen a swastika or portrait of Hitler on any walls in this building, only his picture. Wasn't that proof that the Germans were leaving our little corner of the world alone? Rumkowski said Hitler needed us. What man, even a brutal dictator, cuts off the hand that feeds him?

Rumkowski's voice took on a conspiratorial tone. "We must not upset the status quo. That is why what you do must remain secret. It is not your life alone at stake. Should the Germans even suspect my deceit, it could cost many lives."

A chill shot through me. "Sir, I'm an engineer. What is it you wish me to do?" Did he need more spies? At my age, married, and built as I was, I certainly wasn't suited for being one of his police or agents.

Rumkowski glanced at Neftalin again. "I'm sure you are aware the Germans have been removing Jews from their homes all over Poland and shipping them here." He shrugged his shoulders. "I have done what I can to squeeze these outsiders in among us. I have rationed food and fuel, to keep things smooth, so the Germans feel no imperative to interfere. Giving them an excuse to take over would be the worst fate for us all."

"Sir, you have done a magnificent job," Neftalin interjected.

"Henryk do not patronize me. I know what some think. They do not understand. They do not know what I know." He turned back to me, his voice softer. "The Germans have asked me to designate a number of these new arrivals for relocation to a northern farming community." He glanced at the paper ball on his desk. "I have been assured each will be given a new home and a plot of land to farm." He unfolded the sheet of paper, turned it plain-side up, and ran his hand over it several times against the polished surface of his desk. "I want records kept of these population movements, both in and out of the ghetto."

That was it? How risky could that be? "That doesn't sound difficult, sir," I said, wondering why he was working so hard to flatten the creases on the paper.

Rumkowski sighed. "The authorities prohibit such records. You will be doing this under their noses. You will find a way to disguise this information within seemingly innocuous documents. It must appear to be a routine chronicle of daily events, something that will not attract attention."

What wasn't he telling me?

Rumkowski peered hard into my eyes. "Ostrowski, you are now in our inner circle. Things will be revealed to you that you may not share with anyone, not even your wife. It is for her safety as well as yours, and ours." He pressed down on the creased paper, shook his head, and placed it face up on his desk. He picked up a pencil stub. "I have much work to do. Deputy Neftalin will explain the rest."

Neftalin headed for the door.

I hesitated, waiting to be dismissed, but Rumkowski was bent over the thick pile of papers. His pencil was making rapid checkmarks down the left margin of what appeared to be a list of names and addresses.

"Thank you, sir. I won't let you down." I rose from the chair.

Rumkowski's eyes shot up and met mine. "Ostrowski, there is something else."

"Yes, sir?"

"Can you live with the hate of others?" Rumkowski covered the page with his arm. "When others discover you knew the truth but chose not to share it; they will hate you."

In the dim light, body hunched over his desk, I could have mistaken him for the Devil.

CHAPTER 3

"**I**s the Chairman ill? He looks tired." When I'm nervous, Miriam says I cackle like the yentas, the gossipy old women who complain and spread rumors about everyone and everything. "I'm sorry. I don't mean to pry."

Neftalin glanced around the corridor. "Our Chairman bears great weight on his shoulders." He lowered his voice. "I know some trouble-makers complain he is a dictator, but trust me, his leadership keeps the Nazi wolves at bay. People don't understand how precarious his, our, situation truly is."

"I don't know much about your politics."

"You're better not knowing. The Chairman walks a tightrope protecting our community by convincing the Germans that we are of value to them. He believes we must be a showcase of productivity, such a well-oiled machine they do not feel any need to interfere."

"And you think his strategy is working?"

His tone turned icy. "You do not? It is not too late for you to decline this position."

I had to think fast. Could I sell my soul for a job and the promise of more food? I thought of Miriam. "Sir, I have faith in our leader. I meant no offense."

Neftalin loosened his tie. "Forgive me. We're all under too much pressure. You'll soon see, now that you are one of us. As the Chairman says, our main objective is to not provide the Germans any excuse to interfere."

"I understand." It explained the Chairman's police force. If we Jews

13

did not keep order, the Germans would step in, a fate to be avoided at all costs.

Neftalin's voice became friendly again. "You know, it is easy to be a critic, but I believe the evidence speaks for itself. Our factories have great productivity because of our leader." A cloud came over his face. "The few disruptions we have are caused by agitators, criminal elements, mostly foreigners forced here by the Germans. These trouble-makers arouse the ignorant masses who do not understand that the Nazis will leave us alone if we keep order. If we fail to do so…I hate to imagine the consequences."

"Yes, sir."

Neftalin smiled. "I have faith the war will be over soon, and all will return to normal."

"May God hear your words."

Neftalin shook his head. "When it comes to the Jews, God has potatoes in his ears." He paused before an unmarked door. "This is where you'll work. You should understand this is also the German Administration building."

My heart beat faster at that news. "We're working in their building?"

"Yes. The authorities ordered our offices to be moved here. I suppose so they can keep an eye on us. That is why the Chairman said you will be working under their noses."

"In the same building?"

"Yes." He pushed the door open. "There are no locks. You'll get used to their regulations."

The room had a musty smell and was as dark as the inside of a coffin.

Neftalin pulled a cord, and a light bulb went on above us. "Only a few buildings have electricity. The authorities promised our Chairman to restore power when possible, but I wouldn't bet on it. We're not their priority. You may draw the curtains."

I pulled the tattered green curtains apart. The window, covered in thin layer of dust, was nailed shut. The room was bare except for a large rectangular table and eight chairs. "Will there be eight of us?"

"We'll start with four and see how it develops." He pulled open a box on the table. "Here are paper, pens, and ink jars. Don't waste them. We'll dig up a typewriter from another office." He pulled out a thin envelope. "This is carbon paper. You place it under the sheet you are typing. It makes a decent copy. You will produce three copies. Absolutely, no more."

"We're not using a printing press?"

"Your work is not meant to be published. All copies will be sent directly to me and then forwarded to the Eldest of the Jews at the end of each day. He alone will read and approve your work."

"Are we not producing a newsletter for the community?"

"The Germans regulate our printing presses. Your work is not for today, but for the future. The Chairman knows someday he will be judged." He paused and then added, "I suppose we all will be."

I wasn't sure what he meant. I ran a finger across the top of the nearest chair. The wood seats would be hard to sit on. Could I ask for cushions? Later.

Neftalin walked to the door and peeked outside. "You may get visitors."

"Visitors?"

"The authorities. That's what we call the Germans. They often show up unannounced. If they ask, you are compiling old records for the archives. Be wise. Speak only if you are addressed. Otherwise, continue working. Always look busy. That is your best protection." He looked as if he was thinking of anything he might have forgotten and said, "Any questions?"

"May I ask, with respect, the Chairman said I'd be paid. I'd like to inform my wife of our good fortune."

"You mustn't tell her everything. Tell her you are working with the housing authority."

"She blames them for the crowded conditions here."

"Well, tell her what you wish, but do not divulge your true task, for her safety, as well as ours. Working in the same building with the Nazis, we are on thin ice. Anything else?"

"I'm sorry to ask again. My wages?"

"Oh, yes. The pay is modest, but you will dine in Kitchen #2, known as the Kitchen for the Intelligentsia. It is quite superior to the other public kitchens. You are one of us now."

"Thank you, sir."

"Don't thank me yet. You haven't met the others."

"The others?" My eyes shot to the empty chairs.

"Let me put it this way: If you put two Jews in a room, you have a debate. Three is an argument. Ah, but four? That is war." Neftalin laughed. "It's an old saying."

"I've heard it many times, but not ending that way."

Neftalin frowned. "Trust me, Ostrowski, I chose you, an engineer, as someone who is disciplined. The others are brilliant, wonderful, writers, but you will be the anchor of this little boat. I warn you, it may not be easy to steer safely past the whirlpools, mostly created by their egos."

"Sir, I do not know how to swim." I immediately regretted my effort at a joke.

Neftalin frowned. "Then, my friend, you will drown and take the rest of us with you. Make no mistake, if the Nazis discover the Chairman's true design, drowning will be a blessing."

CHAPTER 4

I thanked Neftalin again, eager to get home and tease Miriam with all the details, especially about the pay. She was nineteen, barely a woman. It hurt me to know how much she had already suffered. Leaving her parents in Lublin had been traumatic enough for her, but now we had no way to communicate with them, no way to know if they were still there. We thought we would be safe in Lodz, the second largest city in Poland, a bustling industrial community where Jews had been factory owners, bankers, and major employers.

I quickly found a job with a Polish building firm and was earning their respect. We were fixing up a comfortable apartment... Miriam cried when we couldn't take the curtains her mother made, a wedding gift, from our apartment in Lodz proper. The Nazis, without prior warning, gave us five minutes to vacate our flat. German soldiers screaming at us, we were rushed into the streets where mobs of Poles taunted and beat fleeing Jews, with fists and sticks, steering us into the maw of the barbed-wire enclosed ghetto. It was a terrifying night. My young wife hadn't gotten over the shock.

"There will be work for an engineer," I'd tried to assure Miriam when we first arrived nearly six months ago. Now there finally was work, but I wasn't sure what was involved. I suspected the Chairman was exaggerating the risk. Should I reveal the possible danger to Miriam? Perhaps a little later. For now, it would make her happy to see her husband employed again. I couldn't wait to tell her.

"I will see you here tomorrow morning, seven, sharp. Unless you still pray with a minyan?" Neftalin asked, closing the door behind us.

17

"Who can find ten men to pray each morning in these troubled times?" I did not want to tell him I'd lost my belief in God, one of the wedges that had caused my father, a Rabbi, to cast me out of his life after I graduated from college. He hadn't approved of my working for a Polish company either, but work was work. I had to grab what I could and now was no different. "I will be here earlier if you wish?"

"Any earlier, the sentries may react." Neftalin's voice dropped. "Incidents, as we call them, have been few, but their police become edgy in the dark."

"Seven it is, sir. Is there anything you would like me to do now?" I wanted to impress him with my industriousness but hoped he would let me leave. I wanted to feel Miriam in my arms after I gave her the wonderful news.

Neftalin smiled. "No. You must go home and tell your wife. She will be pleased."

"Thank you again for this opportunity. I will not let you down."

"It is our esteemed Chairman you must not let down. I know you do not understand the full impact of what he wants, but someday, with God's help, this war will be over, and your work will be a record for all who follow. Go with God's blessing."

Neftalin was religious. Yet, he wore a business suit with no sign of a prayer shawl. He appeared to be about my age and well-educated. I wondered how he could still be a believer. I envied him. I envied Miriam's faith as well.

The Service Order men, Rumkowski's Jewish police, one on either side of the double entrance doors, were focused on the crowd below the steps. I didn't take my eyes off their clubs as I passed between them.

"He's one of them," someone rasped, as I tried to look inconspicuous passing through the mob.

"No. Look at the man's clothes. He's as ragged as we are," another replied.

I held my breath. If these people suspected I was part of the government, would they start trouble? I searched for help.

Two pairs of armed German police scanned the scene from opposing posts on the square. Were they waiting to enforce the law if things got out of control?

I cut through the crowd, eager to get away. I was, as Rumkowski stated, a member of the inner circle now. "Go home and obey your Chairman," I wanted to shout, convinced his strategy was the only way we could hope to survive the storm Hitler had unleashed, not only on the Jews but on all of Europe. Only our skills and hard work would shield us. Why didn't these people understand that? Didn't they see the German rifles and machine guns? All the Nazi bastards needed was a minor provocation, and a storm of bullets would tear into hundreds of these unwashed bodies. Nobody would shed a tear over a bunch of dead Jews.

Once past the Balut Market square, which housed the German and Jewish ghetto administrations, I walked faster. A flash of my Identification card and the Service Order police parted like the Red Sea. I was beginning to understand that I no longer had to be afraid of being stopped by the Jewish police. I was now their superior and had nothing to fear from them.

It was a German policeman who stopped me.

CHAPTER 5

I was walking too fast, almost running. I slammed to a stop as if the German were a wall into which I almost crashed. *Don't speak unless you are spoken to. Don't speak. You've done nothing wrong. Don't be afraid.* My stomach was churning.

"Papers, Jew!"

I know little about guns, but the Lugar has an ominous, appearance. Its black barrel pointing at your face is like seeing a shark poised to strike. I averted my eyes from the gun and handed my new papers into his black glove. My legs were rubbery, bile rising in my throat. I couldn't see his eyes, shielded by the lip of his helmet. I felt like a child, observing every move he made, focused on the gun.

"You are in a hurry?" The officer growled, holding my papers hostage. "Jew, I said, you are in a hurry?"

His German sounded harsh, menacing. "I'm with the government," I said, attempting a smile. "Work. Arbeit." I was too nervous to use full sentences even though my German is half-decent. *What if I throw up? Will he shoot me?*

He scanned me from head to toe, a predator sizing up his defenseless prey. He glanced again at my papers. He was going to shove them into his coat pocket. They'd be valuable on the black market.

I was powerless to stop him. I held my breath, a sour taste in my mouth.

He advanced his hand toward me, and the papers dropped to the ground.

Had I missed them? Did he let them fall on purpose? What do I do?

He watched me, hawk-like, gun in hand.

I wanted to pick up the documents but didn't move. Was the bastard daring me to pick them up? His finger was on the trigger. God, I wanted to pick up my papers but waited.

The thug placed a muddy boot on my new identification card. "No running, Jew. You could be shot." He pulled his boot away and sneered. "You would not want that. Would you?" He waved the gun hypnotically before my eyes.

I didn't speak, didn't move, not without permission.

"Pick up your papers, damn Jew."

Did I dare? Neftalin said there had been only a few incidents. Would bending down to pick up my papers be an excuse for this brute to shoot me? Is that what he was daring me to do with his cold eyes?

"Pick them up! Must I repeat it?" The officer shook his head. "You Jews are all such cowards." He holstered his pistol and turned his back on me. "Now, coward, pick them up."

If I had a gun, would I have shot him? Turning his back on me was insulting. He knew I'd never risk provoking him. I am a coward, I thought, not moving, feeling impotent.

"Damn Jews," he said and walked to the other side of the road.

I would have slumped to the ground with relief but fought to stand until I saw him turn the corner. I still hesitated. Another Nazi bastard could be lurking nearby. It would be my luck to get shot on the same day I got a new job. I thought of Miriam. She was waiting for me. I had to be safe. *Wait a few minutes. Check the street. Is it clear?*

Once I assured myself it was safe, I dropped to the ground, picked up my papers and wiped off the muck. They remained locked in my hand for the rest of the trek to our flat, almost two miles away.

Still shaking, I walked ahead without looking back. Was the bastard again watching me? What if he came after me? No more running, I told myself. *Stupid! Stupid!* I'd be damned if I was going to be the next victim of an incident.

I began to breathe normally only when I reached the front door of our three-story tenement. I decided I would not tell Miriam about the Nazi. They were still rare on our streets, mostly patrolled by Rumkowski's Order Service. Instead, I would give her good news, great news.

As I climbed the steps in the dark stairwell, I became excited again. What would Miriam say when I told her I had a job? How would she react when I revealed it was not just any job, but with the government? I imagined her laughter, so long unheard. In my mind, I could see her eyes sparkle. Oh God, how I longed to see them look so alive again. The thought of breaking this hopeful news hurried my steps. I pushed against the door.

My frightening encounter with the policeman was in the past. Rumkowski and Neftalin's warnings, the angry mob gathered at the ghetto Headquarters —all were forgotten in my excitement. The door was barely open. "Miriam, dearest, I have wonderful news! Wait until you hear—"

Miriam's lovely face was streaked with tears.

CHAPTER 6

"Come inside," I urged, feeling more a father than a husband to my young wife. "Now tell me, dear, what is wrong?" A better question would have been, "What is right?"

Miriam wiped her face with her sleeve. She looked like a stubborn child, dark hair in thick ringlets, hazel eyes almost gray in the dim light of a candle. "How much longer must we take this?" she asked.

I should have told her then about the job, but her face told me the best thing I could do was let her release what was inside.

She let out a deep sigh and took my hand. "Benny, look at us. Look at us."

"Did something happen today?"

She stroked the back of my palm. "This isn't living. We are bugs waiting to be stomped on in this awful place."

"Let us pray the exterminators don't find us then," I said as a joke, but her lips quivered. "I'm sorry. That wasn't funny."

Miriam dropped my hand. "If something doesn't change soon, winter will exterminate all of us. We have no food, no fuel for heat."

"We must be grateful we have each other."

Miriam burst into tears.

I rushed to hold her, but she held up her arms to stop me. "Sarah's baby…died."

At first, her words went past me. I was too absorbed in my news. But then, feeling Miriam's body wracked with tears, her hands squeezing my hand tightly, her head pressed into my chest, I understood. "Oh, Miriam, I'm so sorry. I had no idea." I held her,

23

wishing I could think of something to comfort her for the loss of her friend's infant. She loved that child, often babysitting for her. Once, she even said she wanted a little girl like her someday. Someday.

Miriam quivered against me. She's ruining your good shirt, a voice inside me warned. You need it for work tomorrow. I couldn't bring myself to raise her head. I held her against me and repeated, "I'm sorry."

When Miriam lifted her head, her eyes were glossy. "Hannah was just a tsatskeleh, a little doll, so beautiful, so helpless." She looked as if she was going to cry again. "I loved her," she mumbled. "Benny, I loved her."

"I know." I could almost see Mendel and Sarah's child, tiny hands reaching for something in the air, constantly searching, for what? Food. Water. A little more heat. A warm, full breast. The poor child never knew happiness. There was not one minute when her tiny stomach was not aching, her eyes begging. "I'm truly sorry, Miriam." I didn't ask the cause. Hunger, disease, cold, thirst; the same root cause. We could trace all our suffering to the German invaders, the Jew haters. "It must be terrible for Mendel and Sarah," I said, unable to accept this terrible news, but having to be strong for Miriam. "Talk to me. It will make you feel better."

"There was no crying," Miriam said as if in a daze. "It was as if she was dead before she died...no screaming...no thrashing around. She simply had enough and let go of life." She turned toward me. "I can see myself doing that someday."

I shook her hard. "You must never say that! God put us here, and it is up to God to take us away." She believed, even if I didn't. I pulled her toward me. She really was like a child, arousing my protective instincts, making me press her face against my heart again. "You have just begun life. The war will be over soon, and all this suffering will be a memory. It will make us stronger. Suffering has always made Jews stronger." *Did I really say that? Did I believe that?*

"I'm so tired. Aren't you?"

I was, but I wanted to distract her. "I have news that will cheer you up. I was summoned to the Jewish Administration."

Miriam sat up, a look of alarm on her face. "Did you do something wrong?"

"I said it was good news. I have a job."

"I don't understand."

This wasn't going as I'd hoped. "I have a job! A real job!"

"What kind of job?"

Why did she look anxious? "I'm going to be working in the Administration building, assisting with the allocation of apartments to new arrivals. You always say they need help."

"Why didn't you tell me you were going to the Council?" Fear clouded her face.

"Miriam, don't you understand? I have a job, and I'm going to be paid. We're going to get an increase in rations. This is good news."

"Why did you go there without telling me? I don't like that place. They say the Devil is there."

I saw a flash of Rumkowski, hunched over his stack of papers. "I didn't want to worry you. I thought you'd be excited about my new position."

Miriam looked deep into my eyes. "Do you really have a job?"

I nodded. "At long last."

She let out a deep sigh. "That is good news." She took my hand. After a long silence, she lifted it to her cheek and said, "Maybe this is a sign that it is time for us to start a family."

I thought I heard wrong. "What did you say?"

Miriam aimed sad eyes at me. "Benny, I want a child of our own."

I understood she said this because her friends had lost their baby. It was as if she'd lost Hannah too. Being much older than my wife, I'd wanted a child for a long time, so I didn't think about why she wanted one now. I was just grateful that she wanted what I wanted, a family; our own baby. I loved my young wife and thought a baby would make her happy in all the misery of the ghetto.

As Miriam led me to our bed, for once, I didn't care that we were entrapped in one room, no paintings on the walls, not even space for a couch. I didn't care that my pants were worn at the knees, my shirt smeared with her tears. I saw the back of my wife's dress as she unleashed her hair and let it fall on her shoulders.

Before we married, my wife, brought up in a strict religious environment, was a virgin, and though I was older, my experience with women was limited. Religious restrictions, the demands of school, and the movement from town to town to find work, plus my own lack of confidence made me shy with the opposite sex. Even now, I found it difficult to accept that Miriam, fifteen years my junior, so lovely to behold, could find me attractive. I suppose that is why I rarely asked her and was not dismayed that she showed little interest in love-making. Each night we made love, it was as if it was the first time, tiny steps, tentative, uncertain.

Miriam blushed, turning her eyes away from me as she pulled off her dress and lay it carefully on a chair. Even in her soiled undershirt, I could not look long at her without feeling astonished, awed, and ashamed of my own body. Where she was curved, soft, and blessed with unblemished skin, I was thin, balding, and more scholarly than athletic in physique. As I removed my glasses, I felt unworthy, but she reached for me and pulled me toward her. "Am I still beautiful?" She asked.

I could not answer. My breath had been stolen. I circled my arms around Miriam's waist, praying she wouldn't push me away. In a bed that would not serve in the lowest of hostels, with coarse bedding that had not been laundered in weeks, I stared at the only beautiful thing I still had in my possession. As always, before I touched her, I hesitated, worried I would ruin this joining of our bodies. As always, before I touched her, I fought my eagerness, my urgent need for her, and waited for her eyes to signal that she was ready. Yes, some of my peers would ridicule my deference to a woman, but I had such tenderness for her I had to be assured she wanted me. Her hand brushed gently across my chest. I felt as if I was gazing at the forbidden fruit of the Garden of Eden as her breasts, barely covered by her tan shirt, were tantalizingly near. I had never seen them fully uncovered but now reached to touch. She trembled, and her eyes peered up at me. "I'm ready," she whispered.

I felt her body tense under me as I pried my hand between her legs. I wanted to be gentle, but I was uncertain how much longer I could last. She moved her thighs slightly apart, and then a little more as if asking if this is enough. I rose over her and then slowly, gently, lowered myself. Though we had done this several times before, it was rare, so each time there were questions and doubts. Am I too heavy? Am I too forceful? Am I hurting her? When I heard her moan, I feared she was in pain, but then she clutched me with her hands and held me as I rose and lowered and heard nothing but my heart pounding and our breathing. It didn't last long until I shuddered and let myself drop to her side, my arm dangling across her middle. I was out of breath, could barely move. I hoped I'd given her some pleasure, but she was silent. I wanted her to speak, to tell me she enjoyed it, that it was more than just to make a child.

It seemed hours that we were like this. When I turned to her, my Miriam was still in her shirt, and her lower parts were concealed by the thin coverlet. Her eyes were wide open, staring at the ceiling.

I said nothing. There were pearl-like tears in Miriam's eyes. I thought they were tears of joy. I felt such love for her.

Miriam broke the silence. Her voice was low.

I heard. I wished I did not. The single sentence echoed hours after Miriam closed her eyes and slept. I could not get her words out of my mind. Her question after we made love was, "How can we bring a child into a world like this?"

CHAPTER 7

Miriam's question tormented me. *"How can we bring a child into a world like this?"* How, after making love, could she ask that?

When she fell asleep, her back facing me, her face resting on a pillow moist from her tears, I saw the child she still was. Her hands clutched her pillow, her dark hair splayed against the faded linen. I felt protective but helpless. Nothing I could do would change the reality. The room we were trapped in was too often the home of cockroaches, crushed by smashing down on them with my shoe. I saw the look of disgust marring her face when she saw them. Now she slept, a few hours when she looked innocent, a child again. But her words lingered.

I felt pain in my heart knowing it would not last, praying that roaches would be the only invaders to storm our flat. My heart pounded at the remembered sounds of the youthful mobs, as they attacked, paving the way for the Nazi force. I still heard the screaming and the smashing of windows and furniture, as the viciousness spread like a fire, dragging us from our beds, hurling us into the night. The German soldiers, bashing down doors and screaming obscenities, chased us from the reasonably comfortable flats where Jews had long been integrated into the city of Lodz, out into the night. We grabbed what we could and raced to the ghetto. The Germans living in Lodz were beaters, herding the hunted Jews with catcalls, sticks, and fists, into the ghetto, while the occupying force applauded their actions and goaded them on. I fought sleep in a vain attempt to protect

28

her if I heard the ominous sound of motors, marching, or screams, shattering the night.

The following morning, I did not want to face Miriam after my sleepless night. What if she regretted our love-making? Had I misread her readiness? She said she wanted a family. I'd broached the subject of children many times, even resorting to the ancient exhortation: "God declared that we should multiply." She had always resisted. It was the death of a neighbor's child, the sweet-faced Hannah, that had won her consent. It was that same waste of a precious child's life that ruined it all with that damn question. If only I understood her better, I thought, but her silence made it difficult for me to know what was in her mind, in her heart. How could she ask that question after we made love? How could I answer it and provide a soothing salve to her depression? It was a depression spreading over the ghetto like a shroud over a corpse.

These thoughts tumbled in my brain as I walked past the dilapidated buildings that lined the ghetto streets. A pungent smell made me hold my nose and brought me back to reality.

A cart with two large wheels was being pulled by two adolescent boys. Girls, young, sweat showing on their jumpers, followed the wagons, wood shovels in their hands. A Jewish policeman followed a short distance behind.

I watched as the girls used their shovels to pick up fecal matter and toss it into the back of the cart.

They were prisoners, I realized, oddly fascinated by the scene. I should have been disgusted that girls so young would be forced into doing this kind of work, but the sight of them tossing the stinking clumps into the vehicle, I now viewed as proof of the organizational skill of Rumkowski's administration. I saw it as evidence that all departments, even sanitation, were functioning smoothly under the firm hand of the Chairman. Without the girls, and boys pulling the cart—no horses allowed to Jews—disease and vermin would have been more rampant than they already were. Corpses would be lining the streets. Rumkowski was right. We had to keep the ghetto organized and regimented, or it would become hell, more of a hell than it already was.

There were people already milling about in the square before the administration building. What else did they have to do? I circled around them and climbed the steps that led to the twin doors.

"Your identification," a burly guard demanded, hand extended, while the other guard observed me with his rubber club thumping in his palm.

I handed over my papers. My hands were steadier. The police cap caught my attention. It was blue with a leather stripe around its base. There were more of these caps appearing in the ghetto each day. Rumkowski's Gestapo, the radicals complained, fearing them almost as much as they feared the Germans.

The sentry returned my papers and held the door open. "Good morning, administrator," he said.

Administrator? It had a welcome ring to it after all this time of being unemployed. "Good morning," I replied.

There were more Jewish policemen, caps on their heads making them recognizable, standing in the dimly lit corridor. One was smoking a cigarette. How did he get that? Why did they look so much cleaner and better fed than the people outside the building? One straightened and tapped his club against his leg.

"Good morning," I said, giving him a smile.

The man swung the end of his club toward me.

I jumped and then felt foolish.

He turned to the others, said something, and they laughed.

Brutes, I thought and walked away.

There was a light showing from under Rumkowski's door. Rumors were that he never slept. No wife, no children, he spent nights in his office, always working, no real ties, no other interests. I admired his dedication to the ghetto. I did not envy his responsibility.

The door to the Archives section was open. I entered and pulled the string to the ceiling bulb. The light gave the walls an orange tinge. Which chair to take? The table, dark wood, needing polish, was marred by gouges and scratches that reminded me of tear trails…Miriam's tears last night. Where had this table been before it was demoted to this bare closet of a room? What histories had it witnessed?

I heard the door open. Turning quickly, I saw a long black coat, but in fact, only saw the large yellow star on its chest. I steeled myself for a policeman's cap but instead saw thinning gray hair under a wide-brimmed felt hat.

The man shook his coat and removed his brown fedora. His face was revealed as narrow, hard of jaw and chin, with a neatly-trimmed gray beard. His nose was bony, large and hooked, as hawk-like as I'd ever seen. It gave him a sharp, intelligent look. He reminded me of a neatly combed Einstein, deep creases running from his eyes down his cheeks. "I'm Rosenfeld, Dr. Oskar Rosenfeld," he announced, and promptly sat at the far end of the rectangular table. "We need cushions," he muttered.

"It is an honor to meet you," I said, taking a seat on the side of the table nearest the door. "I am Bernard Ostrowski. My friends call me Benny."

"Thank you. You may call me Dr. Rosenfeld. I believe we must maintain a certain official tone."

I was about to answer when Rosenfeld's eyes jumped to the door. "Germans are in the building," he hissed.

I turned to the door, unsure of what to expect.

"Shalom," a hatless man with long black hair, darting eyes, and smiling lips said, rushing through the door.

"No Hebrew," Rosenfeld hissed. "It is forbidden."

The young stranger removed his coat. "Of course, it is." He laughed. "I'm Oscar Singer, and you are?"

"Oscar? You're both named Oscar?" Why did I find this humorous?

"I'm Oscar with a K," Rosenfeld said. "Dr. Singer, who I know from his writings, is with a C if I'm not mistaken."

Oh God, I thought, I'm in big trouble. Just then the door opened again.

Two Jews are a debate. Three, an argument. Four? War.

CHAPTER 8

"I see you've met the others," Neftalin said, pulling off his fur-collared coat. "Gentlemen. Allow me to introduce Julian Cukier. He initiated your project, with our Chairman's authorization, of course."

"You give me too much credit," Cukier said, settling at the other end of the table.

Neftalin placed his hand on Cukier's shoulder. "Not at all. Some of you may better know my friend, Julian, as Stanislaw Cerski."

Rosenfeld stiffened. "Are you that writer for Republicka? A liberal rag."

"My father says the same." Cukier laughed.

"Your father? Ludwik Cukier, the factory owner?" Singer leaned forward. "You write for that daily? Your father must love that."

"My father often threatened to disown me."

"I've read your work. Cerski's work. Well done. Most of it," Singer said.

"Drivel," Rosenfeld muttered.

Neftalin laughed. "I can see you're all going to get along famously. I'll leave you in the good hands of Julian. By the way, I notice you have been silent, Ostrowski."

I felt out of my league by these learned men, two doctors named Oscar, and a well-known commentator for the Republicka, the only newspaper in the ghetto until it too was banned. "As an engineer, I am goal-oriented, sir. I'm more interested in what we are expected to do rather than in our pasts and philosophies." I added quickly, "With respect, sir."

Neftalin beamed. "Ah ha! That is why I selected Ostrowski. We can't afford endless debate and drifting from our mission. He is pragmatic, grounded, and will serve as our sergeant-at-arms. You will rein in these learned scholars if they roam too far afield."

Wonderful, I thought, a great way to create hostility toward me, the outsider.

Rosenfeld stood. "As the experienced former editor of a great Vienna weekly, I should be the captain of this enterprise?"

"With all respect, Dr. Rosenfeld, you are a foreigner, while Cukier is from Lodz. Secondly, when were you born? If you don't mind my asking?" Neftalin smiled.

Rosenfeld stood at attention. "1884, in Korycany, which is Moravia. I am well known as a writer and publicist. I worked with Herzl himself, the founder of our vibrant Zionist movement for the establishment of a Jewish homeland in Israel."

Cukier was about to respond, but Neftalin stopped him. "Dr. Rosenfeld, your accomplishments are well known to us, as are your credentials as a Zionist leader. The Chairman asked for your participation; however, he made it clear that Cukier will guide this team."

"Why? Why am I being bypassed?" Rosenfeld slipped on his coat. "Everyone knows of the first Jewish theater in Vienna. I, Dr. Oskar Rosenfeld, established it. Does that not prove my organizational skills?"

Cukier's voice was steady. "Doctor, you are a man of great knowledge, and a genuine hero. We applaud you for this. But sir, we can't let your passion for an Israeli homeland influence our work here."

"He's right," Neftalin said. "Oskar, may I call you that?"

Rosenfeld shrugged, his buttons now closed and collar up.

"Oskar, the truth is that we are going to do this work in the same building housing the German ghetto administration. There is no room for the Zionist dream here, at this perilous time."

"Then why am I here?" Rosenfeld held his hat in his bony hand.

"The Chairman requires a consummate editor. He greatly admires your work." Neftalin said. "But if you cannot work under the present conditions, I'd reluctantly have to consent to your declining his generous patronage."

Cukier stepped closer. "Doctor, the Eldest of the Jews wants you. Are you willing to sacrifice the good you can do here? Is it about your pride? I don't believe you will let your ego prevent you from helping your countrymen at this crucial time in our history."

Rosenfeld stared at Cukier.

I wasn't sure if he was angry or thinking over what the younger man said. There was a certain calming quality in Cukier that I liked. I wasn't sure about Rosenfeld.

Neftalin picked up his folio. "My friends, we have no time. Oskar, the truth is, and I won't pull punches, you are the wise owl in the room. While normally that would give you seniority, we need a younger slant to this as well. We welcome your skill, but I must insist you decide now. It is a job with pay and a food allowance. I urge you not to turn this down. Your work will have significance beyond the walls of our community. It may very well be the message in the bottle for the future."

"I too am a well-known writer," Dr. Singer interrupted. "I could serve as our chairman."

"You wrote an anti-Nazi play," Neftalin replied. "Do you wish to call attention to yourself with that, and other things, in your dossier?"

Singer became silent.

I wondered what Neftalin meant by "other things" in the young man's files, but there was no time to inquire, if we were to get started. I hesitated to speak, but felt that someone had to light a fire under these learned men or we'd never accomplish what the Chairman wanted. "I'm the only one here who isn't a famous writer," I interjected. "I'm humbled by you. I envy your skills. I am an engineer, a fish out of the water. But it seems to me we must all start at the beginning, as in a novel. In this ghetto, none of our accomplishments matter. We have all lost so much, family, homes, possessions that we are alike in that respect. War removes all differences in social standing, especially for its victims."

Rosenfeld trembled.

Singer remained unreadable.

I continued, "I respect all of you, but I want to get to work. This is our chance to do something important. The Chairman wants to preserve our culture, our Jewish way of life. Let us set aside our pasts, egos, and differences, and create something that tells the future what happened here."

Rosenfeld unbuttoned his coat but kept it on. "Are you sure you're not a writer?" he asked.

"Heaven forbid," I replied.

Neftalin nodded. "Very well. We are all ready to work now that the preliminaries are over. I might add, in record time." He gave me a smile. "What the Chairman wants is a constant account of everything that happens in our community. He will check your writing personally at the end of each day—"

"Check us?" Rosenfeld interrupted a dismayed expression on his face.

"Yes. The Chairman will check every item daily."

Cukier addressed Rosenfeld, who was still poised to leave. "This is not censorship. We are free to write about whatever we wish. However, we must be circumspect." He looked pointedly at the door.

I understood he was relaying his fear that the Germans could be listening even now. "The Chairman is protecting us. That is why we are in this closet concealed behind the Department of the Archives rooms," I said.

Rosenfeld was silent.

Neftalin walked to the door and creaked it open. He then closed it and leaned over Rosenfeld. "For your sake and ours, always be aware that your work must be kept secret."

Singer raised his hand. "How secret will it be once it is published?"

Neftalin shook his head. "Dr. Singer, I don't know if it will ever be published."

"So why are we doing this?" Singer asked. "Are we so afraid of the Nazis that we self-censor our outrage?" He looked disgusted. "I've written many anti-Nazi opinion pieces. I, for one, will not be cowed by these monsters."

Oh no, I thought, studying this wild-eyed idealist who would recklessly endanger all of us if he had his way.

Neftalin maintained his calm. "We are occupied and completely sealed off from the world. We know the brutality of the Germans and should not want to invite even greater danger."

"This is giving into the wolves," Singer insisted.

"It is saving our community from being devoured by the wolves," Neftalin replied. "What can we do to fight against an army that is terrorizing the entire world? The Chairman believes this is the way we will survive."

"I know his ideas already," Singer snapped. "He thinks he can save the ghetto by proving to the Germans they can't live without our factories. He's wrong. We should be fighting them with everything we have. We should be using this newsletter to arouse everyone to resistance, as we are doing in Warsaw."

"Is that where you're from?" I asked.

Singer ignored the question. "Only in resistance lies hope."

Cukier sighed. "Be practical. Unlike Warsaw, our ghetto is completely walled in. Outside our walls, the city of Lodz has been 'Germanized.' We are wholly insulated by Jew-haters. Even the Poles, those needed for the factories just outside our ghetto, are falling for Nazi nationalistic chauvinism and hate of Jews." He shook his head. "We can't even smuggle in food so tightly are we enclosed. Weapons? Impossible. Our only hope is that the Germans continue to need us. We must do everything to keep them convinced of our value."

"But we must try to resist," Singer pressed on. "We Jews have always resisted tyranny."

Neftalin pounded his fist on the table. "Do you wish to invite the German army, the Gestapo, into our community? Haven't you heard? They shoot Jews. No. Chairman Rumkowski has determined, and the evidence bears him out, that our best course of action is what we are doing. The Germans respect hard work. I support my Chairman, and this work of yours must show support for his efforts in every way possible. He is your benefactor and employer. That is your job."

Singer slouched back in his chair.

Rosenfeld tapped a pen on his pad.

I was grateful the brash young militant was finally silent.

"This is not an easy time for any of us," Neftalin said in a calmer tone, closing the buttons of his coat. "None of us can predict the future, but we can be certain that whoever comes after us knows about our lives. Hitler wants to annihilate every Jew in Europe, so our job is to preserve whatever we may of our culture for our children and grandchildren." He glanced at Singer. "I know some would rather fight, but under current circumstances, that would be suicide, and totally against our Chairman's strategy."

I wanted to cut off this debate. "Do you still wish copies made?"

"Yes, a few. We have a limited amount of carbon paper. Does everyone know how this works?"

"I will show them," I said.

"Ostrowski, be careful not to get the copy ink on your hands, clothes, and especially not your face," Neftalin warned. "If the authorities find the originals, we can hope they will not know about the copies."

"We'll be careful," I replied.

"Any other questions?" Neftalin aimed his eyes at Singer. "I've already said, you are free to write about what you wish. However, the Chairman feels it is most important to have records of the arrival and departures of the newcomers hidden within your other writings."

"How will we manage that?" Singer asked.

Neftalin sighed. "Engineer, you must find a way to disguise this data, in case the Germans do get hold of any of your records."

Singer threw down his gauntlet yet again. "We must be mice before the wolves."

"That is your task." Neftalin shrugged. "If you can't do it, the Chairman will find others who can. I must leave. Take the rest of this session to get to know each other and find out each of your strengths." He dug into his jacket pocket. "I almost forgot. These are your new passes for Kitchen #2. It is called the Kitchen for the Intelligentsia for obvious reasons. You will be eating your lunch there. You will find it a vast improvement over your previous kitchens." He looked a bit embarrassed. "Unfortunately, given present conditions, your new ration cards are delayed."

Singer frowned. "I've heard of this Kitchen for the Elite. I mean, Intelligentsia. So, we eat better than everyone else?"

I was losing patience with the young man's insolence.

Rosenfeld smiled. "I've dined there and can affirm its superior quality. Thank you, Henryk."

Singer shrugged. "I will continue to eat in my district's kitchen."

Neftalin sighed. "Oscar, your kitchen is too far away. You will eat with your team. That is the Chairman's wish."

Cukier stepped in. "Dr. Singer, our friend, Neftalin, is correct. There will be no time for us to go home for lunch. Nobody knows how long we will be able to accomplish our task before the wolves prohibit even something as harmless. Every minute counts. In time, we may be able to take more liberties. What do you say, my friends?"

"Of course," Rosenfeld replied. "As the Chairman states, those who work deserve better treatment than those who do not. A decent meal is hardly anti-Zionist."

Singer was silent.

As we walked the short distance to the Kitchen for the Intelligentsia, I wondered why Rumkowski had assembled such a difficult group.

Months later. I devised a theory: the sly fox did not want us to be cut from the same cloth, so we would not become friends and ally against him. He wanted control, as he commanded full control of all the ghetto departments, factories, and personnel. Did he believe such absolute control was essential to save the ghetto's populace? I wanted to believe that was his motive, but there were many others, such as Singer, who suspected otherwise. I wasn't concerned if he was our savior or the devil. I only knew the food at the Intelligentsia kitchen, served by a staff of well-clad, clean, young women, was a pleasant interlude from the constant bickering around our conference table. When Singer questioned why our food and service was so far above that offered the other residents, I answered, "We are in the inner circle now. We have greater responsibility and risk. To do our work well, we must be fed. That is simple logic."

Singer argued back, "What of our friends and neighbors? They work and sweat for the Chairman in his factories. Do they not deserve this treatment as well?"

Rosenfeld came to my rescue. "Young man, do you not think if your peers were given this opportunity, they would not take it? We are the key to this community's survival. Before you, in this kitchen, are the men and women who make the decisions that make existence possible. Without us, our neighbors and friends, would not even have what they are provided now."

"A Zionist who is also an elitist," Singer remarked. "That's an interesting combination."

Rosenfeld pointed his knife at Singer. "And you must be a Communist."

Singer laughed.

"Look there," I interrupted.

The room went silent.

It was Rumkowski. The Chairman was flanked by Neftalin and two young women. He stopped at the front of the room and surveyed the diners who promptly stood. Removing his hat, he walked along the perimeter of the massive dining room, nodding here and there.

I was already standing. Rosenfeld stood slowly. Cukier was at another table talking to a policeman.

Singer hissed in my ear. "Someday, someone will shoot the bastard."

I shuddered. Not for the first time, nor the last, did I wonder why Singer had been included in our little club.

CHAPTER 9

After lunch, we returned to the conference room in the rear of the Archives section. It had been the best meal I'd had in a long time. I smuggled out half of a roll in a cloth napkin concealed in my coat pocket. I would have brought a little of the stew with real meat chips in it, for Miriam, but that was impossible.

There was a stiff price to pay for eating in the superior dining hall. It wasn't the dust-heavy smell of the long-enclosed workroom, nor the locked-up window that faced another office building with more of Rumkowski's departments. It wasn't even the closeness of the walls. It was the men with whom I was trapped in debate. We were all from different geographic areas and contrasting socio-economic backgrounds. Our philosophies were in constant conflict, which frustrated my goal-oriented nature.

Singer, the vehement anti-Nazi, began the afternoon battle with one word: "Decadent."

"What is?" I should have ignored him.

He aimed his dark eyes at me as if they were gun barrels. "Do you not think it is decadent that the so-called intelligentsia, dines so much better than our brothers and sisters who slave in the Chairman's factories?"

Cukier shrugged. "I don't question the wisdom of the Chairman."

"You have no conscience then?" Singer asked. "It seems to me that a fairer system could be worked out. Engineer, don't you agree that an equitable system could be created to keep up morale?"

I wondered how Singer could bite the hand that was feeding us. "I believe we have work to accomplish, and though I wish all kitchens were run this efficiently, we need to focus on the task at hand."

"Isn't it everybody's task to assure our brothers and sisters are kept as comfortable as we are?" Singer asked, grinning as if he knew he was shooting arrows at us.

Rosenfeld nodded. "But the reality is that can only happen in a true socialist society, such as my friend, Herzl, wishes to establish in Israel."

"Do you think the powers that be will ever allow Jews to have a homeland?" Singer asked. "This is an impossible dream."

Cukier sighed. "Gentlemen, I too pray for a homeland in Israel, but for now, we must concern ourselves with the mission our great leader has entrusted to us."

I'd been writing on a sheet of paper, not being one for philosophical discussions.

"Are you drawing a blueprint, Engineer?" Rosenfeld asked, pulling his coat around him. "Is it cold in here, or am I getting old?" he asked.

Singer laughed. "You are old, but yes, it is cold in here. Is there no heat?" He looked at the lifeless fireplace, a small box in the wall.

Cukier smiled. "You want heat when our brothers and sisters are begging for a bit of coal?"

Singer looked as if one of his arrows had been shot back at him.

I decided to rescue him. "Our friend, Dr. Singer, was not asking for a shovel, but for a lump, fair rations for a room of highly regarded scholars, and one engineer."

"Well said," Rosenfeld remarked, lighting his pipe.

"Must you smoke that in here?" Singer asked. "It's stifling enough in this torture chamber without that awful smell. It's not even real tobacco, is it?"

Rosenfeld took two more puffs, and with his thumb put it out. "I'll save the rest for later."

"Ostrowski, what are you writing? Are you keeping a record of our conversations?" Cukier leaned over my pad of paper.

"No. I think the Chairman would not approve of us keeping such notes."

"Agreed," Rosenfeld said. "It would be impossible to keep track of all the brilliant statements such articulate men spout." He let out a little laugh, still holding his pipe, now unlit, in his mouth.

"I believe that was sarcasm," Singer said. "I didn't know the old man knew how to joke like that."

"There is much this old man can do from which a young man, with any intelligence, could learn," Rosenfeld shot back.

Cukier jumped in. "Let's all agree that each of us has positive attributes that lend themselves well to this endeavor. If we ever get started."

That was my cue. "Sirs, I am only an engineer, but designing structures makes one structured."

"That's a very good play on words," Singer said. "Now, you surprise me too."

"Thank you." I looked at Rosenfeld. He looked curious, so I persisted, "I have been working to define our task, but need your wise help." I held the pad up so they could see my work. "I have listed topics which I suggest we include in our records."

"I see why you were selected to join us," Cukier said, giving me a smile. "This is an excellent start."

Rosenfeld squinted at the sheet. "So, you're saying we should focus on these topics?"

"It's only a start."

"As Cukier says, it is a good start," Rosenfeld remarked and wrote on his pad.

"I said, "excellent start," Cukier replied. "But let's not get into another debate when Ostrowski has given us an excellent framework to begin our discussion."

Singer shook his head. "The weather? The first priority on your list to assure the survival of Jewish culture is the weather?" He shook his head again. "Is that what we are wasting our talent on? Is writing about the weather what earns us this deferential treatment? The weather?" He looked disgusted.

"I think weather is quite significant," Rosenfeld said. "Harsh weather means poor food growth which necessitates a greater need for fuel for heat, warmer clothing, blankets, etc."

"Why did you include the weather?" Cukier asked.

"It is my understanding we must do this work in secret."

"Correct. The Germans can walk in on us at any time," Cukier replied.

"Any time?" Rosenfeld asked, tightening his necktie with a hand that had age spots on veiny flesh.

"We are as Rumkowski aptly put it, "working under the German noses.""

"I understand your plan," Cukier said. "All these lesser categories will serve to mask the important things we need to include."

"They're camouflage," I replied.

Singer smiled. "So, they won't see the tree for the forest." He nodded his head thoughtfully. "I think this is not a bad concept. Mind you, this war will be over soon. The Germans will pay a terrible price for all the suffering they have caused."

"Let God hear your words." Rosenfeld closed his eyes and whispered, "Amen."

"I didn't think you were religious," Singer said.

"I'm a practical Jew. As a realist, I'm not sure God exists, but then again, I'm not sure he doesn't. Therefore, I hedge my bets and pray," Rosenfeld replied.

"Just in case?" Cukier asked.

"Just in case," Rosenfeld replied.

"In that case. Amen." Singer said. "And you, Engineer?"

"Amen," I replied quickly accepting my nickname, hoping to avoid another argument. "So, I suggest we list all the subjects we wish to include and present this list to the Chairman as a skeleton—"

"Skeleton?" Rosenfeld almost dropped the pipe from his mouth.

"Call it a framework. The rate things are going, skeletons we will become if the Germans have their way."

"Framework it is," I said. "Good, now let's begin by listing the topics each of us feels should be included."

Rosenfeld immediately wrote his name in big, bold, letters across the top: Dr. Oscar Rosenfeld, Editor, Zionist Weekly of Vienna. He took great care with his handwriting, whereas Singer had already scribbled more than twenty words all over his page. Cukier's page had a line dividing it in half. He wrote: "Yes," on top of the left side, and, "No," on the right. I was fascinated by how these educated men differed in their solutions to the problem I'd presented.

"Gentlemen, it is time," Cukier said after several minutes.

"I have more to add," Rosenfeld said, his pipe on the table.

"This is not a competition, Doctor. Of course, you may continue. But I believe we should share our thoughts at this time. Ostrowski, would you mind adding the new suggestions to your list?"

I viewed it as Cukier's way of acknowledging my modest contribution. I felt proud I'd gotten us on track. Of course, these learned men argued about each item, but in the end, we compiled a comprehensive list of what we would include.

Cukier reinforced the preeminent requirement: "Remember, the Chairman will want to check each day's work personally."

Of course, Singer reacted. "Censorship, plain and simple. I will not have my work censored by anyone."

By the end of the day, we were all exhausted, and Cukier wisely decided to table the discussion about censorship and freedom of the press until it became necessary.

As I headed home, I could still hear my new coworkers' voices arguing over each point as rabbis of the past deliberated over the meaning of each word in the Torah, the Old Testament. I told myself it was just the first day and things will improve once we get the parameters established. A flash of lightning lit the horizon.

I hoped it was an airplane bombing the Nazis. But the sky belonged to the Luftwaffe and to God, and all the latter had done was given us poor ghetto Jews foul weather. Fearing the impending storm, I forgot it was dangerous to run.

CHAPTER 10

"Halt!"

The command brought me to an immediate standstill. How far was I from home? I'd rarely seen German soldiers on the streets close to our tenement.

"Raise your hands," the voice ordered. "Lock them on top of your hat."

I moved my hands cautiously to the top of my hat. "My papers are in my pocket," I said, hoping my voice wasn't cracking.

The officer was now in front of me. His hat brim was level with my forehead. Built powerfully, he was holding his stick in an upright position. "Why are you running?" He looked up and down the street as if checking to see if anyone would witness him smashing me with the club.

"Officer," I said, trying to sound more confident than I felt. "It is my first day working for the government, and I was excited to return home to my wife."

"Stop! I don't need your life story. Our job is to keep order. If you are in the government, you should know this."

Sonofabitch, I thought, but replied, "Of course, you are right. The rain is near, and I hoped to escape it. May I show you my papers, sir?" Others said the Jewish police could be brutal. Some critics asserted that these men, all hired by Rumkowski, were doing the work of the Nazis for them. I found it hard to accept any Jew would do that.

"Show me your papers. Stop! Move only one hand."

I saw the club was raised. "They're in my jacket pocket."

"Remove them slowly." He raised his club higher.

I held my fingers in the air and opened my jacket, revealing the inside pocket. "May I remove them?" I used two fingers to lift the packet.

He pulled the packet from my grasp.

I dropped my hand.

"On your head!" He eyed me sternly and opened my ID folder.

Hands on top of my head, I was anxious he might think I'd forged the documents, a common occurrence. What would I do then? I thought of Miriam's face.

He slipped the papers back into the folder. "Put your hands down. Everything appears to be in order." He handed the papers back. "You should be more careful. I might have been Gestapo. Then you would not be so lucky."

"You're right. I'll be more careful. Thank you."

"These are difficult times, my friend. There are those who wish to undermine our authority, criminal elements, who care nothing about our survival."

"I understand." Rumkowski persistently blamed criminals and foreigners for any violations of his policies.

"Yes. There are many criminals and deviants among these immigrants," the policeman said, pounding his club in his palm.

As a newcomer myself, I kept my tongue, something I'd been learning to do. I wished he would stop pounding the club.

He looked down the street. "The lowlifes are not native Lodzer like we police and ghetto administrators, such as yourself. Most share none of our values. They will attack and steal anything you possess, including your documents." He grilled me with his eyes. "I hate them. They are vampires, blood-thirsty villains of the worst sort."

I watched him brandish his club. I suspected it had been used, but always in the name of public safety. "We in the government know you police are on the front line. Thank you for your service."

The club dropped to his side. "Order must be maintained, or the occupiers will take over. I must be off. You will be safe?"

"Yes. Thank you." I watched with relief as he walked across the road and turned the corner. "Rumkowski has his own damn army," I muttered, as my heartbeat steadied. As much as I wanted to escape the cold and rain, I stifled my impulse to run and checked every alley for villains who might mug me for my ration cards or my concealed lump of bread. My door did not come soon enough. "Miriam, it's me."

"Did you have a good first day at work?" She peered into my face. "What is wrong? You look strange."

I forced myself to smile. Why worry my lovely wife about something I was already putting in the past. "I'm just tired. It was a long day." I pulled off my coat. "You would not believe the lunch I had. Here, this is for you." I pulled the roll from my pocket and it crumbled onto the floor. "I guess it was in there too long."

To my shock, Miriam dropped to her hands and knees, and with her lovely fingers swept the crumbs into her hand. I could say nothing as I watched her place the crumpled roll back into the cloth napkin, wrapping it up as if it was a precious treasure.

It upset me to see Miriam scrambling for the crumbs on our dirty floor. When she finished gathering what she could, her eyes glanced up at me as if asking if it was all right.

After finishing off a few bits of the roll, Miriam wrapped the rest back in the napkin. "So now, dear husband, tell me about your first day of work." She leaned forward reminding me of an attentive child listening to her teacher.

Instead of filling her with lies about my new job, I described the magnificent Kitchen for the Intelligentsia. "You should see the dishes and the flatware. The servers were all young girls, so clean and polite. It was reassuring to see how smoothly everything operates."

Miriam nestled against me, her head warm against my chest. I was about to suggest we retire to our bed when she lifted her eyes and said, "So you do not believe he is the Devil?"

"Who? Do you mean the Chairman?" Her questions startled me.

Miriam pulled herself off my chest. Her eyes locked onto my face. "My friends say he is willing to sacrifice everyone in the ghetto to save himself. They say he is working with the Nazis and making himself rich while the rest of us suffer." She shivered. "Can such a Jew exist? I'm frightened, Benny. Have you met him?"

I shook my head. This was not the time to tell her the truth. "Everyone in the ghetto administration praises how he is watching over us. He is our father figure, our protector."

"I hope so." She looked uncertain.

"Dearest, you should not worry. I will take care of you." I pulled her toward me again and rocked her in my arms. In seconds, I heard her rhythmic breathing, the breathing of sleep. I did not have the heart to wake her. Painful as this position became, I kept her in my arms, held her against my chest, and refused to let go. I listened to her heartbeats and gentle breathing.

An hour or more passed, and I felt her stirring against me. "Do you want to go to bed?" I asked, still cradling her against me.

She stood up and reached for my hand. "Come, Benny," she whispered, "You've had a long day."

I rose eagerly, following her to our bed. When she pulled off her dress, folding it neatly, I regretted she would have to wear it again tomorrow. The few things we had brought with us when we were chased into the Lodz ghetto—they'd given us so little time to pack our one bag each—did not allow for many changes of attire.

Miriam's shirt covered her breasts, but I wanted to see them tonight. "May I?" I asked, reaching for the thin laces that kept the shirt closed. I saw her nod and gently pulled at the top lace. It took forever to loosen. I could barely breathe as I lowered my hand to the next tie. "Yes?" She nodded again. The tie was frayed. Now I could see her flesh. There was a smudge of dirt. A bath, a shower, once a week, if you're lucky. The third tie was begging to be loosened, but she took hold of my wrist. "What is it? Do you want me to stop?"

51

Miriam shook her head and then said softly, "With the world as it is, I want to taste love without modesty. Does that make sense?"

I didn't really understand, but the pressure was building inside me. "I only know I love you," I said. "It would make me the happiest man in the world to lie tonight with you and nothing between us."

She pulled open the last lace and then pulled the garment over her head. She let the shirt fall to the floor.

I saw her as God intended. I'd imagined how beautiful she would look without the filthy rags that her modesty dictated she wear in our bed, but nothing prepared me for what I felt. I'd never been with another woman and must have looked a fool just taking her in with my eyes and not reaching for her. "You're so beautiful," I stammered, almost unable to speak. "May I touch you?" I lowered my hand to her breast. I was afraid she'd pull away, but she pushed herself toward me, her hand reaching, fingers searching for me. I could not resist, did not want to resist. She led me to our bed.

Her body undulated below me so that each time I lowered myself I felt her flesh against my flesh, her legs tightening around me, her breathing labored, her eyes closed. I could forget the world, Hitler, Rumkowski, all, for a few precious seconds of losing myself in her. When her legs locked around me and I heard her moan, I shuddered, barely able to support myself on arms that were rubber. I rolled onto my back to avoid hurting her. "Thank you," I whispered.

She was silent.

"Are you all right? I did not hurt you?"

Miriam gazed silently at the ceiling for several minutes and then asked, "What do you really do at work?"

"What do you mean?" I was out of breath, and her question surprised me.

Miriam lifted herself on her elbow and gazed into my half-closed eyes. "You used to talk about your work all the time. You'd brag about this project or that. Now, you don't say anything about what you do, or who you work with."

"It's nothing," I replied and closed my eyes hoping she would drop the subject.

"Is it dangerous? I do not want you to do anything that is dangerous."

I mulled that over. "You know me well, my darling, would I do something dangerous? I'm many things, but not a risk taker."

Miriam fell to her back again. "When my parents gave me to you, I did not know if I would ever love you. My parents said you would protect me."

"The past is the past," I said, not wanting to hear her admit she was not attracted to me at first, perhaps not even now. Being she was much younger, I understood she might not love me, but my love for her was enough.

"I was just a silly girl then. It was a natural reaction." She took my hand. "I do not know what I would do if something happened to you."

"Nothing will happen to me. The world will continue spinning long after the insane housepainter is buried and forgotten."

"You mean Hitler?"

"His name should not come from your sweet lips. It will be erased from history, much like the names of the pharaohs and would-be conquerors from the past. None have managed to destroy the Jews. Somehow, we survive." When I turned to see if I'd helped, Miriam was asleep. The thin sheet barely covered her naked posterior. I pulled it over her and stared up at her profile, hair flowing across the pillow. "You have nothing to worry about. I will always take care of you."

Unable to sleep, my mind rushed over too many conflicting thoughts. Gazing at Miriam, I resolved that no matter how insufferable these men were, I would not give up this position. I had to take care of this sleeping child in my bed. When that Jewish policeman stood over me with his club, I did not think of my safety, only of never seeing my Miriam again. "Thank you, God. I don't know if I believe in you but thank you for this precious gift in a world gone mad."

Miriam let out an almost inaudible moan and clutched her pillow as if afraid to let go.

CHAPTER 11

T hough I had promised to remain on the job, by the end of the first week in that tiny room, I was ready to shoot myself. I was discouraged at how supposedly highly intelligent men hammered at each other over one issue after another without much progress. Cukier's insistence on open discussion, while democratic, opened the floodgates of hell. Every time I was hopeful the gates were closing, Singer threw in another monkey wrench.

Friday afternoon, I was eagerly awaiting early dismissal since the others observed the Sabbath when our youngest member erupted. "Why must we always sing his praises? Rumkowski isn't God. He's not infallible."

"No Jew is God," I said.

"Especially not married Jews," Rosenfeld quipped and laughed at his own joke.

I didn't laugh. "Let's get back to work."

"I never said the Eldest of the Jews is God," Cukier said, refusing to drop the argument.

"He acts like a god. Or a king. Yes, a damn king!" Singer tossed down the document he'd been working on. "Yet we always defend him."

And you act like an ass, I thought, staring at the dust-covered window, yearning to be out in the cold air. The cushion-less chairs were making it impossible to sit, but there was hardly any room to walk around the conference table. I'd had enough. "Dr. Singer, don't you think we should do everything we can to convince the authorities that our Chairman has matters under control?"

Singer snapped back, "Nothing is under his control. He's fooling himself, and I did not sign on to be a liar."

Rosenfeld's unlit pipe bobbed in his mouth. "I am not a liar."

I thought of the lies I was telling Miriam.

"You see, Dr. Rosenfeld agrees with me," Singer waved his arm triumphantly. "We owe our people the truth." He turned to me, a sly smile on his face. "And Engineer, you're not a real writer. Are you one of his spies?"

Cukier jumped up. "Singer, you go too far."

Rosenfeld said, "Ostrowski, was selected because we are dreamers. He is a realist, our balance."

"I do not write propaganda for anyone," Singer snarled, casting me an insolent grin.

"Singer, you don't understand our reality." I tried to keep calm, but I was frustrated and suffocating in our tight quarters. "The truth is not always absolute."

"Of course it is," Singer shot back. "Something is either true or it is false. We are writing lies knowingly."

I wanted to go home, but we still had an hour left. "Let me give you an example. When I build a house, all the measurements must be true, or it will collapse. Do you agree?"

"My point precisely," Singer interrupted. "A house cannot stand on lies."

I gripped the back of my chair to control my anger. "Just listen. You are always busy criticizing, but you don't listen to anyone else but yourself." I felt as if I were scolding a child. "We are not building a house with measuring tools and exact figures. In our situation, there isn't any way to know if something is true, half true, or not true at all."

"That makes no sense," Singer said.

Rosenfeld took his pipe from his lips. "I'm not sure I follow your logic either."

"Let me explain. Yes, we can tell our friends and others what we believe is true, but are we absolutely sure of what the truth is?"

"That's double-talk," Singer said.

"No. It is not. How can you criticize what our leader does when we're not able to know everything behind his decisions? We are locked in this small chamber and must depend on others for the truth. The Germans don't tell us the truth, do they?"

Cukier nodded. "And unless we are absolutely sure of all the facts, we will only stoke discontent and fear by our questioning of the Chairman's policies. He is the only one who knows the truths behind his decisions. Therefore, we must trust the Eldest of the Jews, our Chairman or all is lost."

Singer shot back. "Fear triggers action. That is what we need. We need to stir everyone to join the fight against these Nazi pigs."

Cukier threw up his hands. "Singer, the engineer is right. You need to listen to others for a change."

I again thought of Miriam and wondered how she would react if she knew everything I was learning about the state of affairs in our ghetto. "Thank you, Julian. Sometimes, my friends, as the saying goes, "ignorance is bliss." Our people are better off not knowing the truth."

"I disagree," Singer said, glaring at us over the table. "Everyone is entitled to the same information we possess."

I was ready to choke him. "Are you serious? Do you really want to know everything the Eldest of the Jews knows? Could you bear it? No. In our perilous situation, we must support the pillars of the house, so the Nazis don't destroy it."

"With us inside," Rosenfeld murmured.

Cukier leaned toward Singer. "The people would panic if they knew everything. Support is what our Chairman deserves for being the lone pillar of this ghetto." He jotted something on his pad. "I like that analogy, Engineer. We are the pillars supporting the Chairman who is the foundation of the ghetto."

Rosenfeld pointed at me with his pipe. "I understand. To keep our 'house', as you put it, standing, we must do what we can to shore up the Chairman. I see your point now."

Cukier aimed his eyes at Singer. "I believe our personal feelings are secondary to our Chairman's mandate: to preserve what we can for the future. If that means tamping down on editorializing, so be it. We can reserve our criticism for after this damn war is over." He let out a muffled cough.

Rosenfeld said. "I reluctantly agree. Young Singer, Rumkowski is our only option. We must pray he does not fail."

Singer shook his head sadly. "You are all wrong."

I said, "Unity is our only hope. Can't you see that?"

Cukier smiled. "He's young. He'll get it eventually. For now, his idealism will serve as our conscience. But Singer, don't push it too far."

Singer's lips were tight. "I'm outnumbered. Fine. I'll play the game for now. Let's get on with it before I change my mind." He sat back in his chair, a resigned expression on his face.

Cukier slid a flyer across the table. "Our chairman sent this directive to department heads and factory managers, ordering them to report all events and statistics to us."

I worried how long before one of the department heads, or their subordinates, divulged our work to the gossips and I'd have to face a furious Miriam. I read the directive. "Do they know what this is for?" I asked.

"No. Subordinates do not question the Chairman's directives." He glanced at Singer.

Singer groaned. "So, the news we slant to favor Rumkowski is first filtered by department heads who owe their status to his Majesty? What happened to honest journalism and freedom of the press?" He shoved the memo back across the table without reading it.

"The Nazis crushed those ideals with their jackboots and tanks," Cukier replied. "If you can't suppress your indignation, dear Oscar, then this task is not for you." He must have seen the shocked looks on our faces because he added quickly, "But I believe you have much to contribute. You have the fire we need to reflect the views of the younger generation. I share your frustration, but our mission makes personal considerations unimportant. I hope you can accept that."

Rosenfeld placed his hand on Singer's shoulder. "My boy, if you leave, I alone shall be the advocate for truth against these blasted propagandists. Do not do that to an old man."

Cukier nodded. "The good Doctor is right; you are an integral voice in the Chairman's effort to preserve our story for the future. We need your righteous anger. Though I hate to admit it." He gave Singer a warm smile. "You are our gadfly."

Singer shrugged his shoulders. "You should have been a diplomat."

Cukier laughed. "Me? Never. I'm far too honest."

We all laughed at that, even Singer.

"Now, let's get to work," Cukier said.

I was grateful to dive into the pile of departmental reports Cukier placed in front of me. Even Singer was silently poring through his stack of memos.

Maybe this won't be so bad, I thought, if that young man can learn to keep his mouth shut. I suspected the gadfly was not going to last long on our team.

CHAPTER 12

By the end of the second week, I felt we were making progress, but with too many bumps in the road. Each time, I thought our differences were resolved, a new debate would erupt. By the second Friday, I was grateful to have a few moments of peace.

Dr. Rosenfeld broke the blessed silence, waving a calendar. "Do you believe it's been four hundred ninety- two days since this shit began?" He threw the paper calendar on the table.

I was shocked he'd used a profanity. "I thought I was the numbers man," I said, trying to lighten his mood.

Cukier picked up the calendar and studied it. "Hitler wanted Lodz and, he got it.".

Singer cut in. "He wanted our factories. He damn well didn't want Jews."

Cukier nodded. "Our industrial reputation was well known."

Singer kicked his chair backwards. "Screw our reputation! What did it get us? He gobbled up one hundred and fifty thousand dirty Jews when he dragged us into his nightmare. Great news for us Jews!"

I groaned. Singer was on his soapbox again.

"Keep your voices down." Cukier checked the door.

Rosenfeld shrugged. "At least, thank God, we are still here. Hitler, madman that he is, knows our value. Otherwise, why did the Nazis not crush us?"

Singer mumbled, "They may do just that."

"Hitler alone knows the answer to that," Cukier said, pressing his body against the door.

"Hitler and Rumkowski," Singer spat.

Cukier was over Singer like a shot. "Goddammit! Don't mention their names together!" He wagged an angry finger at Singer. "They are not at all alike! Not in any way! Never say that again! Do you hear me? Never!" He coughed into his hand. "Sonofabitch."

Singer looked shocked.

I was too. I'd never seen Cukier lose his temper before. I cut in, changing the subject. "I never realized Jews had such an established community in Lodz."

Cukier was breathing hard, leaning on the wall. "We're the second...largest Jewish population in Poland." He was gasping for air as he spoke. Asthma?

Rosenfeld sighed. "Everyone knows of Warsaw and Krakow, but Jews have been in Lodz for centuries. We're the power behind the factories. Or we were."

Cukier sounded wistful. "We had a lovely house in the city. This section of Lodz, our ghetto, we thought of as a slum."

"The Cukiers were rich capitalists," Singer hissed.

Cukier glanced at him. "We were accepted by the Poles. There were incidents, of course."

Singer sneered. "Incidents? Cukier, they're called pogroms!"

"Well, they were better here." Cukier coughed into his handkerchief.

Singer shot back, "Better? They never liked Jews. They tolerated us because they needed our money. Don't fool yourself for one minute that the Poles liked Jews any more than the Germans. That's the mistake we made...one of the mistakes. Stupid! That's what we were. We should have armed ourselves from the beginning." He made his hand into a pistol and fired the imaginary gun in the direction of the window. "Guns are all they understand. It's not too late."

"They'll mow us down like fleas," Cukier replied.

"At least we'd die like men, like our heroes of old," Singer said.

Rosenfeld pulled at his beard. "For once, Singer's right, at least partly. Once the Germans no longer need us, I'm afraid we are kaput, finished."

"That's what I've been saying," Singer rasped. "We need to get guns and fight."

"Enough. I'm going to Neftalin." Cukier was out the door almost before he finished the sentence.

Singer looked anxious. "I'll bet he's going to report me."

I couldn't believe our brave young warrior sounded worried. Why couldn't he keep his mouth shut and let us get to our work? I wouldn't blame Cukier if he'd enough of this reckless character who took pleasure in egging us on.

"Do you think he's reporting me?" Singer asked. "Not that I care really." He shrugged his shoulders. "I don't plan to be here much longer."

Rosenfeld looked concerned. "And where will you go? We're sealed in here like rats, and you know what Germans do with rats."

"They treat them better than Jews." Singer replied. "I guess I'd better get a few of these done before he returns." He looked like a schoolboy as he finally, silently, began to read the departmental memos.

I slid over to Dr. Rosenfeld. "Doctor, you're an educated man, why did you remain here, when so many left?"

"A good question. I supposed, as most Lodz Jews thought, that war would be averted, and, at any rate, not reach here. We overestimated Poland's strength."

Singer piped up, "Who could believe England, France, the Americans, everyone, would sit on their asses and let Hitler just take Poland? Those imperialist cowards deserve what they get." He rose from his chair and glanced out the doorway.

I ignored his rants, believing his membership with us was about to end.

Singer closed the door. "These so-called great powers thought the bastard would be satisfied with Poland, so they tossed him a bone."

Rosenfeld sighed. "So, Dr. Singer, you knew better in Warsaw? No one guessed Hitler was so strong and our government so impotent. It fooled us all." He glanced sadly at his empty pipe.

"Hitler is a coward. He attacked Poland without declaring war," Singer said, retaking his seat.

"It was naïve to expect Hitler to play by rules. It was war." Rosenfeld laughed. "Engineer, do you remember the news reports that day?"

"What day?" I asked.

"September 1st. A year ago. Is that incredible? It seems a lifetime since everything turned upside down." He shook his head sadly. "The radio reported our troops stormed into Germany."

"Oh yes. I remember now. The radio said thirty Polish planes bombed Berlin."

Singer laughed bitterly. "That's as funny as the reports that French troops were crushing the Nazis. Shit! We all applauded. You should have seen the beer and wine! Girls were throwing themselves at my feet. What a night!"

Rosenfeld pointed his pipe stem at Singer. "You are a bad boy, but we also celebrated victory." He gave Singer a wry smile. "We believed it was all over until German tanks streamed into Warsaw. It was a total surprise. Nobody believed it."

"The damn Germans set us up." Singer said. "It was all Nazi propaganda. And you want us to write that for him?" He threw down his pad in disgust.

Back to that argument again? I groaned. Where was Cukier?

"Propaganda, yes," Rosenfeld said, chugging thoughtfully on his pipe. "The Germans made it appear as if their forces had been beaten by our superior military might. They caught us off-guard and then attacked."

"You mean they caught us with our pants down," Singer said without smiling. "Doctor, they didn't attack. Not one shot was fired when they took over."

Rosenfeld nodded sadly. "Here, pro-Hitler groups living among the Lodz population did the dirty work for them."

"They were Germans and Poles employed by your factories." Singer shot an insolent look at Cukier's empty chair. "Just as I said, these factories will be the death of us."

Rosenfeld nodded. "It's ironic. They were working for Jews like Cukier's father, making good money, but then drove us from our homes into this slum, destroying their meal ticket."

Singer laughed. "But we were a kosher meal ticket. Our good neighbors and loyal employees joined the mob, stealing whatever they wanted." He aimed his eyes at me. "We should have fought then, and we must fight now."

I recalled the night Miriam, and I were rousted from our sleep and chased into the ghetto. I heard the screaming and the smashing of glass as I pushed Miriam into the crowd, hoping the bodies pressing around us would shield her. What would have happened had I tried to fight the young thugs? Miriam would have been a widow.

Cukier entered the room and sat in his chair without a word to Singer.

Rosenfeld asked, "Are you alright?"

Cukier nodded slowly. "I needed air."

We all do, I thought, wondering if he'd seen Neftalin. Wasn't anyone going to at least chastise our outspoken radical?

Singer, apparently buoyed by Cukier's failure to take action against him, took the reins, "We were analyzing how the Poles betrayed their Jewish employers and how we should have fought against them...should fight them now."

Cukier stared at Singer with sad eyes. "Sure. Fight them. You don't know. You were in Warsaw. Here, in Lodz, it was a blood bath, people bleeding from rifle butts, broomsticks, clubs, whatever the Poles could grab. We were all running, running past unconscious bodies. Friends...family members...parents." Cukier trembled, and then coughed into his white handkerchief.

"Julian," I said, noting he never spoke about his parents. None of us revealed much about our backgrounds. It was as if we didn't want to face all we'd lost.

"It is nothing," Cukier rasped, moving his handkerchief underneath the table.

Rosenfeld sighed. "I thought the ghetto would be a sanctuary from the Poles and Germans." His voice quivered. "Our employees, neighbors, friends, had become Nazis, plain and simple."

Singer slammed his fist on the table. "No. That's where you're wrong. They were Nazis all along. We chose to be blind to their hatred."

"No, they were not always Nazis," Cukier said. "I don't know what happened to them, but you can't tell me they were always Jew haters."

"No? They loved working for rich Jews like your father." Singer said.

Cukier's face reddened, and he was about to reply, but a coughing fit stopped him.

"You're upsetting him. Why don't you just leave?" I regretted saying that, but it was too late.

Cukier was coughing harder, covering his face with the cloth.

Rosenfeld was at his side, trying to calm him.

Singer pulled on his coat and looked down at Cukier, "Julian, it is because you are a good man that you can't believe such evil exists. Though I am younger, I know. It does, my friend, it does."

"Where are you going?" Rosenfeld asked.

Cukier was staring balefully at the door over his handkerchief.

I wished Singer would never come back. Without his presence, the rest of us would disagree about some minor things, but not be hamstrung by all these arguments.

After Singer left, Cukier, coughing still, directed us to go home. "Good Sabbath," he managed to say.

"Do you want me to remain?" I asked.

He shook his head, sweat beading on his forehead. "I'm fine. It's just a cough."

I was relieved he didn't need me. I wanted to get home and share my pent-up anger and frustration with Miriam. But then I'd have to tell her the truth of what I was doing for the Chairman. He had warned me that would put her in danger. I couldn't risk that.

When at last I was safely home, Miriam asked me how my day had gone. I made up a sketchy story about how frustrating it was to find decent housing in the ghetto for the new arrivals. I weighed every word, unable to share with her my honest thoughts, fears, and even hopes. There were uncomfortable gaps in our conversation. I was eager to put out the candle and surrender to the enforced blackout. In the dark, Miriam would not be able to search my lying eyes.

That night, when Miriam and I went to bed, I was grateful she showed no eagerness to make love.

CHAPTER 13

It was a difficult weekend. Miriam walked with Sarah and Mendel to the bread line. I remained home, exhausted from a week of battling with Singer and the others. I was most bothered by having to lie to Miriam. I was not a good liar and suspected my young wife sensed I was not honest with her. It made me irritable and yet there was nowhere to go.

By Sunday, I was eager to get out of the flat, to avoid conversation with Miriam. Afraid of slipping and revealing my job, I told her I'd changed departments and was now working for the Department of the Archives.

"I never heard of that department. What do you do there?"

"I work with a small group of men sorting through old records and books." It sounded believably boring.

"So, you are safe?"

"Yes, my love, I'm safe." If I don't kill one of these scholars, I thought.

"That is good," Miriam said.

I was relieved she believed me but worried she'd wangle the truth out of me. By Monday, tired of being on guard, I was looking forward to work. I should have known better.

As usual, Singer started it. "I refuse to call this place Litzmannstadt. It was, is, and always will be, Lodz to me and the hundreds of thousands of Lodzer that have lived here."

Cukier shook the Chairman's decree in front of Singer's face. "Change the name now. The Chairman insists, and so do I."

"What's going on now?" I asked, my head pounding already, wishing

I could hammer sense into Singer's stubborn brain. "It's just a name! Why did the Germans change it anyway?"

Rosenfeld had a faraway look on his gaunt face. "Shakespeare said, "What is in a name? A rose by any other name…'"

Singer barked, "I'll tell you. The Germans want no question about who owns this city, so they changed our name to Litzmannstadt, to 'Germanize' all of Lodz once and for all."

"Litzmannstadt? That's a mouthful. I can't even say it, let alone spell it," I said.

Rosenfeld nodded. "It's a slap in the face for the Poles. Karl Litzmann, a German general, fell in battle near here during the first World War."

"So that is why all the streets and town squares have German names?"

"It's a Nazi plot to erase all signs of Polish ties to Lodz. It serves the bastards right for welcoming the Huns with open arms." Singer said.

Rosenfeld dropped his empty pipe from his lips. "I hope I haven't broken it," he muttered.

Cukier cracked open the door and then closed it, an act of caution whenever we got into a heated debate. "Keep your voices down," he urged.

I lowered my voice. "Ah, that answers the question. In Lublin, I heard that Lodz was a great German industrial city, yet on maps, Lodz is shown as part of Poland. I wondered about that."

Rosenfeld, unlit pipe restored to his mouth, said, "I must admit, in all my studies of world history, I've never seen anything quite like what has happened to us. To my knowledge, no other city, not even Warsaw, has been so totally cut off and transformed in such a short time. It's quite a feat."

Singer hissed. "Lodz is totally Nazified. That's the result of Rumkowski's plan to make us an industrial super-power. Is it a surprise Hitler wants us for himself?"

Rosenfeld nodded. "Again, I agree. The Germans totally encircled the ghetto with more Germans. Even Poles are not welcome. Rumkowski is right, the Germans need our production, but I don't know if he realizes how much importance they place in possessing our facilities."

"So, the Chairman is right," I said, feeling hopeful. "As long as we work we are safe."

Singer looked wild. "Are we safe? Barbed wire is everywhere! German guards have orders to shoot to kill! Rumkowski does nothing. We do nothing to resist. It's a lie. It's disgusting! We never learn. We think we're brilliant because we're Jews. But we're sheep being lured to the slaughterhouse."

"You exhaust me," Cukier said, echoing my feelings.

Rosenfeld spread out a torn map. "See here, our city is no longer Polish, but a part of Germany. So yes, if we do not serve the Fuhrer's purpose, we are, as I said earlier, kaput."

Singer leaned over me. "Rumkowski may have saved us from war, perhaps from death now, as my much wiser friends here insist, but he has doomed us to be slaves for the Reich. Either way, we are doomed. When he no longer needs us, the butchers will be waiting."

I wanted to hear no more of all this gloomy talk. I tried to focus on reading a memo from the housing department.

Rosenfeld slid two photographs across the table. "Look at these, Engineer. The Nazis burned our old Orthodox synagogue on Wolborska Street and our Reformed Synagogue on Kosciuszko Blvd. All that is left is rubble."

"I pass the Orthodox synagogue on my way to work," I said, looking at the black and white photographs.

Rosenfeld pointed his finger at the photograph. "You did not see it in its glory."

I gazed at the photograph. The tall towers had once risen proudly over the surrounding tenements. "It looks beautiful. I'm sorry."

Cukier put his arm on Rosenfeld's shoulder. "In Lodz, the Nazis are hell-bent to destroy our religion. They know that without our faith, we are broken."

Singer's anger exploded. "They can't break me. I have the dream of returning to Zion, Israel. Europe is not a home for Jews. Even before Hitler shook the tree and the hate nuts fell upon us, it was never our home. Our home is only in the land of milk and honey. That is my dream. That should be everyone's dream."

Cukier smiled sadly. "My family was always loyal to Poland. My father prospered here. Lodz was the only home I ever knew. But perhaps young Oscar is right. Hitler could not do what he did to us if many Poles had not helped."

"For once I concur with my young friend," Rosenfeld said, casting a paternal look at Singer. "Hitler's actions against Jews were visible to the world. Nobody did anything."

I remembered when the German laws banned all religious ceremonies, shuttered our temples, and prohibited all our holidays. I'd never cared about those things after attending university, but under attack, we Jews are a stubborn people. I and many others who'd lost our Jewish identity awakened when Hitler took it away from us. Many of my friends—where were they now– prayed in secret, in their homes, in boarded up stores, much as in ancient times Jews prayed hidden in caves. I would have joined them, but I'd lost all faith, despite Miriam's efforts to rekindle it. I envied her child-like belief in God. What peace I might have felt if only I could believe.

Rosenfeld's voice cracked, disrupting my thoughts. "How could the world not hear when the Germans committed their atrocities? They knew. And the righteous nations of the world sat on their hands and did nothing."

"Sat on their fat, capitalist asses," Singer cut in. "It is all about money. It always has been and always will be."

"But they're at war now," I protested.

"Not because of us," Singer replied. "Poland shocked them. It awakened them to their vulnerability. Self-preservation is all they are concerned with. Do you think they'd fight for us, a few million dirty Jews?"

"Nobody protects us." Cukier held up his coat. "We are branded, forced to wear the Star of David, ironically a symbol of biblical glory, on every coat, jacket, and shirt we own. The world does not see this? God must even see this humiliation, but he, for whatever reason, does not send lightning down to smite our enemy as of old. No, my friends, we are totally alone."

I sat back in my chair. Singer's fatalism was contagious and weighed me down. I sought the window, a glimpse of the world outside this cell. My eyes were greeted by the plywood planks that had been nailed to the inside frame per the Chairman's orders.

"We should stop discussing this," Cukier said. "It does us no good. Engineer, will you kindly type our first entries?"

"I'm not a typist sir." I mimed using my two index fingers on an invisible keyboard.

"Then you will make less noise on the keys," Rosenfeld said.

"And don't forget to use the carbon paper to make copies," Cukier added.

"We should print our work for the world to see." Singer said.

Cukier handed me the box of carbon paper. "Let us be grateful for what we are able to do." He coughed.

"My son, you must take better care of yourself," Rosenfeld said, a look of concern on his face.

Cukier laughed. "You sound like my father."

Rosenfeld chuckled. "More like your grandfather."

We needed a laugh, so we all laughed, even Singer.

As I laughed with them, I recalled Neftalin's admonition, "Put two Jews in a room." All we need is one Singer, I thought, eyeing the typewriter and the small pile of papers at its side. "War." So little done. If only he would disappear.

CHAPTER 14

"**W**EATHER"

"*It was ten degrees below zero centigrade. No wind. Sunny.*"

Those were the first words in our record for Sunday, January 12, 1941 after a month of wrangling. Even this entry triggered a debate long after I thought it was settled: "The weather? Who needs to know the weather?" And the opposite: "The weather is a story since there is a shortage of coal and wood." So, we voted. Singer lost, and the weather won. It became the first line of many of our entries. Cruel weather was one more stone hurled at our flagging spirits.

The second item, appearing almost daily, we titled, "DEATHS AND BIRTHS."

Rosenfeld gathered the statistics from the various departments, and we took turns writing the reports, all unsigned.

Singer initially insisted we list the names of each of the deceased as well as the causes of death, but Cukier said, "Soon, there will be room for nothing else."

Rosenfeld mumbled. "Soon there will be nothing else."

"Come, Doctor," I said to lighten the mood, "This too shall pass."

Rosenfeld didn't reply. He read the entry for the day aloud: "Today 52 people died in the ghetto. The principal cause was heart disease, followed by exhaustion from hunger and the freezing cold."

"Such bullshit!"

I didn't have to guess who said that.

Singer had arrived late and hadn't even taken off his coat but was already stirring up trouble. "We all know what is killing them. We should say it, so your future readers know. Hunger and cold are the result of the damn Nazis stealing our fuel and food for themselves."

I expected Rosenfeld to reply, but he was gazing down at his hands, silent as a stone.

It was Cukier who responded, "Oscar, I think everyone knows what is causing our misery. The only people who may not agree are the Germans, and this is not the time to spell it out for them. Discretion, my friend, is essential to accomplish our goal."

I added, "We must remember our Chairman will be the one hung by our opinions if the authorities discover our work."

Cukier added, "If Rumkowski is lost then we are all lost."

Singer shook his head. "This is a waste of time. I'm not sure about any of this."

"None of us are," I said, "but what choices are there?"

Rosenfeld nodded. "And at least we had fourteen kinder newly born, seven boys and seven girls. That is something, is it not? Children are God's blessing, even in dire times. Bless these new arrivals. Amen."

"Yes, children are a blessing," I said, still haunted by Miriam's words after we made love. I returned to my typing, one finger at a time. "Stinky old typewriter," I cursed the black-keyed monster with its loud clacking sound.

"This item is interestingly worded," Rosenfeld said.

"What item is that?" Cukier asked.

Rosenfeld read from the heading, "Demands Made by Members of the Order Service."

"The superior bastards want even more?" Singer asked.

Rosenfeld read the memo: "As if they don't get better than everyone, the members of the Order Service sent a delegation to headquarters to petition for improvements in conditions, food and fuel supplements, wage increases, and so on." He looked at me. "I'm quoting Deputy Neftalin."

Singer closed his eyes. "And so on and so on and so on. It's his own personal army so he should not complain about them demanding more. He created the monster."

"You didn't read far enough." Cukier gave Singer a disapproving look. "The petition was rejected by the Chairman. You see, he refuses to grant special privileges to even the police." He shook the paper at Singer. "Our esteemed leader understands the need for equal treatment. No one is better than the rest."

Rosenfeld shook his head. "Cukier, you are naïve. Look at the last sentences the Deputy submitted: "To ease the lot of the Order Service, the commandant promised to make an effort to enlarge the police mess halls so they can serve the families of the policemen as well."

"That's more than two thousand meals, three times a day," I exclaimed, always the mathematician.

Singer grabbed the page. "They snuck that in at the end so nobody would notice. And we must write to support this unequal treatment? Bullshit! It is favoritism. We should condemn it."

"We are not here to voice opinions, or we may not be here at all," Cukier said.

"So, we simply turn a blind eye to Rumkowski's Gestapo?" Singer asked.

"Singer, you go too far," Cukier warned.

"Listen, Oscar, Rumkowski created this force because the Germans ordered it. The police are Jews like us, forced to wear armbands with Stars of David, reminders that they are nothing but Jews." Rosenfeld said.

Cukier reached for the memo. "Our police protect law-abiding citizens against the criminal elements. If you do not commit crimes, you have nothing to fear from them."

"They have clubs," Singer interrupted. "Is that to protect citizens as well?" He mimed smashing a club on my head.

Cukier threw up his hands. "What is wrong with you? Why is

everything an argument?" He coughed. "Think what the hell you like." He pulled a paper over his face and coughed behind it.

"Their clubs are rubber," I said, taking up the battle for Cukier. "Just like the rest of us the police are forbidden any weapons that could be turned against the authorities."

Rosenfeld placed his hand on Singer's arm. "Think, my young friend, without the police, it would be the Nazis patrolling our streets. The Jewish police force is the far lesser of two evils."

"So, you admit having Jewish police clopping people over the head, even with rubber clubs, is evil?" Singer hopped on Rosenfeld's words.

Rosenfeld smiled sadly. "Such a fighter you are, Singer. Yes, I admit Jews policing Jews, using violence of any kind against our brothers and sisters, is wrong. But I see Rumkowski's point. There is nothing worse than the Nazis."

Cukier said, "Enough, we move on."

"I have something to share," I began.

"I have a news item," Singer interrupted. "If you don't mind?"

Annoyed he'd cut me off, but tired of arguing, I waved him on.

Singer began in a melodramatic style, "Oscar Singer, life-long socialist, was on his way to work at the Jewish Ghetto Administration office when…" He paused, biting his lip, but steeled himself and said, "When he heard someone saying Kaddish, the prayer we chant after someone dies. And… and… as if God threw him from the sky, a body crashed to the ground a few feet away from the cynical Singer."

"Oh, God." Someone exclaimed in our barren room. It could have been me. I don't know.

Our young radical had a pained look in his eyes as he continued, "I don't know what to do with this story." He picked up his pad and read, "Further investigation revealed one Abram Nozycki threw himself to the pavement from a fourth story window at 2 Marynaska Street." He looked up into Rosenfeld's eyes. "Abram is eighteen years old. Eighteen."

"Did he survive?" I asked after none of us spoke for several long seconds.

Singer looked at me with sad eyes and replied, "I was paralyzed. I saw the crushed, broken…" He read from the sheet again, "The emergency physicians arrived. They tried to treat him. One said, "We can't waste our supplies."

"Oh, God," I heard again. This time it was Rosenfeld.

Singer put down the page and said to Julian, "I wanted to curse that medic, but no words came. I was too shaken, still seeing the body falling like a missile toward me." He wiped his face. "I asked the medics, "Where are you taking him?" "What does it matter?" the same fool replied."" He paused. "I ask you, my friends, what does Oscar Singer, the great social advocate, write about this boy to our future generations?" He surveyed our faces. "You don't answer? I don't know either. What should we write when one of us decides enough is enough?" He raised his eyes to the faded ceiling as if asking God for help.

"Eighteen? Does anyone know why he did it?" I asked, not knowing what I could say to console Oscar.

"Are you joking?" Singer glared at me. "He isn't the first, and he won't be the last. Every one of these poor souls should be a clarion call to our plight. Don't you see what is happening?" He threw something on the table. "I stole it from the corpse. Nobody else will know who he is. He lived a nobody, and the poor boy will be buried as a nobody. We all are."

"His parents. You must tell them."

Singer replied, "They're dead. Don't you think I checked?"

Rosenfeld glanced at the identification card, not touching it, as if it was some sort of booby trap. "It is painful to believe that a slip of paper, a few words, is the sum of an eighteen- year old's life. Surely his death should mean something."

Singer replied, "No, Professor, this boy will be but one more number in our list. As you say, just give the facts as they come to you. But from the sky? He fell from the sky." He raised his hand and then let it drop down slowly as if it were a leaf gliding down languidly from a tree.

Rosenfeld's voice was tender. "It is over. Singer, my friend, there is nothing more we can do for this tragic lad."

"I agree with the good doctor," I said. "But there is something in your tragic story we're overlooking."

They all looked at me, perhaps hoping I could make sense of the unfathomable suicide of a young man who in other times would have so much for which to live. "This incident shows the correct thinking of our leadership."

Singer erupted. "How does it show that? A teenage boy killed himself!"

The other's faces showed disbelief as well.

"It is a dreadful tragedy, of course, but the fact is that Rumkowski's emergency service arrived to try and save him."

"What the hell?" Singer looked ready to leap over the table and pound my head into a pulp.

"Don't you see? This proves the emergency service and the morgue are functioning. These are positives that we should include in this tragic story."

"Positives?" Singer looked stunned.

I forced myself to be calm as I defended my position. "It will be reassuring to our people to know that our leader is keeping things functioning. It may prevent others from emulating this poor boy's behavior."

Singer snarled, "Fine! A boy jumps from a building and almost lands on me, and creative journalists, guardians of truth, that we are, we exploit his tragedy to extol the virtues of our government?"

Cukier interceded before Singer had the chance to strike me. "I sympathize with your feelings, but our engineer is right. We have no choice. We don't know why your boy did this, so to blame anyone is pointless."

I grabbed a pen and was writing furiously. "I have written the entry.

"A SUICIDE ATTEMPT": Eighteen- year old Abram Nozycki of 21 Zgierska Street threw himself to the pavement from the window of a fourth floor at 2 Marynarska Street. The emergency physician arriving at the scene determined that Nozycki suffered injuries and after applying first aid brought him to Hospital No. 1 in critical condition."

"I never said that," Singer interrupted.

"The medics would have taken him to the hospital. It's standard procedure. We don't know if he died. Do we?"

Singer closed his eyes. "I don't care anymore. Write what you will."

The rest of the day, we barely spoke.

As I walked home, not only was I on the look-out for Gestapo and Jewish police, but I kept a wary eye on the rooftops of our crumbling buildings.

CHAPTER 15

I was in the conference room, thinking about my rough night with Miriam while the others were working.

The door opened.

A glance at the others told me they were staring at the entry as well. The German ghetto administrators, the Gestapo, could storm in any time they wanted. It was why we had to be careful about what we wrote.

A Jewish policeman entered the room like a hulking black-coated shadow. He stood in the entryway eyeing us with unmasked disdain. "This is from the Eldest of the Jews," he announced in a loud voice. "He wants it included in your work "ver-ba-tim." Those are his exact words."

"That is what it means," I said.

"What what means?" He asked.

"Verbatim."

"Those are his exact words." The hulk replied. "I don't care what they mean. Just do it."

"That means exactly as written," I said, feeling a bit smug.

The officer snorted and handed the document to me, being I was closest. "Verbatim," he repeated and left the room.

"Pleasant fellow," Singer remarked.

I wanted to remind him that the officer was merely doing his job, but what was the point? Singer was a wall. If the Chairman had made any mistakes in his selections; I knew one. I perused the notice. "They're issuing yet another ration card. The announcement says, "it's

79

more substantial because it includes a small number of vegetables.""
I smiled. "Good news for a change."

"I'll bet there's a catch," Singer remarked. "What else does it say?"
I tossed it to him.

Singer read silently then said, "I love the last line: "This proclamation was received very favorably by the populace." How does he
know that? I'm not receiving it that favorably."

"It appears the Chairman is not only the author but also the critic
now," Rosenfeld said, rubbing his hands together.

"Be that as it may, you heard what the officer said." Cukier took
the report from Singer and handed it to me. "Type it verbatim." He
chuckled. "Is there anything else any of you feel we should include?"

Rosenfeld raised his hand. "Yesterday there was another large
demonstration for food and fuel. Shall I write about it?"

"There are protests every day," I said, thinking of the scraggly lot in
our square.

"This is different, Engineer. There has not been a mass demonstration since September," Singer said. "What a mess that one was."

Cukier frowned. "I know where you're going with this. But go
ahead. He may as well understand."

I hated being left in the dark. "Okay, what happened in September?"

Rosenfeld's voice dropped to a whisper. "What was supposed to be
a peaceful protest was taken over by criminal agitators."

Singer snarled, "That's what they said after it was over. I tell you,
they're not all criminals despite what our leader says."

Rosenfeld buttoned his coat. "Perhaps. But Rumkowski claimed he
was ordered by the Germans to end the demonstrations."

"He sent his damn goons to break up the crowd. I was there," Singer
said.

"May I finish my story, Dr. Singer?" Rosenfeld shot him an annoyed
look. "The Jewish Police surrounded Balut Square. The protesters
refused to disperse. The crowd grew larger. Our police swung their
clubs in the air, as a warning. The demonstrators still wouldn't obey."

Singer pointed his pen. "Why should they? There is nothing wrong with exercising freedom of speech."

Rosenfeld sounded exasperated. "This is war. When the crowd ignored the police, the inevitable happened. Without warning, squads of the German police assaulted the mob."

"The sonofabitches shot at us," Singer shouted. "We had no weapons!"

"Quiet, Singer. Let the good doctor finish? We don't want others to hear us." Cukier checked the door.

Rosenfeld sucked in his cheeks. "He's right. The German police shot into the crowd. People were wounded. Some killed."

"Rumkowski called them in," Singer hissed.

Rosenfeld shook his head. "Nobody knows who called the Germans in, but the lesson was learned. There have not been any large disturbances since."

"Demonstrations," Singer corrected.

Cukier cut in, "And it must remain so, or the wolves will intercede again. That is the crux of the matter."

I sat back. The Germans fired on a peaceful demonstration. Rumkowski was right: If the Germans saw we could not control our people, they would not hesitate to step in any way they chose.

Cukier reached past Singer and handed me a draft of a new entry he called, "STREET DEMONSTRATION." I soon understood why he had not delegated it to our young radical. I even had trouble accepting what I was typing: "It is worth noting that since the September incidents, there has not been a single instance of the peace being disturbed in the ghetto." There was no mention of the German police wounding and killing people in the September riots. I read on: "It has been determined beyond question that this action was organized by irresponsible individuals, intent on disturbing the peace and public order created by the authorities who watch over the law, safety, and food supplies of the ghetto dwellers."

Singer was reading over my shoulder. "Engineer, do they really think every person who dares speak up against what is happening to us is an irresponsible individual, a criminal, a Communist, or an ungrateful immigrant? What hogwash!"

My head was throbbing again. "Please let me read undisturbed?" When I finished, I looked at Cukier. "Julian, do you really want me to lay the blame on some unknown group of agitators when we don't know who instigated this?"

"Verbatim," Cukier said and turned back to his papers.

I continued typing but stopped cold when I read, "Several times, the crowd attempted to steal food that was being transported by a wagon but was thwarted by the heroic stance taken by the Order Service. Peace was completely restored by the afternoon." I glanced at Singer. He was watching, challenging me, waiting for me to do something. I did. I finished typing the entry. I handed the completed article to Cukier.

He read it in silence. "You don't like this, do you, Engineer?"

"It is not my place to question an order." He was my superior and provided Miriam and me the little we had.

Cukier placed the typed page on top of our small stack of completed work. "I have another story for you. Perhaps it will help all of us understand why we must support our government. He read loudly, "A crowd of a few hundred residents demolished a wooden shed at 67 Brzesinska Street. While the wood was being stolen, the roof of the shed collapsed."

Singer broke in, "They're desperate. They steal whatever wood they can for heat. The Germans are taking it all. So, they destroyed a shed. Not a big deal."

Cukier looked at Singer. "I was there."

Singer looked surprised.

Cukier continued, "I was walking home when I heard screams from across the street. A teenage boy, arms holding bits of wood, rushed by. I grabbed him. "What is happening?" I asked. He said several people who were sleeping in the shed were trapped in the rubble.

Do not interrupt, Singer," Cukier snapped, and continued, "I heard more cries. Coming closer..." He paused, a sad expression on his face. "I heard pitiful cries for help." He looked at me. "Even hearing desperate pleas, no one in the crowd came to their aid." He let this sink in. "The robbery continued."

"They're desperate," Singer said, but without his usual conviction.

"Desperate. Yes. Lawless? Sadly, yes." Rosenfeld said.

Cukier coughed into his handkerchief.

"What did you do?" Singer asked.

Singer didn't have his usual smug expression nor accusatory tone. I wondered what I would I have done if I had been Cukier.

"I went home." Cukier swallowed hard. "I left. I did nothing to help. It was a mob."

"You were right to not risk your life," I said, reminding myself that Miriam had to be my first concern.

"Can one man stand against a mob?" Rosenfeld said, staring woefully at his empty pipe.

Singer was silent.

Cukier put his hands flat on the table. "Today, I learned a young woman was killed."

"That's terrible," I said. "In the mob?"

Cukier shook his head. "In the shed. She was thirty-six years old. Her name was Frania Szanik. I didn't know her. Two others may not live." He aimed his eyes at Singer. "I saw this with my own eyes. It answered every doubt I had. I am convinced, one hundred percent, that lawlessness will explode without strict enforcement. No matter how we may personally feel, we must support law and order, or all will be chaos. My good friends, our fellow Jews, did this, for scraps of wood."

"They are desperate," Singer repeated. "It isn't their fault. It's the Germans."

"Desperate people do desperate things," Rosenfeld responded and jotted it down.

Two and two equals four, I thought, grateful Miriam was safe at home.

"Julian is right," Rosenfeld said, waving his empty pipe in his hand. "We must present a united front against the criminals, or none will be safe. The people need a strong ruler. Think Julius Caesar, Alexander the Great, Napoleon..."

"And Hitler?"

Rosenfeld and Cukier scowled at Singer. I did too.

Cukier slid his hand-written entry across the table. "Please, type this as is."

I typed Cukier's report word for word, but added a rare personal comment, which I read to the others before laying the entry to rest: "This lamentable instance of moral savagery, a direct result of agitation by lawless elements, clearly illustrates the necessity for an all-out struggle against the parasites of the underworld."

"You're becoming quite a writer," Cukier said. "Well done."

Singer jumped up from his chair. "This is what we've become?" He waved a sheet of paper he'd pulled from the pile on the table. "Just listen to this: "Appearing before the Order Service, an eight-year-old boy filed a report against his parents!"

"His parents? What on Earth for?" Rosenfeld asked.

Singer laughed. "Wait, it gets better. This son charged his parents with not giving him his bread ration. Can you imagine? This boy reported his parents to the police!"

"What did the police do?" I asked.

"The boy demanded a full investigation. He demanded that the guilty parties be punished." Singer handed me the paper. "I'd think it was a joke, but it's not funny. Soon, we'll all be thieves, spies, and worse.

Cukier burst into laughter. "Listen to this police report: "The residents of a building found themselves in a disconcerting situation when, after waking up, they discovered that during the night unknown culprits had stolen their stairs." He looked at us. "Imagine waking up and finding your stairs are missing."

I imagined naked men and women rising from their beds only to find their stairs had been stolen during the night. I could almost hear the cursing and screaming for help. I wished I'd been there when they told the police: "We were making love upstairs and heard nothing. When we awoke, we discovered our stairs were gone." I laughed and laughed. How ridiculous! How insane! But when I stopped laughing. I realized it wasn't humorous.

Cukier said, "We all needed a laugh."

Was it funny, I thought, as I added it to my typing pile. Was anything that was happening to us funny?

CHAPTER 16

I was walking out of the administration building five weeks after beginning our work. After my frightening encounters with Jewish and German police, I made it my business not to run. The Germans had confiscated all our wagons, pushcarts and horses, and stopped our trams and buses, so the streets were silent. I heard footsteps.

I searched the street. Was I being pursued? Was I out past the curfew? Jews were prohibited from the streets from seven p.m. to eight in the morning. Cukier always released us from the Archives in plenty of time to get home.

The footsteps were closer.

I turned the corner and ducked into an alley.

He followed me.

"Why are you following me?" I cowered against the wall, holding up my arm to fend off a policeman's club, a robber's knife. "Leave me alone."

A long black coat and hat. Gestapo?

I peered up to see a face hidden by a fedora, brim pulled down. "Rosenfeld? You scared me half to death," I said, catching my breath. "Don't you know it's dangerous to follow someone like that?"

He looked up the narrow alley. "I'm sorry, Engineer. I need to talk to someone...to you."

"We can talk tomorrow. Curfew begins soon." What was wrong with him? Why was he shaking? "Doctor, are you ill?"

Rosenfeld signaled me to step into a nearby doorway. "I'm ill of heart and soul, my friend. I don't sleep."

"It is difficult to sleep in these hard times." I glanced out the doorway, wishing I was closer to home.

"Do you believe in luck? I know you don't believe in God."

"This is a hell of a time to debate my faith. We should be going home."

"Something happened which I don't know how to deal with."

I thought of our eldest member as capable of dealing with any problem, so I was curious. "Please make it fast? Miriam will worry."

"Yes, you are lucky to have someone to worry over you." He glanced into the street. "I shall make it fast, and perhaps, if you are kind enough, you will think about what I'm sharing with you and offer me some solution." He lowered his voice. "A few weeks ago, the eighteenth of October to be exact, I was to meet some of my friends—we usually met once a week—at any rate, I was delayed by a Jewish policeman."

"That can be frightening." I had a flashback of my own encounter.

"It turned out it was fortunate."

"I don't understand."

"Have you heard of the Astoria Café?"

"I'm new in the ghetto." I was impatient and fearful of being out past the curfew, but he looked so upset, rare for the wise owl in our little club.

Rosenfeld removed his hat and wiped his brow. "The Astoria was a meeting place for our artists, the intelligentsia. You could go there and solve all the world's problems, debate with the great minds of the ghetto."

"I thought the great minds were all in our stuffy chamber," I joked. Rosenfeld didn't laugh.

"Doctor, please? I must get home before the curfew."

"Ah yes, the curfew. There was no curfew then, so we sat and enjoyed our chats about what was best for humanity. But I was delayed that evening. As luck would have it, of all nights, I was stopped by a policeman."

"You've said that already."

He gave me a sad look. "When I approached the café, perhaps a quarter hour late, I heard screaming. There were the sounds of something banging, perhaps chairs, tables, and glass breaking. I thought at first some of my friends had taken their philosophical differences too far, but then I felt a chill and saw them." Rosenfeld paused, rechecking the alley. "I hid behind a stanchion on the opposite side of the street because I saw black cars, trucks, and uniformed men. They were SS, rifles in their hands, driving out everyone from the café. There must have been one hundred Jews. Mostly men, but some women too. Some were holding their heads, blood on their hands."

"They were beaten?"

Rosenfeld nodded. "The SS men were laughing as they pushed the crowd down the street, shouting orders, cursing in their crude language, striking those that lagged behind with rifle butts and their boots."

"These were your friends?" I remembered how Miriam and I were attacked and taunted as we were chased into the ghetto. I still woke up sweating with nightmares of that night.

Rosenfeld nodded. "Yes, I was one of them. But I was delayed by a Jewish policeman."

"What happened to them...to your friends?"

"I never saw them again."

"This happened this past October?"

"October eighteen. I thought the Germans were playing with them, teasing the intellectuals, frightening them. A few, the very rich, were given the opportunity to buy their freedom. One found me. "Where were you?" He cursed me for not being there with the others. "Did you know? Is that why you weren't there?" He screamed at me."

"He thought you knew? He thought you were an informant?"

"I suppose. Yes, that makes sense. Of course, I knew nothing. It was pure luck, and that idiot policeman, that saved me."

"Thank God! What happened to the others, the ones that could not bribe their captors?"

Rosenfeld shivered and wiped his brow again. "Once my wealthy friend believed me, he told me that he, and the few others who bought their freedom, were forced to dig..." Rosenfeld choked.

"Dig what? What did he say?"

Rosenfeld swallowed hard. "My friend had tears in his eyes. "Doctor, you won't believe what I am telling you. We were forced to dig holes, wide holes. They were mass graves for the others."

I froze. "Mass graves?"

Rosenfeld nodded. "Of course, I did not believe him. The Germans are among the most cultured people on Earth. Musicians, artists, philosophers...how could such a civilized nation become so barbaric? Engineer, do you know the answer to this? I do not."

"It doesn't make sense that the Germans would let your friend live after witnessing this."

"He says after he dug the hole, he was chased away. He claims he heard rifles repeatedly firing as he fled the forest. He ran and never looked back."

"Oh, God. Do you believe him?"

"I have not seen my friends since that night. What am I to believe?"

I stared at Rosenfeld. The dignified professor was reduced to a trembling old man in a dark alley. What could I say to him? What could I tell myself? If this was true, it was a hint of what was to come, a bitter taste of what Hitler's hatred for us was capable of unleashing. "My friend, does the Chairman know of this atrocity? Have you told anyone?"

Rosenfeld mumbled something and then, out of the blue, said, "I must go. I must go."

"Have you told Rumkowski? Does he know?"

"Don't you understand?"

"What? What?" I tried to think calmly, always the engineer. Two and two make four.

"There were Elders in the café that night. All were taken. All the other Elders were taken."

A lightning bolt shot through me.

"We all heard the rumors, all unconfirmed. But one fact emerged: Rumkowski became the unquestioned power in the ghetto when the original members of the Council of Elders vanished."

I thought back to my first meeting with the man some called the devil, king, and Emperor of Lodz. I could see his face before me, sharp features, dark, eyes, piercing. I could see his body enlarged by that thick tweed coat, hair overflowing his felt hat. I heard the whispers, "He's the devil. He's the devil." But no Jew, surely not our leader, was capable of what Rosenfeld was insinuating. No human was capable of being so without conscience. "I don't believe he could do this," I said.

"Engineer, you of all people, believe in coincidence?"

"No."

"Nor do I. I want to scream out the truth, but I don't know the truth. I want to rail against the Nazis who could do such things. I want to raise my voice and sing Kaddish for my friends who died in the forest."

"You can't do that. The authorities would silence you. Neftalin is right about that. Cukier, dear Cukier, is right too. My friend, we must stay alive to preserve what is happening. We need your wise head and caring heart."

"But it's all a lie! Rumkowski says we are a "smooth-running machine," but how smooth can we be if the wolves can remove us at will? The Astoria was a demonstration of their power. They wanted a puppet government here. Oh God, what can I do? Engineer, what can I do? I am so confused. I live with this in silence every day. I feel such guilt."

"Guilt that you survived?"

"Luck saved me."

"God saved you. He wants you to complete the task at hand. Perhaps, someday you will be able to raise your voice, once the war is over, which with God's help, will be soon. But for now, you should not feel guilty because God chose you to live."

Rosenfeld laughed bitterly. "So, like most men who profess to be atheists, you believe, when push comes to shove, in God? How ironic, that when God does not hear our supplications, is blind to the horrors we are facing, the most rational of men, those who deny him the loudest, appeal loudest to his deaf ears."

It was true. I was reaching for the God I never believed in. How can a builder of buildings and bridges acknowledge there is a builder greater than all of mankind? "I only said this because you are a believer," I lied. "It is natural to say the words. It does not mean you are a believer."

"It doesn't matter. Nothing you say can assuage my guilt that first, I escaped the fate of my friends, and second, I must remain silent. Is there nothing else you can offer to help me?"

I dug deep into my mental pockets but came up empty. The terror he described was unreal, impossible to accept. I could give no absolution for his confession. I was stunned by the revelation, horrified by his accusation.

Rosenfeld pulled his coat collar up around his neck. "I must write this for our Chronicle. It is the least I can do to honor my friends."

"You can't. Rumkowski reads it every day. The day will come, soon, I pray, when you will stand in the courts and bear witness against the Germans, the true culprits, to what happened to your friends. But, my dear doctor, that day is not now. We all have our secrets that must be hidden until the day we are liberated. And that is what this incident must be for now."

"You are a cold thinker, Engineer. I shall try to become one as well. I just don't know if I can live with this, this guilt, this silence. It goes against my nature."

Before I could reply, he was gone, a shadow rushing to his lonely home.

I gazed up at the stars. I had to hurry. Curfew. I didn't run. I didn't dare. I now knew that the Germans were not afraid to kill. There had been at least one confirmed incident, a mass murder. Were there more? Did Rumkowski know? He knew everything going on in the ghetto. How could he not know?

That night, I kept Rosenfeld's secret secure from my Miriam. I ate in silence, dark thoughts reappearing like racing clouds in my brain. That night, when we lay in our bed, a night when I could not make love to my wife, I curled up against her. It was I who felt like a child, terrified of sleep, fearful I would hear the screams of a hundred people who had been out for a night of friendly amusement, a cold drink, a rare respite from the realities of ghetto life. And as they enjoyed a few moments of escaping their harsh reality, they were interrupted by the brutality of a Nazi raid, followed by a forced march into the forest. Not knowing their fate, devoured by uncertainty, disbelieving what was happening, they were lined up in front of massive holes they recognized for what they were. But perhaps did not believe, could not imagine, these shallow pits would be their graves. It was a terrifying image, a haunting panorama. I'd forgotten to ask Rosenfeld if they'd been killed in their clothes, or were forced to stand, no, parade, naked before their own graves. I'd forgotten to ask Rosenfeld how the few who escaped managed to pay for their freedom.

The clouds kept darkening my brain as I lay against Miriam's back, my hand resting on her belly. It was hours later that her words came back to me, "How can we bring a child into a world such as this?"

In the sleepless night, I had no answer. I only knew I had to keep Rosenfeld's story away from her. I prayed the mass execution was an aberration, a solitary act of rogue violence that our leader was preventing from repeating by his policies. Proving to the Nazi wolves, they could not survive without their Jews, seemed the only strategy open to us. Solidifying his power by any means was essential to our existence. I didn't care how he acceded to his role, or what powers he assumed. I'd never want his responsibilities, the terrible choices. The more I struggled with my thoughts, the less I understood why anyone would want to walk a tightrope so treacherous between the Nazis, Poles, and the rebellious Jews. Rumkowski might have been the devil, but there is an old expression, perhaps invented by long-suffering Jews, "The devil you know is better than the devil you don't."

I ended this sleepless night, resolved, that whatever I believed about Rumkowski, I had to support him, even if it meant silencing Rosenfeld. The alleyway confession was the final nail, convincing me that this old, craggy, man, whose portrait was now hanging in every public building, was our only hope.

When Miriam turned to me in the morning, her lips pressing on my lips, she didn't know I was officially a convert, a loyal disciple of the devil of Lodz.

Two plus two equals four.

CHAPTER 17

"You're smiling," Miriam commented, serving me a bit of crumbled bread and dried pork I had smuggled from the mess hall. "Work is going better?"

I did not want to answer questions about that which I could not share with her. "And what will you do today?"

"The Izbitzka's baby needs caring. Pola suffered much giving birth. You should see the child. He's a big boy with red cheeks. It must have been painful without any drugs and available doctors."

"You will babysit again?" I remembered how long Miriam had mourned Hannah and worried she would become too attached to another child. Hungry children do not survive, and she became terribly depressed when she lost one of her babies. "Someday, you will have your own sweet baby. And more. If you wish?"

She gave me a little smile. "There is a little ersatz coffee for you."

"You may have it. Kitchen 2 has real coffee."

"Real coffee? You, civil servants, are well treated."

"We shoulder great responsibilities."

"I would not want your job. How do you decide who gets what housing? It must be difficult."

"I'm not with housing anymore. I'm with the Department of the Archives."

"Another department? Why does he need so many departments?"

"Rumkowski has departments to make our lives as comfortable as possible."

"Like his police force? Everyone says they are his personal army.

Mietek says they are his Gestapo."

"Don't believe everything you hear, especially not from that idiot. He's a trouble-maker. He's always had eyes for you." I regretted saying that. Stupid jealousy.

Miriam pushed away from the table.

"I'm sorry. I didn't mean to say that." I reached for her hand, but she dropped it in her lap. "Miriam, I'm exhausted. I don't know what the hell I'm saying." I let my eyes beg for forgiveness. "There are things you don't know, things that are happening. Please, don't listen to what some malcontents are saying? I'm part of the inner circle now."

Miriam stopped to look at me. "What does that mean?"

I was giving too much away. "I'm only a small fish. I'm new, but already I am getting a clearer picture of what our Chairman is trying to do." I reached for her hand. This time, she didn't pull away. "I believe he sincerely wants to help us."

"Some say he's protecting himself and his wealth."

I stroked her hand. "Could I work for such people? Could I? You know me, Miriam, am I the kind of man who could work for such people?"

She shook her head. "No. I don't believe you could, under normal circumstances. But if it isn't true, why do so many people say it?"

"I think, when people are frustrated, afraid, they look for a scapegoat, someone they can blame for what is happening."

"Like Hitler blames us?"

"We Jews are always given the blame. Yes, that is right. I think too many of our neighbors, especially those who lived and prospered for many years, many generations, in Lodz, blame their poor conditions on the newcomers, on us. Whose fault is that? Rumkowski, they say, because that is all they know. They are clutching at straws. It is logical. But wrong."

"Everyone knows it is the Germans who are to blame," Miriam said. "I hate them. But I also don't trust Rumkowski and his crooked family and friends. The whole system is corrupt."

"Shaa, Miriam. Don't let others hear you. They'll turn you in like a shot, and what will become of me?" I tried to smile. "But yes, you have hit the nail on the head: it is the Germans at the root of our misery. As for the other assertion, the more I work with the administrators, the more I believe they are risking their own lives to keep the ghetto safe. Yes, some do live better than others, but is this so terrible? Rumkowski sleeps in his office many nights. I can't imagine bearing his responsibility."

Miriam studied me with her dark eyes. "You were critical of him before."

"I didn't understand. Nobody who is not there can understand what it is like. It is a balancing act over a pit of swords. Rumkowski is trapped between the demands of the Germans, the Poles, and of course, our own people. It is quite a performance, and he does it all without a safety net."

"You make it sound like a circus. It probably is. You'll be late for work. I understand what you are saying. But what if he's wrong?"

"What do you mean?"

"You know how you always say, 'Two and two make four?'"

"It is how I think about things. Yes."

"What if it doesn't?"

"It always does. All science, math, and logic depend on this foundation."

Miriam frowned. "But humans are not always logical. Don't you always say that about me?"

"It's a joke, we old married men make about our wives."

"Is Hitler logical?" She didn't take my humorous bait.

"What a question. No. Maybe. I never thought about it."

"Don't you always say he's insane?"

I nodded. "But maybe there's a logic I don't understand behind seemingly crazy actions. Stick to the subject. Please?"

"Very well. If human behavior isn't always logical, then you can't say that two and two, when we discuss human actions, are always true."

I burst into laughter. "I have to get going. What's the point?" I was amused, but she had a serious expression on her face. "Go on. I'm listening."

"Your arguments about the government of the ghetto make sense, but you're basing everything on your assumption that Hitler, and the Nazi leaders, are logical, and will always adhere to your two plus two formula."

This was too much. "I surrender. My pretty, little wife, is now a philosopher and logician." I laughed.

"Please, don't make fun of me?"

"I'm sorry. I just find this charming."

Her brow furrowed. "I'm serious. Rumkowski is basing his actions on the Germans being logical. He is betting Hitler will spare us, for his benefit."

I was amazed by her astute analysis. "That's right. Only a fool will destroy that which makes him rich."

"Yes. But what if he's wrong? What if Hitler is so insane that he will destroy even those things that benefit him and Germany?"

"You're driving me crazy. Nobody is that insane."

"You always say he is."

She had me on that. "Okay. Let us say Rumkowski is wrong, what other options are there?"

"I'm just your pretty wife," Miriam said. "You already know the options."

"I don't see any."

"Fight them," Miriam said in a low voice. "Resist. Get weapons. Sabotage them at every turn."

Was this my wife? She sounded like Singer. "We can't fight them. We'll lose. You don't know, my innocent one. We have no army, weapons, training. We're totally sealed off from the rest of Poland, the rest of the world. We'll all die. Is that logical?" Where had this idea come from? Was it her own? Who was she listening to while

I was at work? Mietek had shown interest in her and was always spouting off such nonsense. No, she would never see him. It wasn't proper. Her upbringing was too strict. What was I thinking? Miriam would never betray me with anyone.

Miriam smiled. "But you see, my dear husband, some of our neighbors say Rumkowski has chosen the wrong answer. Instead of obeying the Nazis, doing their dirty work, we should be obstructing them, forcing them to divert their military and treasury with every ounce of our strength, with every bit of our ingenuity."

She looked so passionate, but on impulse, I grabbed her toward me. "Oh, Miriam, my child, I love you." I held her tightly, her head against my chest, trying to keep her from speaking such dangerous ideas. "I love when you talk about these things. You are truly adorable."

She pulled away. "You're making fun of me again."

"No. Of course not." The truth is I was. I really wasn't paying much attention to her arguments, nor did I see her lips quiver and her face become determined. "You know," I said, "If I didn't have to go to work today, I would grab you in my arms, carry you to bed and show you how much I love every word you said." I kissed her forehead and wishing I could stay, said, "Who do you get your ideas from?" Laughing, I hurried through the door.

It wasn't until days later that I'd recall the strange look on her face just before I kissed her good-bye.

CHAPTER 18

"There is something we must discuss," Cukier said.

The work was going a little more smoothly, fewer arguments, less tension, a growing tolerance. I was, more, or less, resigned to typing and getting a little faster with my 'hunt and peck' at the keyboard. Incredibly, Singer seemed a little less obnoxious as well.

"We need to address the resettlements," Cukier continued. "As you know, the Chairman considers this a crucial matter."

"It's a difficult subject," Rosenfeld said, no longer wearing his coat and scarf as if ready to bound out of the room at the slightest provocation. "Some greet this relocation of segments of our population with relief since the people who are leaving us are mostly immigrants and volunteers."

Singer sounded surprisingly calm when he asked, "Am I correct the Germans asked the Chairman for a list of fifty thousand Jews who were to leave Lodz?"

Cukier nodded. "Yes. But that was way back in November of '39." Ages ago."

"And he supplied them their fifty thousand?" I asked, getting a flashback of the chairman, looking like an old man, as he labored over papers on his desk the first morning that I saw him. Is that what he was working on? What did he say to me that day? "Can you deal with their hate?" I shuddered. Could I designate human beings to leave the ghetto?

Cukier replied, "He told me that he had negotiated with the

authorities that the list would be of volunteers only. My God, he offered each volunteer fifty zlotys from the ghetto treasury."

I breathed a sigh of relief. "So, everyone who left was a volunteer."

"No," Singer jumped in. He looked at Cukier. "That's not true. The German police took over when there were not enough volunteers. It was brutal. All the people who lived on Zgierska and Lagiewnicka Streets were forced from their homes. Kosciuszko Boulevard, named after the great general who helped the Americans in their war for independence, a hero to the Poles, was emptied. That is what happened."

Cukier coughed into his handkerchief.

Rosenfeld said, "Singer is correct. The Germans stepped in." He pulled his pipe from his teeth. "All the people to be resettled were herded with only the clothes on their backs to the railroad station. I saw them. A pitiful sight walking through our streets." He looked at his hands. "I hid. We all hid. No reason, but it is as you say, the devil you know."

Singer nodded in agreement. "I was told they were loaded into cattle cars. There were hundreds per car."

I was shocked. "Where were these hundreds of people taken?" I asked, doubting they were cattle cars. Singer's artistic license. Mathematically, moving hundreds of people would take an enormous number of train cars. No, it was impossible.

Rosenfeld looked thoughtfully at the empty bowl of his pipe, and said, "We were told by the Chairman they were being resettled in rural towns in northern Poland."

Singer frowned. "Nobody cared much since we were overcrowded. Food and fuel were in short supply. Most of the deportees were foreigners anyway, and the originals didn't care what happened to them."

Rosenfeld pointed his pipe at me. "I think most people felt these immigrants were to be housed here temporarily anyway. As I've said before, the Lodz residents needed someone to blame for their hardships, so the removal of a few immigrants was a relief, even if we found the German methods of recruiting disconcerting."

"That's an understatement," Singer said.

"He's right," Rosenfeld agreed.

Cukier nodded. "We expected more deportations. Some hoped for more, but for some reason, the Germans never demanded more than the original fifty thousand. Our Chairperson told me he believed he had been successful in convincing the authorities that our workers had to remain in Lodz or Germany would lose a valuable supplier."

"I expect," Rosenfeld said, sounding like the college professor he was, "the Germans realized that moving Jews, hither and yon, to new homes, even if they needed more labor in other areas, was a huge expense during war."

"Thank you, Professor," Singer said. "Don't you understand? The Germans hate Jews. If they want to take over Lodz's industries for their war effort, they will find a way to relocate as many of us as they want. This is just a lull. Don't fool yourselves. No matter what our Chairman believes, Germans will never find Jews indispensable. We will all eventually be moved to the coldest and most barren farmlands in the north." He laughed. "I can't imagine us as farmers."

Rosenfeld studied Singer, thumbing his pipe bowl. "If Singer is right, and they plan to someday restart these resettlements from Lodz, having Jews all locked up in a walled-up area would certainly make it easy, when they are ready, to move us."

Cukier sighed. "We were free to live anywhere in Lodz until the ghetto was established."

"I thought it was established long ago, like the villages Jews settled in throughout Europe," I said.

Rosenfeld thought back. "I know the Lodz chief of police, whatever his name was– Johannes Schafer—I can't believe I remember that one but can't recall what I ate for breakfast this morning—my memory is not as good as it was–ordered its establishment in February of 1940."

"So, you were all ordered to move here then?" I again thought to how we had five minutes to pack up and were hounded through the gates by the jeering Poles and German residents of the city.

"Ordered? We were pulled out of our homes throughout the city and terrorized to relocate here, most without possessions." Rosenfeld replied. "We called it, Bloody Thursday."

Cukier spoke softly, "They shot hundreds of us in the streets, even in our homes. The damn German police and SS shot everyone they found. Some SS were in uniforms, but many others wore civilian clothes. We ran into the ghetto to escape the madness."

"Then the bastards ordered the Jewish quarter to be sealed." Singer said. "It was the dirtiest, most neglected part of the city. We had no facilities, water pipes or sewerage. It was a slum. Look around you. It still is."

Rosenfeld said, "Some 200,000 of us were squeezed like worms into this horrible hole."

My math brain was working. "How many kilometers is the ghetto?" I asked.

Cukier shook his head. "You and your math. For once I agree with Singer. What is important to know is that 15 to 20 people were living in one room. It was horrible."

Rosenfeld sighed. "Yes, it was, but we were grateful to be alive."

"Like I said, they wanted all their fish in one pond so they can catch us in one sweep of their net," Singer replied. "They're shrewd bastards."

Cukier coughed and then said, "Let us hope young Singer is wrong. Nobody can manage what he is suggesting. It's humanly impossible."

Rosenfeld said, "Amen."

Cukier nodded. "I almost forgot why I brought the resettlements up. Neftalin wants me to remind you that we must do everything possible to record any more of these resettlements."

"Did the Chairman receive more orders for deportation?" Singer asked, looking alarmed.

"No. Not at all. Our leader just wants us prepared to get any potential incidents in our records without the German authorities knowing about it." Cukier coughed again.

"How can we include the fact that 50,000 of us were taken for resettlement without saying exactly that?" Singer asked.

"I don't know," Cukier replied. "I only know what my superior has requested."

"It seems to me the Germans accomplished an amazing feat," I said, after studying this shifting of populations.

"What the hell are you talking about?" Singer asked.

"What are you talking about, Engineer?" Cukier held his hand up to quiet Singer who looked poised to take a poke at me.

I showed them a worksheet. "Think about it as an engineer."

"I'd rather remain human," Singer said.

"I am human, but that doesn't mean I can't assess a thing objectively."

"You evaluate this atrocity objectively. I prefer to get drunk," Singer said.

Cukier looked annoyed at Singer. "Tell me, Ostrowski, "What are you talking about?"

I pulled another sheet of paper from my briefcase, battered from our escape to the ghetto. "This ghetto was selected by the Germans for a good reason. It is the most neglected part of greater Lodz. Is it not?"

"It's a shithole," Singer said. "We all know that."

"Thank you. I was about to get to that. The ghetto within the barbed wire is about 11 kilometers in total area, four square kilometers habitable." I pulled out a chart I'd made.

"You're not telling us something we don't know," Singer said.

"Stop being rude," Cukier admonished. "The Engineer has clearly done his homework. Let's hear him out."

"Thank you. In the ghetto, we have, approximately 32,000 apartments, but what you didn't say is that most of these have only one room. And that only seven hundred and twenty-five have running water."

"That is why we all smell so lovely," Singer mumbled.

I ignored him since Cukier punished him with another glare. "Additionally, most apartments do not have electricity."

Singer laughed. "It doesn't matter, we're not allowed to use lights from eight P.M. to 6 A.M. anyway. And without food and fuel, electricity? Shit, that's the last thing we should worry about."

I was becoming irritated with our young friend again. "I fully agree with you, but here's the amazing part. In all of Lodz, there were approximately 200 thousand Jews, and every one of them was poured into this ghetto within a relatively short period. In strictly objective terms, this was a logistical and organizational puzzle of immense magnitude the Germans solved."

"The forced relocation of masses of innocent men, women, and children is not something I want to celebrate. It is sick." Singer said.

"Yes. But do you realize the Germans engineered the relocation of fifty thousand Jews in mere months? Do you understand the planning and logistics of such a move? I would not be surprised if it is unprecedented in human history."

Singer slammed his hand on the table making Rosenfeld jump out of his seat. "Engineer, the German tools for this miracle of yours are intimidation and violence. And they had help from the Chairman and his Jewish Service Order, those self-serving bastards. That's me being objective."

Cukier rose from his seat. "Singer, calm down. Ostrowski is just being himself." He gave me a slight smile.

"Everyone knows the Nazis are bastards," Singer replied, "But that doesn't excuse our Jewish police force for doing the Nazi's dirty work."

"Perhaps you would prefer a trip to the Kripo headquarters?" Cukier sounded as if he was losing his patience.

I interrupted. "Am I correct that the Shutz are the guards at the ghetto entrance, while the Kripo are the criminal police within the ghetto?"

Cukier replied, "Basically yes. The Kripo are headquartered in a parish building, the Church of the Most Blessed Virgin Mary."

"Nothing religious or virginal about that place," Singer said. "The cellars are now prison cells and the Germans torture captives there. They call it the Red House. Some say because the bricks are red, but you can imagine for yourself why it is called that."

I shivered at the image of young Jews, any humans, being tortured.

Singer angrily added, "The Kripo are merciless with smugglers."

Why would Singer care about smugglers?

"The Kripo are also in charge of the deportations," Rosenfeld added. "They swarm in on the street and force everyone out of their flats. Then they tear the places apart searching for anything that may have value." He shook his head. "Beware if you see them. They clean everyone out like we're cockroaches."

Cukier coughed. "I dread the Gestapo most. All the other forces are subordinate to them. Their cruelty is unimaginable." He coughed into his rag and stopped talking.

Rosenfeld pulled his pipe from his lips. "Nothing happens here without the Gestapo's approval. They are the final authority on all Jewish matters. I fear them the most too."

Singer leered at me. "They run the resettlement logistics you so admire, Engineer."

I felt as if he had a knife pointed at me. Rosenfeld and Cukier stared at me as well. "Let me clarify this. I'm not saying I admire these inhumane actions. The precision with which Jews from greater Lodz were taken from their homes and imported to the ghetto is quite a logistical challenge. Nobody could have ever conceived of something like this on such a grand scale."

"They had help," Singer said. "You know who I mean." He eyed Cukier.

Cukier exploded, "Don't start that again."

I knew who Singer meant. Was it true? Was any of it true?

Cukier put his arm on my shoulder. "Rumkowski is the ghetto,

Engineer. No matter what anyone else thinks." He looked at Singer and burst into a terrible bout of coughing.

I aimed my eyes at Singer. "It's enough. It is time to get back to work. We must find a way to satisfy our benefactor." I returned to my typing. Usually, the clatter of the keys kept me from thinking, but today I was drifting, reflecting on my coworkers' heated exchanges. They were such opposites: Cukier, fully committed to our Chairman; Singer outspoken in his distrust and urging militant resistance against the Germans. The two dueled continually, with dear Dr. Rosenfeld siding with one or the other at various times. I was torn, wishing I could have blind faith in Rumkowski, but perhaps because of Singer, and now Miriam, finding my certainty tested. I stared over my infernal typewriter at Singer.

Our gadfly was bent over his work, a benign figure for a few blessed minutes. His thick black hair, long and wild, matched his playboy personality. It was ironic that though he was our youngest member, he dominated our dialogue and his discourse troubled my brain. I envied his bravado but viewed him, and his kind, as a threat to our survival. Returning to my typing, I vowed that if that reckless anarchist did anything even slightly to endanger Miriam, I'd report him myself.

CHAPTER 19

Miriam was more depressed each day. I thought it was understandable given the widespread sense of hopelessness enveloping the ghetto. Food was scarce, as was fuel. I'd laughed at the renters whose staircase was stolen as they slept, but with thievery rampant, it was no longer funny. I rushed home after each day of work to offer what protection I could for my wife. I couldn't protect her from the sadness all around us.

"Tell me about your Chairman now," Miriam challenged, her beautiful hazel eyes locked on me so hard I had little choice but to answer.

"Why do you want to trouble about him?" I was exhausted from discussing his latest actions with the other chroniclers. It was a daily debate, argument, war.

"I value your opinion."

"You do? Well then, frankly, I think the Chairman is doing an excellent job."

"You do? Do you know he failed in business twice?"

"I didn't, but it doesn't matter. The Eldest of the Jews was elected by the Elders."

"That's not what I heard. The Germans wanted him and threatened the other Elders."

"How do you know that?" I recalled Rosenfeld's suspicions and was grateful Miriam was unaware of that horrifying event.

"I just know." She curled her legs under her.

"Well, all I know is that before he took over all the coffers were emptied by the Nazis, all bank accounts frozen, and the right to move around, even in daylight, was curtailed."

"And you think he changed all that?"

"Miriam, my love, look around you. He has set up departments to find housing, provide supplies, food and fuel. He established public mess halls for dining. Most importantly, he has restored law and order."

"He helped in the creation of this ghetto. Did you know that?"

"I'm sure he was forced to do that, threatened with terrible reprisals for the people. Without him, there would not be a fire department, as enfeebled as it is by the Germans taking their vehicles, a post office, emergency services, hospitals and more."

"And, of course, his own police force," Miriam said.

She sounded like Singer and I resented her sarcasm. "Miriam, I don't understand your hostility. He has suffered too. He lost his wife before the war, has no children, and in his position, has none or few friends. But he's a good man. He started an orphanage on a farm just outside of Lodz. He loves children. He protects them as if they were his own."

"My friends say he used the orphanage solely to build his prestige, not out of a good heart."

I was furious. "What do your friends know? Who are these friends who fill your head with such unfounded allegations?" I assumed it was that Mietek, or a bunch of old yentas, gossips, who had nothing better to do than spread rumors and fan flames of discontent. "You shouldn't bother with such nonsense."

"So, you're saying none of it is true? He does not live like a king off the sweat of the workers?"

"Miriam, I just know that without Rumkowski we might not have survived this long. These are old accusations from malcontents. Who are they to judge him? I work for the Chairman now. Haven't you heard, "Don't bite the hand that feeds you?" Miriam, I have a good job because of Rumkowski. That should be enough for you. It is for me."

"So, it doesn't matter that nobody seems to know how this man with a minimal formal education got such a high-and-mighty position?"

"What are you talking about? He's one of the brightest men in the ghetto. Only Rosenfeld may be more knowledgeable, but I would not leave the responsibilities of running this community, with all its criminals and malcontents, to the good Doctor. Rumkowski needs to be tough, organized, and brave. I don't envy him. You shouldn't criticize what you don't know."

"And you know?"

I was sick and tired of this. "Yes, I know."

Miriam's face got smug. "Rumkowski may be bright, but he only attended four or five years of elementary school, and not even in Lodz—"

"He's an immigrant?"

"That is your concern? Did you forget your roots?" She gave me a scornful look.

"It's just a surprise. I assumed Rumkowski was old Lodz."

"He grew up in Tsarist Russia. Nobody knows how he became our leader. Perhaps the Germans do."

"Miriam, if you saw him, even once, you would understand. He is tall, elegant in fashion, and a powerful speaker. He stands out when he comes into a room." I remembered how small I felt next to him.

"A wolf in sheep's clothing is also well-dressed."

"Oh, for God's sake! He is our leader. How can you say such things?" I would have left, but where could I go? It was after curfew too.

Miriam smiled slyly. "He is now single-handedly controlling every aspect of our lives. He is a one-man government."

"As were Julius Caesar and Napoleon. This is ridiculous."

"I wouldn't know about them. The Nazis closed all the Jewish schools. Remember you are much older and could get an education." Miriam trembled. "I wanted to be a teacher. What am I now? I was robbed of my childhood by these Nazis, and now I am a prisoner in a ghetto that makes products for those who want to destroy us."

I no longer felt like arguing about Rumkowski, an argument I had learned I could not win with her. I thought she was about to cry, and I didn't want that. "Dearest Miri, when the war is over—it will end soon— I will gladly pay for your lessons, and someday, you will make an excellent teacher. The children will love you as much as I do."

That calmed her. She sat on the chair next to mine, the fire of the debate extinguished, until she said, "Did you know that less than a month after Rumkowski was ordered to select a Council of Elders, all but eight of its thirty members were arrested and killed? It happened all on one night."

"I'm going to bed," I said, worried that she knew of the mass arrest and execution that Rosenfeld had revealed to me.

"You go. I can't sleep." Miriam walked to the window. Without lights, because of the black-out declared by the authorities, via the Chairman, the streets were dark.

"Don't you want to come to bed?" I asked, wondering when all this arguing was going to end.

Miriam stared at me.

"Miriam, I'm asking you to come to bed with me. Please?"

"I'm pregnant."

I was nearly asleep.

"Benny, I'm pregnant. I think I am."

My eyes were closed. My addled brain didn't register Miriam's words. But then, as if a light flashed in the room, my eyes popped open. I searched for her by the window. "I did not hear you right. I'm so tired of all this stress and arguing."

Miriam approached the bed and pulled my hand to her belly. "It's true. I'm pregnant. You're going to be a father."

I didn't feel a heartbeat. "I don't hear anything?"

"It's too early."

German trucks passing outside were too loud for me to hear anything anyway.

CHAPTER 20

J **ANUARY 14, 1941:** A SEARCH
A search was conducted today by the authorities on the premises of the United Engravers firm located at 2 Brzesinska Street. Gold objects were confiscated.

I had just entered our workroom. The short entry was handed to me by Cukier even before I got my coat off. I wanted to shout out my good news but decided to keep it to myself. Why? I don't know, but maybe it was because my sweet Miriam's words still haunted me, "How can we bring a child into a world like this?"

"What is this about?" I asked. "Who conducted this search?"

Rosenfeld replied, "As usual, details are missing."

Singer replied, "Almost all the private Jewish businesses were shut down by the Nazis months ago. Only the Chairman's enterprises are still running."

Rosenfeld added, "They weren't just shut down. Everything was confiscated by the authorities, and now one of the Chairman's sources of pride is also gone."

Cukier looked up from what he was reading. "All gold was seized by the Gestapo."

"So why don't you say that?" Singer asked. "You deliberately left out the name of the enemy who steals everything we desperately need: Germans, Nazis and the rest of the rotten swine."

Cukier coughed into a handkerchief. "You know why. We've been through this too many times before—"

"So, the Emperor can fool everyone into thinking the wolves will leave us alone. Last week, they took all our furs. Today, they take what little we have of our gold, and yet, we remain sheep, waiting to be butchered. What else will they take from us before we fight back?"

"This is getting stale," I said. "You know we have nothing with which to fight."

"But we don't have to help them," Singer said.

"Let us go on," I said firmly, taking the role assigned to me by Neftalin. "What other news is there?"

Rosenfeld sifted through his files. "You'll like this one. A woman who tried to arrange a funeral for her mother complained, 'You can't die these days since with the current increase in the death rate there is a huge delay at the cemeteries.'"

"And we know who is causing that," Singer remarked.

Cukier coughed into his handkerchief. "It is early in the day. Can you please stop?"

"Are you okay?" I asked, seeing Julian's face was red.

He waved his hand in a signal to Rosenfeld to continue.

Rosenfeld looked concerned about Cukier but continued reading the report from the head of the Mortuary Department, "This poor woman has a legitimate complaint. Jewish tradition requires burial one day after death, but now it can take as many as ten days."

"We'll need lines at the cemetery," Singer said. "So, what's the problem? What's causing all this crap now?"

Rosenfeld sighed. "The director says besides the drastic increase in the death rate, the cause is that there are three horses left in the entire ghetto to pull the hearses."

"They took our horses for the hearses?" Singer burst into laughter. "Horses for hearses. That's funny. Give me this one. I'll write it up."

"There's nothing funny about this. If bodies aren't buried, the resident dying from disease will be worse than it is now," I replied.

Rosenfeld held onto the report. "Let me finish. The director continues to report, 'There was such a backlog in the transporting of bodies that a new type of wagon had to be pressed into service. It can be loaded with dozens of corpses at the one time." He looked sadly at me. "Singer is right. We will have to wait in line to be buried."

My mathematician mind was working. "Does anyone know how many died daily before the ghetto was established and how many are dying now?"

"What difference does that make? The fact is our Jewish requirement is that bodies be buried in one day, but even this, the last event of a person's life, has been taken away from us by the beasts." Singer held out his hand for the paper.

"Rosenfeld discovered it, so he will write it up," Cukier said firmly. "As for your question, Engineer with the mathematical mind, Singer, go to the archives and dig up the figures."

Singer looked about to protest this errand, but Cukier coughed again.

Rosenfeld said, "Wait. The Director supplied his statistics. He states that before the arrival of winter, where the death rate is now 25-30 cases per day, the average death rate was..." He paused, swallowing hard. "He says only six."

There was silence as we mulled that over.

"There is another factor," I said, "Before this brutal winter, the population here was two hundred fifty thousand. Correct? Now, our latest figures, for January 1941, are one hundred fifty-four thousand."

"Always the number man," Singer said.

"And you're the cynic," I shot back.

Rosenfeld stepped in. "Singer, the Engineer is right. Before we were entombed here, only six died daily out of two hundred and fifty thousand, but now twenty-five to thirty of us die daily out of only one hundred and fifty thousand. That is one hundred thousand less, so the percentage is that much more."

Singer became quiet as the mathematics of our increased death rate struck home.

Rosenfeld read the rest of the note and then said, "There is more.

The director writes, "There were twelve gravediggers employed at the cemetery. Today, there are two hundred, and it's still not enough."

"Two hundred?" I couldn't imagine two hundred men digging graves would not be sufficient.

Rosenfeld continued, "In spite of such a horrendously large number of gravediggers, no more than fifty graves can be dug per day. The reason: a lack of skilled labor, as well as the ground being frozen."

Singer burst into laughter again.

Why was he laughing?

Rosenfeld waited for Singer. "The director closes with, "And this causes the macabre line to grow longer."

"Lines to be buried is definitely a macabre story," Cukier said. "Give it a title, write it up and hand it to Ostrowski for typing. I've had enough for the day."

Singer said, "I've got your title: "Sad but true: Lines are also obligatory for the deceased."

Cukier nodded. "Fine. It is sad and true, so go ahead with that title." He stretched his body and burst into a fit of coughing.

"Do you want me to go with you?" I asked.

He waved me away. "No. Continue. I'll be back."

He closed the door behind him, leaving us staring at the raw wood. I returned to my chair. "Anything else?" I asked.

Singer held up a page and said. "This is interesting. The Council wants us to announce that a shipment of coal has arrived. They claim it is a 40 to 50 percent increase."

I said, "We should definitely include that good news. It will raise spirits considerably."

Rosenfeld nodded agreement. "That is good news."

Singer shook his head. "I should have read on. Apparently, the coal delivered is not very good quality, and I quote, "distribution of the coal to the people of the ghetto is unfortunately still out of the question."

"What? All that coal and we don't get any relief?" Rosenfeld shouted.

"We're freezing to death! What the hell is going on? Why aren't they distributing this huge increase as they call it, to us?"

I'd never seen him so angry before. "Singer, does it explain?"

Singer read further and replied, "The coal is needed for the workshops and the community kitchens, as well as the..." He made a wry face. "the departments and institutions of the Eldest of the Jews." He let the article drift to the table. "There you have it, my friends."

Rosenfeld sat down. "Does it say anything at all about when ordinary people will get help?" He rubbed his bony hands together.

I noticed earlier the good doctor had not removed his coat. He said, "Old people feel the cold more." Feeling it myself, I understood his frustration.

Singer skimmed to the end of the Energy Department memo. "Here's all it says, "This week, the fuel shortage has still not been overcome, but there are prospects for a resolution of the most urgent issue—the distribution of fuel to the populace. This will come in the very near future.' That's the last line. I'm sorry, Doctor."

Rosenfeld nodded slowly. "This will come in the very near future. That is hopeful." He rubbed his hands together again. "Perhaps we will get it here sooner," he said.

"Singer, please write it up. Be sure to include the last lines. We need to offer hope when possible," I said, and began typing again.

Singer was staring at Rosenfeld, who was still rubbing his hands together while bundled up in his tattered coat. The rascal had a tender look on his face I had not noticed before. I guess he likes the old gentleman, I thought.

"Oscar," I said, hating to break the spell, "Please compose the entry about the coal."

For once, he didn't argue. He was staring at Rosenfeld's hands.

CHAPTER 21

T UESDAY, JANUARY 21, 1941
Big news! Bread ration increased to 400 grams. Supplemental bread rations will stop. "*The increase in the bread rations, by relieving the greatest complaint of the population, caused universal and intense satisfaction among the starving masses who inhabit the ghetto.*

"Are you really letting that go like that?" Singer asked.

"Why not? It is the truth." Dr. Rosenfeld replied.

"Am I the only one who sees they're stopping the supplemental bread rations?"

"I saw it," I said, but the important point is we're getting more—"

Singer erupted, "You sound like the Chairman. I'll tell you what I witnessed last night on Brzesinska Street."

"Here we go," I grumbled.

Singer ignored my comment. "I was walking home when I heard a noise by Epstztajn's grocery. Someone was screaming. I was about to walk over when the Jewish police came running. So, what do you think happened?"

"I have no idea."

"A man was trapped under a heavy wood door."

"The door fell on him?" Cukier asked.

"No. Well, yes."

"Is it no or yes?" Rosenfeld asked.

Singer was obviously enjoying our curiosity. "Have you heard of Mogen?"

"That means the stomach, Cukier said. "What does the stomach have to do with a door falling on a man?"

Rosenfeld replied. "Isn't he a thief?"

Singer nodded. "His real name is Frajlus Kiwe. Well, apparently he was stealing the door from Ep's store, to sell for wood on the black market, when somehow it fell on top of him."

"They'll steal anything these days," Rosenfeld said.

Cukier smiled. "We need to include that. It will give people a much-needed belly-laugh." He laughed at his pun.

"I see. Mogen means stomach. Yes, it is a belly-laugh, but not for the thief. He was sentenced to three months in prison." Rosenfeld shook his head. "Maybe he'll steal the prison doors and let out all the hungry and cold Jews sentenced by Rumkowski's hand-picked judges."

"You sound sympathetic to the thief," I said, taking a break from my typing.

Rosenfeld rubbed his hands. "I'm so damn cold I'd consider stealing a door for firewood. Wouldn't you?"

Cukier replied, "These thieves are criminals, undermining the Chairman's efforts at order. The only answer is harsh punishments and no sympathy for—" He broke into a fit of coughing, but still gasped, "We are all suffering. These criminals make it worse."

Singer snuck in, "Some are suffering far more than others."

"What do you mean?" Cukier asked.

"It doesn't matter."

Cukier grabbed Singer's arm. "Say what you mean." He coughed again.

"Stop goading him, Singer." Cukier's coughing got worse when he was upset.

"I'm sorry," Cukier stammered, letting go of Singer's arm and coughing into his handkerchief.

I helped Cukier back to his seat.

Singer looked contrite. "I'm sorry, Julian. I meant no offense to you."

Cukier waved his hand.

"I only meant that the courts are not what we used to know. What happened to being allowed to offer a defense? I have friends who were sentenced for protesting peacefully in the square. They were given no chance at a trial. No lawyers. No defense. One got three months of cleaning cesspools! All he was doing was asking for coal for his family. He has young children."

"I saw some young girl prisoners picking up excrement and tossing it into wagons pulled by male prisoners," I said. "When I asked the Service Order guard escorting them why these girls were doing this, he said it was not my business. I showed my identification, and gritting his teeth, he spat out that they were "common criminals" being punished. My God. They were only young girls."

Cukier looked surprised at my taking Singer's side. He was still breathing hard but was able to say, "Both of you need to understand the only way to stop crime is by punishment. I don't like it. Nobody likes it. It is a fact."

"Are you sure nobody likes it?" Singer asked.

"There you go again. I know we need a gadfly amongst us, but sometimes I wish you would try and see the opposing point of view." Cukier said, a handkerchief over his mouth.

"How can you justify such punishments for young girls?" Singer asked.

It was Rosenfeld who answered. "You know me, my friend, so you know I hate such stories. I ask you this: if we did not punish such behavior, what would the Germans do? What punishment would this door thief have gotten from the Gestapo? Imagine what German police might do to a young Jewish girl in their custody. They think we are not human. Perhaps they would want to find out what our girls have under their dresses."

"Stop! Stop it already!"

"Engineer?" Rosenfeld looked at me as if he couldn't believe I had emotions.

I was shaking, my head throbbing. I had an image of young girls standing with their dresses raised by prying German hands. I thought of Miriam and was terrified at the thought that a German soldier or policeman, Gestapo, could stop her on the streets for no reason, and subject her to any cruelty he wished. It was an ugly, horrifying picture. I couldn't stand it.

"Ostrowski, what's wrong, my friend?"

Cukier's voice penetrated my dark thoughts. I let out a deep sigh. "My wife is going to have a baby," I said, wondering how they would react, wondering if any of these learned men would ask, "How can you bring a baby into a world like this?"

Cukier smiled and extended his hand. "That is wonderful news. Wonderful. I'm happy for you. Mazel tov!"

Rosenfeld put his pipe down and rose from his seat. "Give me your hand. In a time of so much unhappiness, you, Engineer, bring us a ray of hope. Much joy to you and your wife! Such good news!" He shook my hand.

I waited to hear what our resident cynic would say.

Singer didn't smile. He reached into his pocket and handed me a card. "It is my ration card. Your wife must eat."

I looked at the card with disbelief. "Are you certain you don't want it?"

Singer shook his head. "I have nothing else I can give you. Please, tell your wife I wish her well."

I extended my hand and thanked him for his kindness.

Rosenfeld put his hand on Singer's shoulder. "You're quite a mensch," he said.

"I agree. You're quite a man," Cukier said, smiling at Singer for the first time in days.

And for the first time in days, Singer's act of kindness made me realize, that even in such terrible times, a baby meant hope. Singer's card meant much more to me than the extra four hundred kilograms of bread, the extra kasha, the extra milk, coffee, ersatz coffee, it would buy. That card was the most precious gift anyone had ever given me, hope that a child might bring light to the darkness of my world.

That night, I made love to my Miriam. For a few minutes, I forgot that we were living in limbo. When her body coiled around me, I did not want to let her go. When she said, "You were so passionate tonight. Did something good happen?" I kissed her neck, then her cheek, and finally her lips, and whispered, "Yes. I'm with you."

CHAPTER 22

I pulled open the door and was grateful to see my friends were already at our work table. I never knew if one morning I would show up and one would be missing, perhaps permanently. Jews vanishing from the ghetto was a fact of life, and this morning, I had a genuine reason to be afraid.

"What is going on? Why are there so many policemen by the workshops?" I asked, having passed by the factories on Drukarska Street.

"It's a strike," Cukier said. "Have you seen Singer? I'll wring his neck if he's with the strikers. That young man is driving me crazy."

Rosenfeld laughed. "He's restless and spirited. His idealism is good for us old men."

"It will get him in grave trouble one day," Cukier said. "Don't you agree, Benny?"

I bristled at the word, grave.

Just then, Singer came charging into the room and promptly placed a chair to block the door. "You should have seen it. There were hundreds of police," he said between gasps.

"Where? What is going on?" I asked.

"On Drusarska Street. The carpenters went out on strike yesterday, and today the Chairman has locked down the factories. All hell is breaking loose. The workers have had enough."

"Enough of what?" Rosenfeld asked, "They get better treatment than most."

"Remember when we read of the supplemental bread allowance

121

being eliminated the other day?"

"That was because everyone's regular bread allowance was raised. Do these workers expect more than everyone else?" I thought of Miriam on her hands and knees scrubbing up crumbs of the roll from the floor.

"Here is the list of their demands." He handed me the list.

"An increase in pay. We'd all love that."

Rosenfeld muttered, "They already got that, so what else do they want?"

"Afternoon meals provided without using their ration coupons. That's a nice deal when everyone else is starving," I said, perusing the list.

Singer looked excited. "More than three hundred carpenters joined the strike. It was amazing. Workers united against the Chairman and bosses."

"What's amazing?" Rosenfeld asked. "They are strangling everyone else with their incessant demands. What if these strikes spread?"

Cukier had been silent. "What did the police do?"

"They surrounded the building. There were a hundred police. The officer in charge demanded the building be vacated."

"Did the workers listen?" I hoped they did. Rosenfeld was right, the Chairman could not let this strike set a precedent, but on the other hand, I hoped violence had been avoided."

"No. The Order Service moved in on the first floor and began to evict the workers by force. The workers barricaded the doors on the second floor. After breaking in the door, the police managed to expel all the workers. It took about an hour."

"Was anyone hurt?" Cukier asked.

"I saw some workers injured. Police too."

Rosenfeld sighed. "Both sides are right. The workers deserve a living wage, but the Chairman can't afford to allow strikes of any kind, or the Nazis may step in."

There was a knock on the door. Singer removed the chair.

A police officer entered without waiting for a reply. "This is for immediate attention." He eyed us curiously and left.

"I hate when they just barge in like that." I froze whenever anyone came through our door. Our office, drab cubicle that it was, had become my security, but it was as tenuous as every other place in our ghetto.

"Don't you get it? They can do exactly what they want," Singer said.

"Shut up, Singer." Cukier examined the note and let out a deep sigh. "There you go. Today all workshops are closed on orders from the Chairman."

"He closed all the workshops?" Singer asked. "He's ruthless."

Rosenfeld shook his head. "He has to make a stand. If this protest spreads, the Germans will descend on us like vultures. Let me write this up?" He reached for the note.

Singer grabbed it. "No. I want to write it. We should be fair to both sides."

Rosenfeld looked to Cukier. "Our first duty is to the Chairman and the populace, not to these workers who are making demands without regard for others."

"They have a right to feed their families," Singer argued. "There is rampant inequality here. The administrators and intelligentsia are parasites living off the workers. They have a right to strike."

Cukier broke into a fit of coughing. "No. They do not have the right to strike, not in such dire circumstances. Singer, give the note to Doctor Rosenfeld. He will write it."

"You support the parasites?" Singer asked, holding the notice out of reach.

Cukier could barely speak for coughing but replied. "We must support the Chairman. Doctor, write it. Read it to us when done. Let's move on."

Rosenfeld took the note from Singer's hand.

"This is bullshit," Singer muttered.

Cukier turned toward Singer. "And by the way, I'm glad you didn't get hurt in the melee. From now on, steer clear of these things. We need you safe. I have a feeling we'll have more strikes if this war doesn't end soon."

Singer replied, "It's more dangerous just to walk the streets. Have you seen the ice?"

Cukier nodded. "On my way here, I saw people sliding all over the place."

"It's worse at night when darkness covers the streets. I almost fell myself. I could have broken my leg." Rosenfeld said, looking up from his paper.

"Okay, write it up, young Singer, but we need a positive conclusion. Try this: "Under these conditions, the campaign for ice and snow removal in the ghetto, so energetically undertaken by our Chairman..." Cukier was fishing for words.

I stepped in: "is enjoying universal approval."

Cukier nodded. "Good. I like it."

Rosenfeld smiled. "I've done it. Want to hear?"

"I can't wait," Singer mumbled.

Rosenfeld cleared his throat. "Today all workshops were closed on orders from the Chairman."

Cukier coughed. "Please skip what we heard."

Rosenfeld nodded. "This shuttering of the factories was due to agitation by irresponsible individuals. Incidents were incited whose intent was to disrupt the normal course of work."

Singer shook his head. "I don't believe you are writing this."

"Continue," Cukier said, giving Singer a wilting look.

"As a result of these unruly incidents, it was necessary to resort to the forcible expulsion of workers from the building they unlawfully occupied."

"That's a nice way of putting it," Singer said.

"Let him finish," I said, leaning back in my chair to rest my fingers from pounding on the stubborn typewriter keys. I should have gone on strike against this infernal machine.

Rosenfeld gave me a nod. "According to information in the Chairman's possession, similar incidents were planned on other facilities. The Chairman points out that he has already warned the workers several times against resorting to any methods that disturb the supplies for the army—"

I interrupted. "The workshops are making goods for what army?"

Singer replied, "Guess."

The sarcasm was dripping like sweat from Singer today, so I wasn't sure whether to take him seriously.

"What choice do we have?" Cukier shouted. "It's all that is saving us."

"Making supplies for the Nazis is one hell of a way to save us. That's like making teeth for a shark about to bite off our legs," Singer stormed.

"It's true? I'm sorry. I didn't know." And yet I should have. Who else could give us orders large enough to keep all of the Chairman's factories going? We were working for the German military to save our skins. I prayed Miriam didn't find this out.

"And you say I'm naïve," Singer muttered.

Rosenfeld shook his pipe at Singer. "Do you want me to finish or not?" When he saw we were silent, he continued, "Being personally responsible for all disturbances in the workplace and for the resulting losses, the Chairman cannot tolerate such offenses."

"He can't tolerate such offenses?" Singer tapped his pen on a pad of paper. "I wish you'd let me write the truth."

"Who knows what the truth is?" Cukier gave Singer a paternal smile. "When I was your age, I also thought I knew the truth. The truth is we have no truth other than that which helps us survive."

"So, all we need to care about is survival?"

"Yes, young Singer, that is all," Cukier replied, studying his handkerchief.

"Do you wish to hear my closing or not?" Rosenfeld asked.

"Please?" Cukier fished in his pocket for a fresh nose rag.

"And Singer, no comments until the end," Rosenfeld eyed our sulking critic paternally and read from his entry, "In his concern for assuring the livelihood of the workers, the Chairman has spared no efforts in organizing his workshops, making it possible for thousands upon thousands of people to work in peace. Furthermore, the Chairman promises that he will make every effort to supply the populace with food as regularly and plentifully as possible. It should be taken into account that a series of reasons, including weather, often makes it impossible to keep all promises—"

"You're going to print this shit?" Singer snarled at Cukier.

"Listen to the end, boy," Cukier snapped.

"I can't. I just can't." Singer rose from his seat.

"These are not my words," Rosenfeld said. "This is what the Chairman said. Now sit down and be a grown up."

Singer, not used to hearing the old man speak to him like this, zipped his lips but remained standing.

"These are the Chairman's own words," Rosenfeld said again. "Like it or not, this is what he wants to be included: 'Irresponsible elements exploit this factor. The individuals creating this discord were arrested and to avoid such incidents, there will be further arrests until peace has been completely restored.'"

We got quiet. The implication was clear.

Singer broke the silence. "Now, do you see? He will do everything and anything until peace has been "completely" restored. That should scare the hell out of us."

Cukier held up a small memo. "The Chairman has placed the Order Services on emergency alert. He commends the police for their effort."

Singer buttoned his coat. "I'm sorry. I have to go."

Cukier glanced at him. "Fresh air will do you good. See you tomorrow morning."

Singer nodded and left the room.

"For the young, expediency is difficult to accept," Rosenfeld said, looking doubtfully at his entry. "Julian, do you think we're doing the right thing?"

Cukier reached for another sheet of paper. "There was a song recital by the gifted tenor Nikodem Sztajman today at Soup Kitchen 2, the Kitchen for the Intelligentsia, at 41 Zgierska Street." He broke into a fit of coughing and handed me the rest of the note.

"Teodor Ryder provided the accompaniment. Arias from the operas of Puccini, Verdi, Tchaikovsky, Leoncavallo, and Meyerbeer were sung." I shook my head at the last sentence and then read it aloud, "The large audience applauded the performers warmly." I was grateful Singer wasn't here for this one. I could imagine what he would say.

CHAPTER 23

J ANUARY 31, 1941
Seventy-three people died in the ghetto yesterday and today. No births were recorded.

Singer returned today. He was oddly silent. There were no good mornings, not even his usual sarcastic rants against Rumkowski. He simply sat down and stared at his hands, which looked raw from the frigid weather of this cursed winter. If I did not have Miriam's body warmth next to me in our cold flat, we both might have frozen to death.

Cukier was smiling. "There is some good news. There is more fuel. The allocation is for six kilograms of coal dust and two kilograms of wood. You can purchase this package with coupon 3 of your food ration card at the police precincts. You see, things are looking up."

Rosenfeld sighed. "So, we must choose between food and fuel, but at least now we have a choice." He rubbed his hands together.

I had seen him do this hand-rubbing often. "Doctor, I have something for you." I pulled two wool gloves from my coat pocket. "Here. Please, take them."

He looked incredulously at the gloves, held them up before his eyes, and then slipped them onto his bony fingers.

I saw tears in his eyes. I barely heard him thank me. I ignored his question, "How did you get them?" When I didn't answer, I think he knew. If he'd protested, I would have replied, "the dead no longer need such things." I wrote on my pad, "Chaim Bielajew died from exhaustion, cold and hunger at 268 Marysinska Street." I knew this for a fact. I'd stumbled upon his frozen body, and with nobody else around, pulled off his gloves. He would no longer need them. I would honor him by including his name in our journal. There were already too many dead to list all their names, but Chaim's gloves bought him this dubious honor.

After I read the entry aloud, Singer stood and walked to the window. Though it was boarded up, his facial expression was unusually calm, as if he was staring at a peaceful scene. For once, there was none of his anger, his passion. It was as if a vampire had found him in the night and robbed him of his life juices, the same life fluids that had caused him to remain away from us until today. "Oscar," I said—we rarely called him by his first name—are you, all right? Did something happen?"

Singer turned from the window and looked down at us where we sat before piles of unread papers, the reports from so many departments, the endless toilet paper of statistics that I so loved. "Have any of you smelled a dead body?"

Nobody answered.

Rosenfeld nodded. "Unfortunately, too many times."

Singer sat down. "I was at my friend Sammy's house. A knock on the door came, and we both jumped. You know what such knocks can mean. We crushed out our cigarettes. And yes, I got them from the black market, but you won't tell."

I often thought of asking him how he managed cigarettes. I wanted to surprise Miriam with some real coffee and sugar but had never dealt with the black market. Later, I'll ask him, I thought, wondering if I'd have the balls to risk such illegal activity.

Singer looked at me. "It was a young girl at the door. She was half frozen. We invited her inside, but she resisted. I said, "It's okay. Nobody will hurt you here." She shook her head and said, "He's in the basement," and ran off."

"Ran off?" Rosenfeld looked like he was really into the story.

"Wasn't she half frozen? So, you said?"

"I would have run from Singer if I was a girl," I joked, but nobody laughed. "Did you chase her?" I asked, thinking that would be natural for someone with his reputation.

Singer shook his head. "I guessed she was more frightened than frozen. We couldn't chase her. She was gone. We walked down to the basement. It was dark. The bulbs had been confiscated. It didn't matter. The stench led me to the corner. "Get someone. Get help," I said, covering my mouth with my sleeve, but unable to remain."

"You, poor boy," Rosenfeld said. "The first is always a shock. Before that first glimpse of death, we perceive humans as handsome or beautiful, the flesh providing camouflage, concealing what lies beneath. It is like looking in a mirror, seeing merely the surface. Then you cut it open and see what ugliness lurks beneath."

"Doctor, you are not helping," Cukier said. "We have all seen too much death lately, and I'm afraid we will see more."

Singer sighed. "It was a boy. Maybe fifteen years old…younger. He had died of hunger, or cold, or exhaustion, in the basement."

"You, poor boy," Rosenfeld repeated, his hand resting on Singer's arm.

Singer gazed at Rosenfeld's eyes and continued. "The Order Service arrived. A patrolman ordered us to stand guard. He said so none of the other tenants would steal from the corpse what little he had."

I thought of the gloves. Was Singer relating this nightmarish story a coincidence or God's punishment for my violating a corpse? But Rosenfeld needed those gloves, and the departed soul did not. Do we not owe more to the living than to the dead?

Rosenfeld said, "Criminals will steal anything today."

Singer gazed at him. "Doctor, they can't all be criminals. Don't you see, just like this boy; they're desperate. While our leaders attend concerts and enjoy warm meals—"

"You blame everything on our Chairman," Cukier interrupted. "Look, I sympathize with you for the death of the boy, but we're all in the same boat. We're all in the same damn boat!"

Singer shot back, "Are we?"

"Yes, dammit, we are!" Cukier burst into a fit of coughing, covering his face with his handkerchief.

Singer lowered his tone. "I can't argue today. I found out from snooping around the neighborhood the dead boy's name was Kleczewski Hersz. May I write him up? May I please include his name? He was only a boy."

Cukier nodded behind his nose rag. "You may honor his name, but state only that he was found in a state of complete exhaustion from cold and hunger."

Singer nodded. "Everyone knows who is to blame anyway."

Cukier smiled bitterly. "It is the Nazis who are to blame. And while you are at it, I want you to check out something for me."

"What is it?"

"It is probably just another rumor, but there is talk that the Authorities plan to remove a large quadrant of land from the ghetto. With your connections, you are the best one to find out if it is true." Cukier placed his hand on Singer's shoulder. "I'm sorry for your loss."

I stopped typing. If the rumor was true, what would the Germans do with all the Jews living in that part of our ghetto?

CHAPTER 24

FRIDAY, FEBRUARY 28, 1941

Forty-five people died in the ghetto today. No births were registered.

The rumors were spreading with lightning speed. Even Miriam had heard that the Germans were planning to remove a large corner of land from the ghetto. "Is it true?" She asked, shortly after I arrived home.

"Is that how you greet the father of your baby?" I reached to touch her stomach, but she pulled back. "Are the Nazi pigs taking away part of our community?"

"Where did you hear that?" I hadn't said anything because I didn't want to worry her.

"Everyone is talking about it. Mietek says you would know."

"Mietek is an idiot." I wished she would stop seeing him and whoever else was influencing her.

"Do you know or not?" Miriam's eyes were fiery.

I was exhausted. "You mustn't tell anyone. But yes, I think the rumors are true."

She fell onto a kitchen chair. "What does it mean?"

"You mustn't worry yourself. The area in question is not near us."

"What do they need our land for? That is where our gardens are."

How did Mietek and the others find this out? There had to be an informer in the administration, but who? I couldn't risk lying to her. "Yes. That, unfortunately, is true as well."

"He's allowing this?"

I knew who she meant, her favorite target. "Allowing it? I doubt it very much. The chairman established our largest fruit and vegetable gardens there after great effort. The Germans fought him all the way, but he finally won. It was quite an accomplishment. The fact that these fields were so productive was amazing since they had been used for dumping rubbish." I shook my head. "I won't lie to you, having these gardens taken from us will be a serious loss."

Miriam nodded. "What about the people who live there? Do you know where the Germans will put them? There must be thousands of Jews there."

She wasn't letting up. Who had given her all this information? "I estimate that approximately seven thousand people live by the gardens, most farming them."

"Seven thousand growing food will now be lost to us?"

Now Miriam sounded like me, the numbers man. "Something like that. I'm sure they will be resettled. It is the loss of the gardens that will cause the most pain."

Miriam shifted on one of our two cushionless chairs. I'd thought of burning one for fuel, but thankfully, we received the coal allocation in time to save the chair's miserable life. "Benny, we have so little already. Why do the Germans want to take away our gardens?" She leaned back and rubbed her stomach.

"Are you alright?" I asked.

She aimed her eyes at me. "Don't try and distract me," she said, still rubbing her stomach.

"I wasn't. The supposed cause is to put a tramline on Franciszkanska and Brzezinska streets. The Germans already started to extend the barbed wire."

Miriam, hand clutching her stomach, stood. "Already? There's no discussion? The almighty Chairman can't save his precious gardens?"

I rose to steady her, but she waved me away. "Miriam, he is doing his best. We are all at the whim of the Germans."

My wife, twenty years of age, but already with dark circles beneath her lovely eyes, peered at me and asked the question I had been asking myself ever since I'd heard the rumors, "Why Benny? Why do they want to build a new tram line in a ghetto, while in the middle of their stupid war?"

"Only the Germans know," I said.

I thought about that most of the night. Even the following morning, when I was waiting for the others to arrive, I could not think of an answer. I also could not lie. After my talk with Miriam, I ended the entry with, "The news about the reduction of the ghetto had a disquieting effect on the populace." I was staring at that sentence when Cukier arrived. "I have had a difficult night," I began.

"I have news," Cukier said. "Let me tell you before the others get here."

What now, I thought, fearing the worst, but praying to the God I didn't believe in, that nothing else was happening to us.

"I found an article in the Litzmannstadter Zeitung."

"You know that's banned to Jews."

"Just listen. This article predicts that the quarter of the city of Lodz, the land in which our ghetto is located, will be turned into parks and gardens."

"More rumors now spread by a Nazi rag," I said. "You mustn't pay attention to such propaganda."

"Is it? The article continues to say, that after the entire area is leveled, beautiful new buildings will be constructed here." Cukier held his handkerchief to his mouth but didn't cough. "Engineer, don't you find that humorous? The Nazis want to build beautiful buildings here."

I found nothing humorous about more baseless rumors. "I would ignore it," I said, praying the newspaper was wrong.

Cukier waved the article in front of me. "There's more. It says, the first stage is already occurring: the buildings on Ogrodowa and Nowomiejska streets, which abut the ghetto, are being razed."

"Is that true?"

Cukier bit his lip. "Yes. A few Jews allowed out for business have returned with reports to the Chairman that several buildings around the ghetto have been demolished."

What did it all mean? Was the war over? Had Hitler won? Was Lodz now in actuality a German city? What would happen to us? Miriam must not learn this.

Cukier leaned closer, his voice a raspy whisper. "Here is the scary part, Engineer. I have the last bit here with me. "As to the Jews inhabiting the ghetto, they will vanish from Litzmannstadt faster than they expect." Can you imagine the reaction when others learn of this?"

I hated this ghetto, but what this article portended was terrifying. Was it true? "This would explain the tramline too," I said. "Such a line would make removing thousands of Jews much easier." I was stunned. "Julian, the rumors are spreading through the grapevine already. My Miriam confronted me last night about the gardens."

"She knows of this article?"

"No. I don't think so. Miriam only questioned the loss of the gardens. I don't know how these things get out."

Cukier crushed the article in his fist. "Then it is not too late. The news of this article will cause terrible alarm. We must say it is false."

"But is it?" I was tired of hiding the truth, especially from Miriam. She acted as if she did not trust me anymore. "Julian, much of this is already known. If we deny it, everyone will know we lied. It will all be out in the open."

Cukier coughed hard into his nose rag. "Okay. Write it this way: "the contents of the article were for the most part falsely reported. In general, all information, whatever its source—the newspaper, private correspondence, and even events from life inside the ghetto—is spread in a distorted and exaggerated way."

"Julian, this is what you want me to type?"

Cukier nodded. "As far as we know, it is all rumors. God, the panic it will cause if people believe it is true." He shivered. "I don't believe it is more than Nazi wishful thinking. We must counter such irresponsible and reckless rumors."

I remembered Rumkowski's question: "Can you stand the hate of others when they find out you knew?" How would I live with the anger, the hate, when Miriam finds out? "But what if it is true?"

"Engineer, the truth won't help them. Nothing can. It will only spread fear and make people commit more desperate acts."

"But Miriam will never forgive me."

"When she understands, she will." He turned back to his work.

I stared at what in other times would have been a joyful announcement: the replacement of a slum with beautiful buildings and parks. If only I could have been the engineer of such a new city? If only I knew what that meant for all of us, lodged so miserably within the barbed wire. Perhaps if I knew the ramifications, instead of fear and panic, I would feel joy and anticipation. I typed the entry just as Cukier wanted it, still wondering if squashing the rumors was the best course of action. I knew what Singer would urge.

As soon as I finished typing, still troubled by doubt, I watched helplessly as Cukier tore the sheet from the typewriter and raced from the room. I'd seen him do this several times previously with controversial entries. I suspected he was taking it to Rumkowski or Neftalin. I guessed that what I'd written was to be used as propaganda, to stifle rumors that I had good reason to believe were true. I felt angry that I was part of a conspiracy to hide something so important from my fellow Jews, from Miriam. "They will hate you..."

That night, when Miriam asked me for news, I refused to speak. When she asked me what was wrong, I shouted, "Don't you think I have enough stress at work? Why do you interrogate me? Just leave me dammit alone!"

Instead of the tears I expected, her face froze into a mask that I recognized as hate.

That night was the first I let her go to bed angry. As I sat in the dark, the claustrophobic black-out dark, I heard a child weeping into her pillow.

In the distance, I imagined hearing demolition machines. My engineer's brain pictured the metal sheen of the German's futuristic construction equipment. I envisioned towering cranes, men risking death at their helm. I calculated how many bricks of the old tenements they might blast apart with each smash of their black wrecking balls. I saw the balls smashing through the crumbling walls of our ghetto as operatic music overwhelmed all. It was the crashing of cymbals, the thunder of drums. It was Wagnerian in its power and majesty. And in the intervals between the sounds of explosions and cannon fire, I counted the seconds between the sporadic sobbing of my pregnant wife.

CHAPTER 25

MARCH 1, 1941
I left for work early. I didn't want to see Miriam. I was ashamed of my behavior toward her but couldn't bring myself to apologize. The truth: I couldn't bear the risk of her rejecting my efforts. Rumkowski had warned early on that others might hate me. He did not inform me that Miriam might hate me too. Nor that I, the logical engineer, might someday hate myself.

The apartment was a one-room box. Our conference room, its rectangular table, taking up almost all of the space, was another box. The streets were forbidden after curfew, so I went from one box to another, and then back again. The lack of freedom and the stale air was getting to me. I was never claustrophobic before, but now I dreamt of escape. There was none. The invaders had sealed us in this tin can of a ghetto. My only distraction was work. Statistics, cold, unfeeling, numbers, were a refuge from contemplating the terrors rising around us like barbed wire, cruel, sharp points waiting to tear into flesh.

I dug through the pile of papers and came up with the figures for February. I was happy to be writing naked statistics without adding words and explanations that were lies and propaganda.

February 1, 1941- ghetto population =153,995.

Rooms fit for human habitation (as if any were)- 49,864

My brain calculated three people per room. "I must tell Miriam how lucky we are not to have to share our palace with others." Would that bit of good news smooth things over between us?

Weather: the mean temperature was 2 below zero.

Deaths for February:

I paused before that figure. Even to an engineer, death has to mean more than a number. I thought of the boy Singer had found; the hundreds of bodies left to rot in mass graves by the Nazis; the man who had thrown himself off a building and almost landed on Singer, and the bodies left in the street. I thought of the man and the gloves I'd taken off his frozen hands. It was safer to focus on numbers...no names, no faces. Numbers...number...numbers.

Deaths in February- 1,069

Births- 52

I was searching for more data when I heard someone at the door. It was too early for the others. Gestapo?

"Do you sleep here?" Singer asked, looking surprised to see me.

"Why are you so early?" I asked, my breathing returning to normal. "I'm reading the Chairman's summary for February."

"Where are the others?"

"They'll be here soon. You're never this early."

Singer smiled. "I like those gloves you gave our friend, Rosenfeld."

I tensed. Did Singer suspect what I did?

"Don't worry. I don't care how you got your gift for the old man. He certainly didn't." He laughed. "Now that you have a baby coming, perhaps you will let me help you and your wife. There are things you need."

"Thank you, but no. We are doing fine as is." I had no intention of getting caught buying stolen goods from the black market and leaving Miriam and my future child without a father."

"Just let me know when you're ready. I take care of my friends."

"Thank you." He'd never called me his friend before. I wasn't sure I wanted to be friends with someone with his questionable connections.

The door opened, and Rosenfeld arrived, shaking the snow off his coat, but leaving it on as usual. He left the gloves on as well. "A terrible story in court yesterday. I tell you, we are all becoming savages."

Singer looked concerned. "Humans aren't savages. Desperation is the result of the savagery of the Nazis. What upset you, dear, Doctor?"

"I will tell you, so you see why we must stop this madness. I was called to examine a body at 42 Franciszkanska Street. When I arrived, I saw the remains were covered with rags. I determined death had occurred at least two weeks earlier."

"Two weeks?" I thought of the stench.

Rosenfeld nodded. "Naturally, I was puzzled by this, as were the Order Service officers who picked up the little one's body."

"You said, little one?" I hated stories about children dying and thought of what Miriam had uttered after we had made love. That seemed eons ago but still nagged at me.

"Yes, the boy was only seven." Rosenfeld sighed. "The police questioned the father. "What is your name?" "Hersz Aragier, sir." He seemed surprisingly calm given the circumstances. "What is your profession?" "I am a batkhn," the father replied."

"An entertainer?" Singer asked.

Rosenfeld nodded. "He explained that he sang mostly at weddings. The policeman asked the man, "Why has your son not been buried?""

"I should hope he'd ask that," Singer said. "Even the most incompetent boobs would ask."

Rosenfeld sighed, "Quiet, Singer. The father refused to respond. Over and over the policeman asked him, and the father would not reply. Finally, the policeman arrested the father."

"Of course. What crime did he commit?" Singer asked.

"Not answering a policeman's questions is a crime," Rosenfeld said, rubbing his gloved hands together.

"So that's the end of the story?" I asked.

"No. I went to the courthouse to testify about examining the boy and finally heard—I can't believe it—the boy, this beautiful seven-year-old child, died of hunger and cold." Rosenfeld shook his head sadly. "The father didn't bury him. Why? So, he could continue to claim his ration coupons." He trembled as if he was going to cry. "He lets his beautiful son's body lie rotting away, so he can get more food. What is the world coming to?"

I stole gloves from a dead body. Singer deals with the black market. A child dies without food and heat, and his father...and I let Miriam sleep alone last night because I was overcome by anger. I swore I'd apologize when I got home. Rosenfeld was right, savagery was rising amongst us. I would not let it take me. "Doctor, Cukier isn't here yet. Would you honor this boy by writing an entry?"

"I can't. I'm sorry. My friend, Singer, you always have such compassion, will you do this for me?"

Singer nodded. "You'll have to give me the information."

Rosenfeld dug into his pocket. "This is the official court record."

Singer read the report. "You forgot about the mother. It says here she was set free."

Rosenfeld nodded. "Read more. She was set free because of her "mental illness."" He laughed bitterly. "That is what we say now when someone commits an act that seems incomprehensible."

"Or commits suicide," I added. "The cause is nearly always blamed on mental illness.

Singer smiled sadly. "In a way, it's true. We're all suffering mental illness."

For once, I agreed with my young anarchist. The whole world was insane.

CHAPTER 26

I left work early, eager to make things right with Miriam, and with a little surprise. When I entered our apartment, I felt alarmed. Where was she? Why was she not here? I thought of running to the neighbors but knew none of them. I didn't want to know them. Rumkowski's warning echoed in my brain, "They will hate you." Not if they don't know me.

"You're home early." Miriam walked past me without a hug.

"I have a surprise for you, something special."

She kept her coat on and sat on the chair. "Do you know about Proclamation 222?" she asked, her face stern.

"Miriam, forget about all that for now."

"It was posted on the walls today. Do you know what it says?"

"No. Let's get it over with. What does it say?"

"It is a summons by the Eldest of the Jews to surrender, in strict confidence, any articles and objects of value that have been hidden in the city, even outside the ghetto." She glared at me. "Your Chairman is taking everything for himself and his cronies."

"He has no choice. The Germans ordered the Chairman to do this."

"Do you believe him?"

"What do you mean?"

"He says they are going to pay for the objects and there is no reason to fear." She unfolded a copy of the proclamation."

"Where did you get that? It is against the law to tear a posting from the official billboards."

"What does it matter? I'll read you one part: "All parties can come forward without fear since they are not subject to any criminal sanctions."

"We have nothing to fear since we own nothing."

"Do you believe him?"

"Yes, I do."

"I hope you're right." She sighed. "I don't know anymore who to believe." She looked at me and pulled her coat around her.

Bundled-up, she looked like a frightened child. I was losing her trust. "I'm sorry, Miriam."

She looked up. "For what?"

"I'm sorry about last night. I guess it's all getting to me too. We are being driven insane by the wolves. I'm truly sorry." I felt tears welling in my eyes, but as always, fought them back. I had to be strong for her.

Miriam stood and walked toward me.

I was about to rise, to meet her but she draped her arms around my head and held me against her coat. She was rocking me like a mother cradling her child. I felt myself slipping away, losing my sense of the present. It was all a nightmare, and mother was, here again, to make it go away.

"I love you, you know," Miriam said softly.

"Just hold me. Please?" Suddenly, I remembered my surprise. I lifted my head from her breast. "Thursday, you must dress nicely. You are going to lunch with me."

She released me. "What did you say?"

I gripped her hands. "I want you to go to lunch with me. It's a special day. My superior has given me a ticket for you."

"I can't go."

"You must. There is a special surprise. I won't take no for an answer."

"Tell me the surprise."

"Don't you want to be surprised?"

"I hate surprises now. Please tell me?"

I didn't see any other way. "We are going to have a concert, and you, my dear, are invited."

"A concert? Live music?" Her eyes lit up. "I love music. You know that."

"Well, tomorrow, we will pretend for one hour, that there is no war, no Hitler, no Germans. Tomorrow, you and I will enjoy a well-deserved bit of pleasure."

Her face darkened. "I don't know."

"I do. It's my way of making up to you for what I did last night."

Miriam smiled sadly. "I've done much worse to you." She rubbed her stomach. "Being pregnant isn't what I expected."

"It isn't you. It's all of this. But now we have a chance to forget. Music gives us hope. It will transport us back to the past when none of this existed. You will see. It will make you happy."

"Will you come to bed with me tonight?"

The way she asked, I could not resist. "I can't make love to you," I said, "not as you are."

"We can tell stories like we did as children."

"I never knew you as a child. I think I would have liked to have known you back then."

"You wouldn't have looked at me. You were fifteen when I was one." She laughed. "That would have been some date."

"I like to hear you laugh." I also liked feeling her hand.

"You don't laugh much," she said.

"No. Engineers don't laugh much. Maybe when the war is over, you'll teach me."

"When the war is over? It is two years already."

"It will end soon. It has to."

"Tomorrow, I'll hear lovely music. Let's not talk about anything sad tonight."

I felt her turn over, and soon her gentle breathing told me she was asleep. I listened to the music of her breathing next to me, something I'd missed last night. I thought about the concert we were going to share. Abruptly I heard Singer's voice, shrill and accusing, "How can they have a concert for the elite in the middle of all this misery?" How many times had I wondered that myself, but tonight, it offered me something to look forward to, something that brought my Miriam back to me. "Shut up, Singer," I shouted at the voice in my brain. "For one day, I want to be free to enjoy a few songs with my wife. So just shut up!"

CHAPTER 27

"I can't go to the concert," Miriam said, making me a cup of ersatz coffee.

"Why not? You love music. It has been a long time since we've enjoyed a day together." Her eyes looked red. "Did you not sleep well last night? Is the baby causing you discomfort?"

"No." She hesitated. "I know it's silly at this time to think of such things. I know I shouldn't be such a bother to you."

I put down my cup. "Please, tell me what is wrong? I will try to make it right. You seemed so happy last night."

She brushed back her hair, one of the most enticing things she did without even knowing it. "I feel terrible even saying it. Benny. I don't have anything to wear to such a fine event. We left without time to bring anything."

It was then I understood. I had not once thought of using some of my pay to buy my wife a dress. What man thinks of such things? "Don't worry. You will look beautiful in anything you wear. Have you seen some of these other wives? You have nothing to worry about. You will be the prettiest wife there."

"I only have schmatas, rags. Nothing is clean." She sat down on the chair and once again reminded me how much she looked like a pouty little girl at times. I was a sucker for that look.

"Miriam, we are going to the concert even if I have to dress like "The Little Tramp" and you like the lovely girl you are."

"But I'm pregnant. I'm fat."

I laughed, not a great idea in front of a woman who just shouted

146

she was pregnant and fat. "You are pregnant, but trust me, compared to the other administrators' wives, you are lovely."

She let out a sigh. "As always, my husband with terrible vision, you are being kind."

"No. I'm being honest. Now, forget about the dress. Just be ready for the nicest time you've had in many months." I kissed her forehead. "Whatever you wear, I will be the proudest man at the concert."

She let out a little grunt. "Also, the craziest."

"That too." I smiled and left the apartment. I had already made up my mind what I would do but wished there was another way. I was deep in thought when I noticed a small crowd gathered around the wall where notices were posted. As always, there were groans and complaints. I expected that. While it bothered me that many of our neighbors could not understand the problems faced by the Eldest of the Jews, Chairman Rumkowski, I knew better than to try and assuage their anger. I waited and then read the posting on the wall. I was surprised that it was unusually short: "All the inhabitants of the ghetto must immediately inform family and friends in writing that they are no longer to mail any parcels of food to the ghetto since the Chairman must confiscate all parcels on orders from the authorities."

"This is shit," a woman next to me shouted.

"It is more of the crap from the Chairman," a man to my right complained.

I decided to correct him. "Don't you see the notice says, "on orders from the authorities." This isn't the Chairman's choice."

The crowd surrounded me. Why did I speak? Rumkowski was right. These people couldn't understand the pressures he was under. Most of those milling around me were vagrants, malcontents, who could never appreciate anything we were doing for them. A few men formed their cold hands into fists.

"Are you in the government?" A tall man in a ragged, stained, coat asked, face inches from my nose.

"He's Miriam's husband," a woman said. "You know, the poor little

147

girl who is carrying a child. How could you do this to her at such a time?"

"I asked, are you with them...with the Chairman?" The man had large hands and a terrible odor from his mouth when he spoke.

I wanted to back away, but several men were circling me like wolves.

"His wife is a good girl," the same woman said. "Leave him alone. They're poor as church mice, like the rest of us. If he were a government man, would he look like this?"

The man looked doubtful, but I saw his fist.

An old man, gray beard scraggly and streaked with grease streaks, had been listening silently. "You had something to say. What is it? Nobody will hurt you." He turned to the big guy who was too close for comfort. "Jack, back off. Have we come to the point where we beat up a fellow Jew because he wishes to speak his mind?"

The man called Jack replied, "He sounds like he was defending that bastard who takes the bread from our children. We starve and freeze while Rumkowski and his band of crooks live in luxury."

The old man, a bag of bones, nodded. "In Russia, where I am from, we also had such a ruler. He was called the Tsar. When the people became too hungry, too cold, too angry, they rebelled against this all-powerful ruler, and do you know what happened?" He crushed a bony hand into his palm. "Yes. The people rose against him and executed all of them, his whole family."

The old man was more menacing than the young hot-head because everyone was listening to him. Unlike Jack, ready with his fists, this soft-voiced old man was speaking with such calm authority that nobody could ignore him. If he merely whispered for them to kill me, I suspected, everyone in the crowd would pounce at his command. My ears were attentive to every word.

"I will tell you something, my young friend," he said, "No matter how mighty the Pharaohs, Kings, Emperors, Hitlers are, eventually, they all crumble to dust."

"I wasn't defending—"

"No. Of course not," the old man said. "All I am saying is one must always be careful. No sheep is safe sleeping with wolves." He smiled benevolently. "Always remember that."

I still felt threatened, so I didn't answer.

"We must go." The old man gripped Jack's elbow and pointed his nose toward the corner.

It was a policeman. I recognized his hat and armband.

"Disperse," the officer ordered in a gruff voice, his club in his hand. "You know the rules. No crowds may gather at any time, by order of the Chairman."

I thought of thanking the officer but didn't dare in the mob's presence. I nodded to the old man, grateful he had interceded in what might have been a beating. I had to learn to listen to Miriam. She always said I open my mouth too much. For a young woman, she has the wisdom of the sages, sometimes.

"Remember what I said," the old man rasped and hobbled away.

Even with the crowd gone, I did not relax until I got to our conference room. I sagged into my chair. It had been a close call. I should have thanked the old man. I didn't even know his name.

As had become his habit of late, Singer was the second to arrive. "Did you see the latest proclamation by our great Chairman?" he asked, throwing off his coat. He was too young to feel the cold. "Now, we can't even get some relief from our families. My uncle is in America, in Chicago. How do I tell him he can't send me even a book?" He leaned closer. "The noose is tightening, my friend. The noose is tightening."

Singer looked his indignant self, so I hesitated before I finally got the courage to do something I knew was wrong. What choice did I have? "Oscar, I have a big favor to ask of you. I understand if you can't...are unable to do this for me."

Singer smiled. "You are a good man, Engineer, what can I do for you?"

After I told him what I wanted, he did not give me that "I told you so," grin I expected. Instead, he studied me for several seconds and asked, "Are you sure you want me to do this?"

I handed him my mother's ring. Because my father had been orthodox, the gold band had no stones to add to its value. "It's all I have. I hid it in the wall." I shoved it into his closed hand. "If it is not enough, I understand."

Singer examined the gold band. "It will be enough. But can you live with this after you condemned it?"

"You often say, desperate people, do desperate things."

He nodded.

I handed him a folded sheet of paper. "I think everything is here. If not, improvise."

"I always do. It is how I survive."

The door opened, and Rosenfeld entered.

Singer pocketed the note and my ring. It was as if nothing had happened.

For a second, it hit me I had trusted Singer with my last valuable possession. What if he lost it? What if he gambled it away? How well did I know him? When he called me his friend, was that the ploy of a desperate man? Rumkowski said everyone was capable of being corrupted, even his chosen few. Oh, my God, what have I done? But Singer was still here. He was bent forward, his coat on his chair, listening to Rosenfeld. I forced myself to try and focus, to hear what the good doctor was saying, but all I could think about was that I had given someone, who was a stranger, someone who had shown frequently that he had no respect for the rule of law…I had given him my mother's ring.

"Singer, I tell you, the Chairman only posted this hateful proclamation because the Germans demanded it," Rosenfeld said.

Listening to Singer fighting back, self-righteous and stubborn as always, was oddly calming to my doubts.

"You always excuse his actions," Singer shouted.

"And you always see the worst in him." Rosenfeld characteristically replied.

Their arguing, more like banter, was comforting today. I drifted away, the sound of their debate transforming into Miriam's voice. She was singing. I heard Miriam's sweet voice singing to the tiny being in her belly. And yes, she'd begun to sing lullabies to our unborn child. They were songs my mother had sung to me. The familiar melodies should have comforted me, but I wondered if someday our child would also not know what happened to his parents. Jews disappeared and were never heard from again.

Rings disappear too.

CHAPTER 28

All the way home, I questioned my decision. Singer had my ring. There was no reason for him to fulfill his part of the bargain. Would a gold ring be sufficient to bribe his way out of the ghetto? I'd heard of such things happening. Friends and relatives turning against each other, stealing from each other to survive. Why did I trust him? He will gamble it away or spend it on some whore. Maybe it isn't enough, and he has no choice but to try and win more. He's a kid, no common sense. No sense of responsibility or loyalty.

By the time I got home, I'd decided it had been a foolish idea by a desperate husband. Even Singer, wild as he was, would not risk breaking the curfew to fulfill his part of the deal. So that was that.

Miriam held up two dresses. "Which do you think looks cleanest?" She asked.

"How should I know? Men don't know such things."

She put them both on the table. Leaning down, she studied them top to bottom. "I can't see with only one candle."

"It's the blackout," I reminded her of the German orders.

She picked up the first dress and brought it to the window. She returned it to the table and repeated her actions with the second dress. "They're both schmatas," she said, letting out a deep sigh. "But I promised I would not act like a spoiled brat." She made a funny face, scrunching her cheeks, and held up the dark blue dress with a stained white collar. "This one. I have nothing else."

"It will look beautiful on you," I said, even though the white collar looked stained, more beige than white.

"Did you hear that?" Miriam pushed closer. "The step creaked."

"I heard nothing." And then I heard the door open. I rose to my feet, nearly throwing Miriam to the floor. The chair was my only weapon. I lifted it and then put it down. Why give the intruder an excuse to shoot me?

"Ostrowski, is this you?"

"Singer?"

"I can't see very well."

"You know all lights must be out by eight." I turned to Miriam. "It's okay. It's my friend, Singer."

Singer came closer. "This is your wife? How lovely to finally meet you. Your husband is always talking about you." He leaned toward her, taking advantage of the candle's illumination.

Miriam looked frightened. Her hand squeezed my palm.

I put my arm around her shoulder. "Miriam, my love, this is Dr. Singer. I work with him in the Archives, sorting books."

Singer nodded. "It's a dirty job, but someone has to do it." He gave Miriam his boyish grin.

Miriam's back lost its tension. She released my hand.

"I have something for you," Singer said.

"You can show her." I prepared myself, anticipation building inside me. "Miriam, I love you."

Singer pulled a thin package wrapped in brown paper from inside his coat. "Do you want to see it?" He teased.

Miriam looked curiously at me.

"Open it, you fool," I said, worried about what he might have picked out.

"Only if she says please?"

"Please," Miriam said. "Mr. Singer, please?"

Singer laughed. "I haven't heard anyone say that word so sweetly in years. Very well." He pulled open the paper and unfurled a dress that was black and cut to a vee in front. A thin line of faux pearls accented the vee. Of course, I noted some pearls were missing. "I hope I picked out the right one," he said, as Miriam touched the fabric looking like Cinderella when she first saw her magical gown for the ball. "Do you like it?" Singer asked.

Miriam ran her hand over the fabric. "It's so smooth. It's beautiful." She turned to me. "You did this?"

I was beaming. I made the right decision after all. Singer surpassed my wishes.

"I had some small part in this." Singer sounded like a neglected child.

Miriam's eyes met his. "Thank you," she said in a barely audible voice. "It's amazing." Her hand touched the pearls. "It is beautifully stitched. Where did you find it?"

"That's not important," I hurried.

Miriam looked at Singer. "You didn't do anything unsafe?" This time her eyes remained on his. "If you did, please take it back." She replaced the dress on the brown paper.

Singer looked dumbfounded. For once he didn't know what to say.

"He did nothing unsafe," I lied. "I did it for you."

Miriam turned her eyes to me. "It is a lovely dress, but…but I can't wear it."

"You're worried we can't afford it? I have a job." I dug into my pocket. "Look, Rumkowski dollars." I placed a few newly printed bills, all with his face, on the table. "Soon, we will have a nicer place in which to live…for our child…for you."

Miriam stroked the dress again. "That would be nice, but I can't wear this dress. It will make us look like we are rich."

"Miriam, it's only for the concert. One afternoon." Why did I feel so irritated by her reaction?

Singer was silent, his eyes fixed on Miriam's face.

Where was my eloquent friend when I needed him to help me convince her? "You will be the most beautiful woman there," I said. "Put it on, darling. See for yourself."

"She already is the most beautiful woman." Singer thankfully found his voice. "Please, try it on?"

"Can you take it back?" Miriam asked.

"Take it back? You're being ridiculous! You are being a child!" I instantly regretted saying that, but I had risked so much in asking Singer to get her the dress from his contacts in the black market, breaking my vow never to resort to dealing with these criminals, that I was angry at her refusal to wear it.

Singer kept a calm head. "It will look lovely on you. I would like to see you try it on. Please?"

Miriam glanced at him and then back at me. "If you wish me to, I will try it on."

I felt a chill when she spoke to me. I should have apologized right then and there but in front of Singer?

There was no place in our one-room flat for Miriam to change. She stood behind the table and pulled her soiled dress over her head.

Singer was staring at our front door.

"Thank you," I whispered. "She will be fine once she tries it on. You did well. I'm grateful."

Singer's eyes darted to where Miriam was changing, but then jumped back to me. "You are a lucky man, Engineer. Most women I date would screw my brains out for such a dress."

Had Miriam heard him? I thought I heard her gasp. "Are you in need of help?" I asked her.

"No. I'm ready. You may turn around."

I knew my wife was beautiful but had never seen her dressed up. There had been no formal wedding, just her mother and father giving her to me in the hope I might take her to America. That had been my plan. Unfortunately, I was too late, and we were transported to Lodz, where now I saw my wife standing before me in a black gown that made her look like a woman, no longer a child. I could not believe my eyes. "You're stunning," I stammered. "You are beautiful."

Singer was silent.

Miriam glanced at him and then focused her eyes on me. "Benny, it is a lovely dress, but please, don't make me wear it?"

Singer turned to me. "I can't return it. I may be able to sell it." He smiled at Miriam. "Your husband loves you."

Miriam looked embarrassed. "Thank you," she said. "With so many of my friends struggling for food, how can I wear such a dress?"

"I give up," I said. "Singer, Oscar, thank you. You may leave now. I wish to talk to Miriam alone." I walked over to my friend—I thought of him, after this kind deed, as a friend—and guided him to the door. "Thank you. I mean it. You did more than I expected."

Singer stopped before leaving and turned to Miriam. "I hope you enjoy the concert."

Miriam nodded but didn't reply.

I walked Singer out the door. "Thank you. You truly are a good friend." I pressed some Rumkowski bills into his hand.

He clenched his fist. "No. I don't want your money. She's special. Other girls would kill for a dress like this. You are lucky, my friend. I envy you."

I watched him descend the stairs and slip out into the unlit streets. Only a madman like Singer would risk violating the curfew. I laughed thinking most likely the shrewdie had bribed every officer in the ghetto.

When I returned to the flat, Miriam was standing in her under-things, the dress hanging on a hook on the wall. "If you wish me to wear it, I will," she said.

How can she make such an issue from something so simple? In some ways, she is still a child, I thought, imagining all the eyes of the administrators staring in awe at my bride. They'll all wonder how someone like me could have such a dazzler at my side. "It is only one day," I coaxed, trying to be patient. "Singer risked much to do this. It would be a sin to waste his effort." I did not tell her I'd given him my mother's gold wedding band. She would never have allowed me to sacrifice my last remembrance of my parents.

"I'm going to bed," Miriam said.

I walked with her to the bed. "It really is a beautiful dress." I watched her change into her nightshirt, catching a glimpse of her breasts. They had grown slightly in pregnancy. I hadn't expected that. It made me realize how inexperienced I was with women, especially pregnant women, particularly with their emotions. I curled up against her, feeling secure, thinking her rejection of the dress was a result of her mood changes from carrying our precious child. When she didn't move away, I felt reassured that all would be well. Oh God, she looked so lustrous in that dress. How could any man not fall in love with her? Singer was right, I was a lucky man.

CHAPTER 29

It was the morning after the concert. I was trying to write a record of the memorable event. "Today, the first symphonic concert, conducted by David Bajgelman, took place in the auditorium of the House of Culture at 3 Krawiecka Street." I paused my pen, distracted by the image of Miriam on my arm as we entered the House of Culture. I was right, all eyes were on her.

"They will look at my shoes," Miriam said, standing in the black sheath, arms bare, breasts highlighted by the pearl-accented vee neck.

I glanced down at her feet. I hadn't thought about shoes. New ones were even harder to obtain than dresses. Leather was among the first commodities confiscated by the Germans. "Your shoes are lovely," I said, "Not everybody wears high heels at these things. Besides you would be too tall for your short husband." Her shoes, low heels, were black but scuffed. I picked them up and buffed them with a rag. "Nobody will look at your shoes once they view your lovely body." I stared at her cleavage. "I only wish I had my mother's gold and diamond necklace for you." My father had traded that for tickets out of Poland. That was the last I'd heard from him and my mother. Jews disappeared.

"I could not wear that. Even this dress is too much." She pulled the dress down by the hips. "It barely fits over my little bump," she said.

Looking at her in the black dress, I'd almost forgotten she was pregnant. Most pregnant women looked much larger by this time, I thought. How could she gain weight, feed our unborn child, on the rations in the ghetto? I would talk to Neftalin and demand more. Now that I was in the inner circle, we could get a little greater allowance to assure the health of my child.

There were no cars in the ghetto. Only one horse-drawn coach. Miriam insisted on covering herself with her coat, a ratty thing that made me wish I'd asked Singer to purchase a dressier wrap from his connections. Perhaps that would have been too much, I thought, as I helped Miriam walk on the cobblestones.

It wasn't long before we were joined by other concert goers. I noticed Order Service officers stationed along the route. The Chairman thinks of everything, I thought, as men in suits, women in gowns, made their way to the House of Culture. I gripped Miriam's hand tighter. I felt as if we were being watched by hidden eyes. From windows, from barely open doors they were watching. Was it envy, anger, or hate in their eyes?

Miriam's eyes were darting to the various groups of on-lookers.

"Don't look at them," I said, walking faster.

As we neared the House of Culture, I noticed more police. A commander surveyed the crowd and signaled his men to spread out and block the street from both sides.

It was then I saw the Germans. Unlike our force, they wore uniforms, helmets, and carried rifles with bayonets. I must have been staring at them because suddenly Miriam pulled me awake.

One of the men, an SS officer, was staring at her. His eyes looked hungry, lustful. I was glad she was covered in her shabby coat. I was relieved when he moved on.

"Ostrowski, is this your wife?"

I turned and almost banged into Rumkowski, a young woman on his arm. "I have heard you are doing good work," he said.

I noted two burly men in trench coats, on either side of him, thick truncheons in their hands. "Yes, Miriam, allow me to introduce the honorable, Chairman Rumkowski. Sir, my wife, Miriam Ostrowski."

Rumkowski removed his hat. "It is a pleasure to meet you. Your husband is a great supporter of our cause. You should be proud."

Miriam smiled politely but was silent.

I wished I could read her thoughts. "Thank you, your Excellency," I said. "I am proud to serve you."

Rumkowski nodded. "Enjoy the concert." He gave Miriam a smile. "Please, come to our other cultural events. It will be my pleasure to host you again."

"Thank you," Miriam said.

I was afraid she was going to overcome her natural reticence and unleash some of her pent-up frustrations, but she behaved like a lady, much to my relief.

I watched Rumkowski walk off, bodyguards scanning in all directions. I stared past him. The German soldiers were watching his every move as well.

Miriam didn't speak. I wondered what she thought of the 'old man.' She had been contemptuous of him, accused him of greed and elitism, but here he was, with the masses, waiting for the concert hall to open. In his thick tweed coat, a brown scarf around his neck, white hair tumbling down from his felt hat, he looked like a grandfather, I thought, as Miriam shared none of her thoughts to me.

I expected the German soldiers, without warning, to throw themselves in front of the door and declare the concert forbidden, but they remained on the outskirts, hawks, staring down at us from their assigned positions. They were apparently content to observe us, at a slight distance. It was the Jewish police who actively forced curious bystanders to stand behind the barricades or risk being 'thumped' by their clubs.

"He's very tall," Miriam said, breaking her silence. "Perhaps that's why the Germans chose him."

I was about to respond when the doors swung open. I assisted Miriam as we climbed the wide concrete stairs. I'd never been in the House of Culture before and was surprised by its size and opulence. Reddish wood covered the entry walls. I was amazed it hadn't been stolen for firewood, or burnt to the ground by the Germans, as they had done to our synagogues.

"Are any of your coworkers here?" Miriam asked as I helped her off with her coat.

"I don't see anyone." I was disappointed they could not see her in this dress.

Miriam clutched my arm as we walked deeper into the hall.

"Ostrowski, you're here?" Doctor Rosenfeld approached. "And this is the lovely wife you are always talking about. Charmed, my dear. You are even more beautiful than your husband described." He removed his glove, and bowing, kissed her hand.

"This is my good friend, Doctor Oskar Rosenfeld," I said, pride swelling inside me.

Rosenfeld smiled. "Thank you, Engineer." He turned to Miriam. "Is this your first concert here? You will enjoy it. It is one of the rare treats left to an old man like me."

I noticed he had replaced the gloves on his hands.

"You don't look a day older than when I first met you," Miriam said.

"But we've never met before," Rosenfeld replied. "I would have remembered. I'm not so senile yet to forget such a lovely smile."

"Exactly," Miriam said and gave him the first warm smile I'd seen from her all evening.

"How does the Engineer like the hall?" Rosenfeld asked. "Is it up to your standards?"

"It's remarkable." I leaned closer. "I'd have thought the wolves would have torn it down by now."

"Shhh. Don't give them ideas." Rosenfeld pressed closer. "The Chairman convinced them it was essential to the smooth operation of the factories. Nearly all management and ghetto administration are here tonight. It is one of the few cultural vestiges left us. How I used to enjoy listening to my radio. Even that pleasure is banned."

"I loved my music," Miriam said, "but tell me, Doctor, how can you enjoy such lavishness as this when others cannot even eat?"

Rosenfeld looked surprised.

"Miriam," I said, dismayed by what might be perceived as rudeness.

"No. It is fine," Rosenfeld replied, giving Miriam a smile. "As an old socialist, I too share such thoughts. But you see, my dear, I have come to believe this ghetto, in which we are all imprisoned, is living on borrowed time. You don't understand? You saw the Germans outside? I am convinced that if one misstep occurs in the smooth operation of our factories, they will crush us under their boots like matchsticks."

"I've told her this same thing many times," I said. "I've explained to her that though there are some things I may disagree with the Chairman about, on the whole, I believe he is the only thing saving us from whatever fate Hitler has in store for the Jews of Europe."

"Do you agree?" Miriam asked.

"Yes. But I'm an old man bewitched by a beautiful young woman, so what do I know?"

"You won't win her over with flattery," I said.

Rosenfeld laughed. "The truth is not flattery." He turned to Miriam. "My dear, will you do me the honor of helping this old man up the stairs?"

Miriam clutched his elbow and walked with Rosenfeld up the grand staircase, past the glass doors that led to the auditorium. I sat on one side of her, Rosenfeld sat on the other.

Miriam was in awe of the proscenium arch and the carved figures that decorated the posts along the high walls. Her eyes scanned the audience. "Everyone is so well dressed," she said. "How is it possible?"

The musicians began tuning up, and suddenly there was silence, as the great Dawid Bajgelman crossed the stage. He looked older than I expected. The lights dimmed, and the music came from all around us. First, there was Bela Keler's Overture. Miriam's hand tightened on mine. When I dared a look at her eyes; they were closed. Popa's Suite Orientale next transported us to the Far East. I envisioned exotic dancers in fluid movement as the music swelled. I was sorry when it ended. It was followed by "Shabes Nokhn Kugel," "After the Sabbath

Meal," also by Popa, a reverential piece that reminded me of Sabbath meals long ago. I refused to let sad thoughts ruin my evening, not with Miriam's hand in mine.

After Bajgelman accepted a thunderous round of applause, he proudly returned to the orchestra, leading them in two of his own works. I was not fond of either, but it had been so long since I'd shared the passion of an orchestra that I even enjoyed these pieces, especially glancing at Miriam and seeing how she was transported by the music.

"I wish I could play like that," Miriam said.

"It is just mathematics," I replied.

Rosenfeld leaned over. "Do you hear yourself, Engineer? Your sweet wife is transported by the passion of music, and, you ascribe it to the cold mechanics of mathematics?"

"It's the way he thinks," Miriam said, her eyes scanning the galleries again.

After the intermission, the orchestra played the overture from Massenet's Phedre. The last piece was about to begin when a spotlight revealed Rumkowski walking with great dignity across the stage.

"Even in a concert?" Miriam asked.

"Shaa, Miriam." I looked around. This was not the time and place to criticize our leader.

Rumkowski took center stage and spoke in a booming voice, "Ladies and Gentlemen, I will take only a minute of your time. Is this not a magnificent program?"

The audience burst into applause.

"We must thank our performers, under the very able direction of David Bajgelman, a gift to us from Kielce Province."

Bajgelman bowed as the audience applauded again.

The Chairman waited for silence. "This wonderful event is the result of the work of your Elders, of whom I am proud to be the Chairman."

There was more applause.

"I will tell you that your great Council has arranged two more performances for today. The great violinist Miss Bronislawa Rotsztat, accompanied by Teodor Ryder, performed today in Kitchen 2."

"That's the dining hall for the Intelligentsia," I whispered to Miriam. "You see, the Chairman provides for all of us."

"Shaa," she shot back at me, listening attentively to the Chairman, whom she had never heard speak before in public.

"And today on the premises of the soup kitchen at 16 Berek Joselewicz Street, there was an evening dedicated to our young poets, while at the soup kitchen at Masarska Street, the fifth consecutive Oneg Shabes, "Joy of Sabbath," was celebrated with happy songs. The Council hopes this is the start of many more cultural events, our token of appreciation for your cooperation in making our ghetto the industrial core of Poland. Our reputation is known throughout Europe! So, thank you all, and enjoy the rest of this wonderful program." Rumkowski was beaming from the stage.

I saw his bodyguards on either wing. I did not see the German police, but they could have been lurking backstage.

The applause was loud and long. I applauded with the others.

Miriam applauded politely, but whispered, "He even steals the spotlight today."

I would have answered, but the music was about to begin for the last song.

Miriam was humming some of the lighter melodies as we walked home. I was checking the narrow alleyways and scanning the upper windows and roofs. I wanted nothing to ruin this outing.

As we undressed for bed, Miriam was silent.

"Did you enjoy the concert," I asked.

She smiled and kissed me on my cheek.

In bed, she lay on her back, staring up at the ceiling. "I wish I could see stars," she said softly.

It made me realize that I had not seen the night sky for months. "Someday," I vowed, "I will show you and our child the most beautiful starry nights ever."

It had been a good night. The music had soothed my precious wife. While we were both too tired to make love—I was tempted, even in her current state—we nestled in our bed together until she fell asleep. She looked as if she was smiling. Perhaps she was still listening to the music or envisioning the stars.

The next morning, I left early. I wanted the memory of last night to last. I was afraid with the passage of night, Miriam might say something that would puncture our temporary joy. I did not want to risk our horrid reality cutting into my good feelings. The interlude made me feel more optimistic that the war would end soon and Miriam, our child, and I, would enjoy many more concerts and star-filled nights.

The conference room was empty when I arrived. I set about documenting the gala. I found it difficult to describe its impact on my emotions, so I listed all the performances around the ghetto and thanked the Chairman for sponsoring such diversions. Of course, I mentioned Rumkowski's short speech, "so well received with thunderous applause." It was the least I could do to thank him. I was about to type my entry when Singer came in. His hair was disheveled, coat unbuttoned, necktie hanging.

"How did you enjoy the concert?" He asked, pulling out a chair and almost falling onto it.

"Were you there?" I wondered if he was drunk.

He laughed raucously. "I wouldn't be seen dead in one of these posh events." He brushed back his shiny black hair. It looked as if he had been in the rain. "Did your wife enjoy it?"

"Yes. Of course. I should have thanked you right away. I'm sorry. You made yesterday very special for us. I'm grateful."

Singer smiled, but his smile looked strange to me, not a full smile. He slurred his words. "If I can do anything for you, or for your wife, please ask." He reached for a pile of notes from the various departments. "Let's get to work."

I gazed at his head bent low over the pile of papers. Sheet after sheet he skimmed and placed flat down on the table.

A few minutes later, I looked again. Singer's head was down, resting on his arms. Was he asleep? I was typing, the keys making their usual racket, but Singer didn't stir. When Rosenfeld and Cukier entered, I signaled them to be quiet. "Oscar is asleep," I whispered.

"Our 'teen-ager' must have had a fun night," Rosenfeld said.

Cukier frowned. "He's nearly thirty and should act it."

I was reading the entry to my two co-workers when I realized Singer was listening as well. He did not voice his usual objections, nor raise the expected questions about the propriety of holding a concert with everything going on in the ghetto. He didn't offer even one slightly sarcastic remark about the Eldest of the Jews. In fact, he remained quiet most of the day.

It was one of the most pleasant days I'd experienced on this job. As I walked home, I thought, that at last, our young revolutionary had joined the team. And then I laughed, thinking it was more likely that Singer had exhausted himself with a night of debauchery. After what he did for me, I felt he deserved whatever pleasure he could get.

CHAPTER 30

*S*UNDAY, MARCH 2, 1941: *AN INSPECTION BY THE GERMAN AUTHORITIES*
Took place today at Precinct I of the Order Service at 27 Franciszkanska Street. The inspectors acquainted themselves with the progress of that institution's work and also visited the jail at the station.

"Is that it?" I asked Rosenfeld who had written the entry based on a note in his pile.

Rosenfeld had already slid his always cold fingers back into his gloves. "That's all the commander wrote."

"It's frightening," Singer said, "All we need is for them to start taking over. Then the shit will really hit the fan."

I laughed. "It's good to have the old Singer back!"

"This isn't funny. We should find out if this so-called inspection was known about by the Chairman in advance." Singer flipped through his pile of memos, searching for any related to the inspection.

"So, you've come to our point of view at last?" I asked.

"I have no idea what you mean, but this could be the tip of the iceberg."

"I will ask Neftalin if he knew of the inspection, but here's one for you, Doctor." Cukier let out a laugh. "You have to love it. "A Mirla Dancygier addressed a letter to the Chairman. She requested he make it possible for her to live to be one hundred years old."

We all burst into laughter. "How old is this enterprising woman now?" I, the numbers man, asked. Staring at the blank walls, feeling them closing in on me, I couldn't imagine wishing to be here until I was one hundred. Even the large photo of Rumkowski would have been a break from the barrenness of this torture chamber in which I'd so willingly entrapped myself.

Cukier scratched his head. "It says here she's 97."

Singer gasped. "She must already be the oldest person in the ghetto! Nobody I know is that old. Not even Rosenfeld."

"You little brat," Rosenfeld said, smiling. "But seriously, I also know nobody that old. She must be the oldest in all of Lodz, perhaps Poland."

"That's what she says too. Listen to this, "As the oldest person in the ghetto, I am counting on the Chairman to summarily order a supplemental food allocation for me in the name of humanitarianism and out of pity for an old woman."

Rosenfeld clapped his gloved hands. "Good for her! I hope she got it?"

Singer frowned. "We should all be treated exactly alike. That is the problem with the ghetto now. The Chairman makes a great pronouncement that all are impacted equally, but—"

Cukier interrupted, "She's 97, Singer. Give her a break! Give me a break too!" He shook his head and read silently. "Oh no."

"What is it?" I asked, wondering if the rest of us would ever reach anywhere near our nineties.

Cukier held the paper toward me. "You have to read this. I can't."

I continued reading, "Investigation revealed that the petitioner had increased her age by eighteen years." Now, I was scratching my head.

"She lied about her age?" Rosenfeld looked shocked.

"All women lie about their age," Singer said.

"Yes, but they usually make themselves younger," Rosenfeld replied. He shook his head. "Desperate people do desperate things."

I glanced at Singer who always said that to excuse some of the illegal acts of the Lodz residents.

Cukier said, "Let young Singer write this one up. He needs to know about old people, and we all need a good laugh."

"Here's one you'll love, especially Singer. "A sick-five-year old boy was brought to the hospital. When he was being undressed, a little sack tied with a string around his neck was found under his shirt.""

"A smuggler at five? Our Chairman is right, crime is everywhere. But five?" Rosenfeld shook his head.

"No. The lad wasn't a smuggler. Not exactly. The sack contained a good-sized portion of bread. He fought the nurse when she tried to take it from him, even after she explained he was going to be fed at the hospital. He proclaimed that the bread was his property, bought with his own money. When the nurse asked how he got the money, he replied, "I have my own money because I'm on welfare.""

Cukier burst into laughter again. "The poor boy should be a lawyer."

Singer shook his head. "Poor boy? Poor everybody."

I hissed to Singer, "He's a future black market, trader, like you, my friend."

Singer didn't reply.

I was beginning to worry about my young coworker. He had lost his sense of humor yet was more diligent than he'd ever been. He was moody lately, as if he was keeping something back, some new secret. His old ones, his past, we'd given up on learning ages ago.

"Let's write it up. Singer, how about you, performing the honors?"

Singer nodded.

"Wait," Rosenfeld said. "May I see the note about this boy?" He removed his glove and read it silently, his lips moving. "Where are the child's parents?" He asked.

"It doesn't say." Why hadn't I thought of that?

"Exactly," Rosenfeld said softly. "Exactly."

"What does it matter," Singer said. "There's nothing we can do."

We never found out what happened to the parents. We didn't look. People were disappearing from the ghetto every day. There were too many young boys and girls sheltered in Rumkowski's orphanages. Nobody ever asked what happened to the parents. Too often, there weren't any answers.

The paper floated to the table with almost a hundred other stories for us to read, discuss, write up, and type. I was fine as long as I kept myself from feeling anything for the rising number of victims of the war. They were all just numbers. It was better that way.

When I went home, I locked all the terrible stories of the day in our ten by twelve-foot workroom and prayed they would stay there rather than haunting me when I was with Miriam. But, as usual, my prayers were rarely answered, and the sadness of what I knew, but could not share with her, permeated our relationship. Not being able to tell her what I was doing because I couldn't be honest with her, restricted me from asking how she spent her days. As long as the grumbling had decreased, I was happy to not ask too many questions. She was home when I got there. I assumed the pregnancy had lightened her mood. As she sang lullabies to our unborn child, I fooled myself into thinking that everything would be fine.

CHAPTER 31

MONDAY, MARCH 3, 1941: *A DAY OF JOY IN THE GHETTO*
The first of March brought the populace a pleasant surprise in the form of supplemental food rations, vegetables being especially plentiful. Equally pleasant surprises were the denatured alcohol and vinegar, neither of which had been available for a long time. Moreover, the populace received sausage and meat, and the coal allotment came to 20 kilograms. In addition, the youngest ghetto dwellers each received one cauliflower...

"Things are looking up," Neftalin said, after handing us the Chairman's report. "What the Chairman has said in his recent public addresses about conditions improving is coming true."

I read further. "The crowning moment came on March 3, "a day which will long remain in the memories of all ghetto dwellers." What happens today?" I asked.

Neftalin smiled. "A new proclamation will inform everyone that their electric lights may be kept on after eight in the evening."

Rosenfeld's eyes showed surprise. "If this is true, it is like a ray of light in the hopeless bleakness of everyday life."

Singer came bouncing into the door. "What's going on? I have not seen such smiles in days. Is it true? The lights may remain on at night?"

Neftalin beamed. "Yes, my friends, our darkest days are behind us. Our faith in the Chairman is being borne out by all this wonderful news."

Rosenfeld laughed. "I must write this up. When was the order first given by the Germans that we could not use lights after eight? Engineer?"

I searched my brain. "November 14, 1940. Am I right?"

Singer searched the proclamation book. "You're amazing! Exactly right. I don't know how you do it."

"Everyone has a gift, my friend."

"I wish I knew mine," Singer muttered.

"Just imagine what a difference this will make," Rosenfeld said, tossing his gloves into his coat pocket. "Our workers will no longer have to eat in the dark."

"With the food we have, we're better off in the dark," Singer remarked.

Rosenfeld wagged his finger at his protégé. "Young man, having light will make many things easier. Mothers will be able to feed their children by light."

"Also diaper them," Singer threw in. "Imagine, Engineer, trying to change your squirmy, shit-covered child in the dark." He looked at me. "You'll know that pleasure soon enough."

I hadn't thought about that. What kind of father would I be?

Neftalin was smiling at our banter. "Gentlemen, friends, the Chairman is waiting for me. I must go, but please carry on your good work. Someday soon, this will be over, and the future will know of our valiant struggle to defeat the occupiers with hard work and Jewish organizational skill. Someday, our Chairman will be regarded as a hero, equivalent to the Maccabees, David, and Solomon."

"I can't believe we're going to have lights at last," I said to Cukier. "Now, if we can get electricity."

"I shall enjoy being able to read by light again," Rosenfeld replied. "It is strange how you take such things for granted."

Singer was silent.

"What is it, Singer? Have you found something sad to write about

172

even in this?" I asked.

"We are fools," he said in a low voice.

"I'm not a fool!" Rosenfeld shot back.

"We all are. Don't you understand? The Chairman passed a proclamation allowing for electric lights after eight and we are all celebrating and heaping praise on his Solomon-like wisdom and policies."

"So, what is wrong with that?" Rosenfeld asked. "Our darkness is being relieved when we were all losing hope."

"Don't you get it? Of course, they're letting us use lights after eight... just as the days are growing longer." He shook his head. "It's all a big con. It's all another crock of bullshit!"

"No. It is not!" Cukier shouted and burst into a short fit of coughing. "Get out! Get the hell out, Singer! I'm sick and tired of you poking holes in every good thing that happens to us." He doubled over, grabbing the table, coughing hard into his hand.

Singer jumped up, looking unsure of what to do. "I'm sorry. I'm sorry. I didn't mean anything by it." He looked at me. "I've said worse."

Cukier was still coughing, Rosenfeld holding him up. "Get him out of here," he croaked between wracking coughs.

I put my arm on Singer's shoulder. "Go out for a while. He'll calm down. He always does. You did nothing wrong."

"Get him...out...of...my...sight," Cukier repeated, choking on phlegm.

"I'm sorry, Julian. I was wrong." Singer said standing awkwardly behind his chair. "I didn't mean to upset him," he said to Rosenfeld.

Rosenfeld whispered something into Singer's ear.

Singer grabbed his coat from the chair and carried it to the door. "I'm really sorry, Julian. I would never hurt you. Not any of you." He pulled open the door and left.

Cukier sank back into his chair. He was hacking, choking on his coughs which he covered with his cloth. "I'm sorry. I'm sorry.

Go…get him back."

"Are you sure? He can be damn annoying." I knew that too well.

Cukier nodded, panting hard. "Not…his…fault."

"Doctor, will you see if he's in the hall?" I didn't want to leave Julian who was still leaning on the table, eyes bulging, sweat beading on his face.

Rosenfeld rushed to the door and peered into the dimly lit corridor. "I don't see him. I'll check outside. Knowing him, he's mingling with the malcontents."

Cukier, still gasping for air, muttered. "I shouldn't have lost my temper… like that… but he punctures… every… hope…every damn…hope. We must have…hope."

"He knows you didn't mean it. He's probably smoking outside." I wondered when Cukier had cleaned the handkerchief. It was covered in green and brown stains. "Are you having many such coughing fits?"

"It is difficult to give myself injections in the dark," Cukier said, still struggling for air.

"Don't talk. Breathe deeply, my friend."

I watched with care as his coughing leveled off. He kept the handkerchief enclosed in his fist.

I had a spot of blood on my hand. Oh God, Julian, what next?

Rosenfeld returned. "He's nowhere to be found."

"I'm sorry," Cukier said, "Singer didn't deserve…that."

"Don't worry, Oscar has skin like a rhinoceros…a thick head too." I joked but wondered if that was true.

Cukier leaned on the table. "I'm going for fresh air." He wiped his nose with the handkerchief. "Will you two finish this, please?"

"Do you want me to come with you?" I was half out of my chair.

Cukier rasped, "I'm not a cripple."

The door closed behind him.

"I never meant to imply he was," I said.

Rosenfeld held up a gloved hand. "We're all under too much

pressure."

I began to type. I turned to Rosenfeld. "You do know Singer is right."

"Yes. I know. The Germans passed this blessing to us just as the days are growing longer. Maybe, they didn't know that?"

"You and I both know they did."

Rosenfeld nodded and ducked back into the safety of his notices.

I wrote up the entry, ending it with, "What is more important is the fact that this proclamation came just as the days were getting longer." Maybe something of Singer's cynicism was rubbing off on me, or it may have been Miriam's questioning finally making inroads on my attitude. Whatever it was, I was finding it difficult to justify and applaud every action of the Chairman, as I had sworn to do since the beginning. Cynicism appeared to be the price I had to pay for being in the inner circle.

When Cukier returned, he read my entry. He didn't comment but added the following: "The slogan, "Work and Peace," constantly underscored by the Chairman in his speeches, has again taken on the glow of life. The lifting of the ban on using electricity will allow people to live in more normal conditions and, consequently, create an atmosphere which favors the carrying out of the Chairman's slogan."

As the day ended and Singer did not return, I walked home thinking, "The Chairman said, "Let there be light." Now if only the Germans would give us electricity.

CHAPTER 32

T UESDAY, MARCH 4, 1941: *TRESPASSING IN THE GHETTO*
Today, on the grounds of the ghetto, agents of the Order Service detained a Pole, a resident of Pabianice, near Lodz, named Bronislaw Fogt, who had entered the ghetto illegally. He has been put at the disposition of the criminal police.

We had just returned from the funeral for Henryk Neftalin's father. The makeshift room, serving as a synagogue, now that the Nazis had set fire to the original, was packed. I was in the back with Rosenfeld and Cukier. Singer hadn't returned. I could see the Chairman, his white hair and hat towering above most of the people between us.

It was a long service. Rabbi Fajner and several other dignitaries spoke for such a long time, people began to fall asleep. I wondered if the Chairman would offer one of his orations, but he remained next to his Deputy. He did not stay for the reception line but shook a few hands and then hurried into his black, horse-drawn coach parked outside. I looked behind the coach and saw Order Service guards. A short distance away, two black cars with German police stared at the crowd.

Rosenfeld was having difficulty walking. "How did your charming wife enjoy the concert?" He asked, pulling on his gloves though it was no longer as cold as it had been during our frigid winter.

"Very much, I think." She wasn't as overjoyed as I'd hoped. She was silent as she hung the dress in the closet, straightening it with care.

"Yes, she loved it," I said.

"It was a rare diversion." Rosenfeld sighed. "Even funerals are diversions from day to day monotony. Hell, most dead today can't afford a coffin, let alone such an affair as this."

"I can't think of funerals as diversions. We have more and more of these diversions every day."

We walked silently for several blocks, storefronts, boarded-up, "Jude," painted in yellow letters across their naked plywood skin.

"They're always here," I said, seeing the usual crowd in front of the Chairman's offices.

"We'd be there too if we were not employed," Rosenfeld said.

"You'd be out here with them? Next, you'll tell me your name is Singer." I laughed at that idea but wondered where he was. I'd wanted him to disappear many times but now was worried about the rascal.

Rosenfeld saw someone he knew and waved. The other man nodded. "He hates me because I work for the Chairman."

"They don't understand the good he is doing for them. Just look at how our food has improved. I think our kitchen is doing a great job."

Rosenfeld flashed his identification card at the sentry and passed into the dimly lit hallway. "Have you eaten at the other kitchens lately? The food is terrible. We're fortunate to dine at Kitchen 2. It is Rumkowski's gift to his most loyal workers. Did you know his sister, Helena Rumkowska, heads it?"

"His sister?"

Rosenfeld stopped walking. "You didn't know. I think this would make a wonderful story. Tell Julian, I'm being a reporter." He laughed. "Who knows? Maybe I'll find a few Jewish skeletons in the dining room's closet."

I thought he was walking faster as he headed toward the massive dining hall. I walked toward the Archives, eager to have some alone time and write up my observations of the funeral. When I opened the door, I froze in fear. Someone was here.

Singer was bent over the table reading through the usual departmental memoranda as if he had never left.

"You missed a splendid funeral," I said, not wanting to give him the satisfaction of inquiring where he'd been.

"How is Julian? I didn't mean to upset him." He placed the papers flat on the table.

"Oscar, you always find something to complain about. Normally, we accept it. It's just you, being you." I sat down. "I think Julian was so happy about the lights, and then you—"

"I know. I should learn to keep my big mouth shut."

"Only sometimes." I gave him a smile. "So? Any news?"

Singer pulled a folded paper from a seam in his jacket. "Tell me what you think of this."

I read the brief memo. "It says the Order Service turned an illegal alien over to the Kripo." I looked at him. "This is a first if it is true?"

Singer nodded. "It is true. Jews are—"

"We're giving up people to the German police."

"It looks that way."

"Let me reread it?" The brief report was hidden in a long list of incidents the Jewish police had supplied to Neftalin. "From what I read here, it says he's a Pole, not a Jew."

"Does that make a difference?"

"Wouldn't it be much worse if the man was Jewish and the Jewish Police turned him over to the Nazis?"

"Would it?"

"You're answering me by throwing back questions?"

"Well, be honest. Does it make a difference that it is not a Jew who we are turning over to be tortured, murdered, or whatever they do to those they label criminals?"

I didn't want to answer. I reexamined the memo. "It's genuine. Okay. But note here. It says this Bronislaw entered the ghetto illegally. He's a thief or a smuggler. He could even be a murderer of Jews."

"Then he should get a fair trial. That was our procedure until the Chairman changed it."

"But he has no choice. Crime is rising like a serpent with many heads. If he doesn't cut off these criminals, it will spread until the Germans will take the law over and it will be much worse. They hate us Jews. You know that."

Singer smiled. "I only ask questions." He pulled out his pad and began to write.

Of course, he did. He upset me, made me ponder the morality of Jewish police turning over a non-Jew to the Kripo, and then ducks the question by burying himself in his work. Typical Singer. "So, tell me, Socrates, what do you think of this?"

"You really want to know?"

I hated when he grinned like that. "I have a feeling I know already, but yes, I want to know."

"I think you already know and agree, even if you won't admit it. It is very frightening. It is a dangerous precedent. We've turned over a fellow human being to the cruel hand of Nazi justice, injustice. Jew, non-Jew, legal, or illegal, we are collaborating with the devil."

"Stop exaggerating. This is only one case. The man is most likely a smuggler, a vicious criminal, who deserves to be punished."

"Trust me, dear Engineer, he will be. He will be. That is one thing you can be sure of when you turn a sheep, even a black sheep, over to the wolves, he will be severely punished. Is your conscience that dead that you can accept such a travesty?"

The door opened. It was Rosenfeld. I expected to see him excited and jubilant about his first major internal investigation. Instead, he walked in and pulled out his notepad. "Where have you been?" He asked Singer. "I was worried."

"You never have to worry about me," Singer replied.

Rosenfeld shook his head and muttered, "Youth."

"Did you get the inside story?" I asked, trying to cut them off before they meandered into a heated debate about the pros and cons of being young.

"Mr. Singer, I'll talk to you later." Rosenfeld gave Singer a paternal smile and then turned to me. "It's quite an operation. It serves more than one thousand people each meal. The director is our Chairman's sister. She gave me this leaflet explaining the function of the kitchen. The introduction is revealing:

Anyone who was in Paris between 1920 and 1925 and took a cab from the railroad station driven by a former Russian grand duke, or was given his room key by a liveries porter who had formerly been a chamberlain at the Tsar's court, would certainly recall those moments when you cross the threshold of Kitchen No 2, the so-called Soup Kitchen for the Intelligentsia.

"Whoever wrote this should write for us," I said.

"She's comparing a ghetto kitchen to that of the decadent Tsar." Singer sighed. "It's far too wordy. It's decadent. Okay. Forget I said that."

Rosenfeld chuckled. "There's more:

The Soup Kitchen for the Intelligentsia is a likely place to find people who once were something, who at one time held important positions, living life to the fullest, and who have today been torn away from all of that.

"They were once "something?" Does that mean the rest of us are nothing?" Singer asked.

"He'll love the rest," Rosenfeld said.

"I love it already," Singer replied, "But don't mind me, I'm a 'nothing.' This is insulting."

Rosenfeld shook his head and read the rest of the kitchen's official introduction:

"It is only when we look at the regular customers of Kitchen No 2 that we can appreciate what the kitchen gives them besides food. It is there and only there that they can find even the illusion of what they had once been accustomed to: a measure of politeness in people's behavior and in the way they are treated—they who are no longer of the elite classes, and now pauperized—a clean and well-set table, dishes that are not nicked, and, finally pleasant surroundings and good company."

"Bullshit!" Singer shouted. "Is that polite enough for the parasites?"

"Singer!"

180

"Fine. I'd rather suffer with the rest of the working class than dine with these selfish parasites. God, I hate this."

Rosenfeld looked annoyed. "It is a sort of club where these people who once were something meet for the midday meal. What is the harm? They have lost far more than most."

"As I said before, to these once high-and-mighty elitists, these "somethings," we are nothing. So much for equality in Rumkowski's ghetto. It is all a myth."

"But they are nothing now too," Rosenfeld said. "We have all fallen. Some from greater heights than others, but we are in the muck together."

"Amen," Singer said. "But their muck is coated with Rumkowski dollars."

And so the argument went until I drowned it out pounding the typewriter keys. Even that monster was a refuge from the bickering. After Rosenfeld's report, each day when I dined at Kitchen 2, I couldn't help noting the clothing and faces of the men and women, eating from their un-nicked plates, with their shiny silver utensils, and try to guess which of them were once something."

Singer had begun to disappear before most of our meals. I assumed he was protesting the favoritism provided for the privileged few at Kitchen #2. Rosenfeld said he was just being Singer. No one asked where he was or why he was late coming back. At times, the rascal brought us firsthand accounts of incidents in the ghetto. Often, he looked out of breath and disheveled, as if he'd been running or had dressed quickly. I even thought perhaps he'd found a female friend. But the braggart would have let us old married men know that.

CHAPTER 33

WEDNESDAY, MARCH 5, 1941: *THE CHAIRMAN*
This morning, accompanied by the director of the Central Workshop Bureau, the Chairman spent some time outside the ghetto. Among other things, the Chairman inspected the work being performed by local residents demolishing the buildings which abut the ghetto.

"Apparently, the rumors are true then," I said to Singer, just before heading out of the building. "But why, in the middle of a war would the Germans devote assets to destroy buildings around our ghetto?"

"Don't you see? They are making permanent their control of the city." Singer said. "This could be disastrous for us."

"It reminds me of when I was a teacher at the university," Rosenfeld said, sucking on his tobacco-less pipe. "They used to give me every shit job because I did my tasks too well."

"What does that have to do with this?" I asked, still mulling over the idea that everything around us was being turned into a kind of 'no-Jews land' where we would be marooned on an isolated, shrinking, an island called the ghetto.

Singer put down the paper he was working on. "I agree. Rumkowski has done his job too well. By turning us into the manufacturing powerhouse of the Reich, he has awakened the Germans to how much they need to possess all of Lodz. Is that what you mean?"

Rosenfeld nodded. "It's a paradox. Our continued existence as a community depends on our factories, but if we screw up, the Germans have the perfect excuse to take over. On the other hand, the better we do, they have even more reason to want control." He sighed. "It's a paradox. Did I say that already?"

"Good night, Professor," I said.

Singer helped Rosenfeld button his coat. The old man was still wearing his gloves. "Would you like me to walk you home?" he asked.

"Do I need a babysitter now?" Rosenfeld barked but immediately added, "Thank you, dear boy. I am fine."

I smiled at Singer and left. I was pondering Rosenfeld's paradox theory when I heard a great deal of commotion as I approached Miynarska Street. A young woman carrying a child handed me a handbill. I have no idea how they got these printed. I could, however, guess most of their demands.

Loud shouts interrupted my reading. Angry voices of men and women were condemning the ghetto's government. Young leaders were conducting a chorus of "Down with the Chairman! Up with the people!" I estimated the crowd at about several hundred and swelling. A few scattered placards were waved in the air as the young ones incited the crowd to shout louder.

They are peaceful at least, I thought, making my way through the mob, glancing to see if I knew anyone.

"Welcome brother," a young woman said, handing me another flyer. I began to read it, but the mob was enveloping me in its stench. Claustrophobia was a problem for me after being in our stuffy conference room. I was sweating, finding it impossible to move through the teeming throng, fists in the air, shouting, and reinforcing each other's protesting. "Excuse me. Excuse me." I tried to forge my path through, but the crowd held me in its grip. I was mired in the mass when I sensed a change. I wheeled around.

Eyes were aimed toward both ends of the street.

"What is happening?" I asked. The sight of a phalanx of Order Service caps at both ends of the road sent an alarm bell off in my brain. "Excuse me! I must get through!" I weaved past the young, old, sane and insane, shouting and waving their arms and a few signs. "Pregnant wife! I must get to her! Please, let me by?"

The police were advancing in a straight line from either end. The formation's pace was controlled, deliberate, meant to be authoritative and menacing. A man I took to be a Commander shouted into a horn, "By order of the Eldest of the Jews, you are to go home immediately!"

I want to. I want to, my brain shouted, as the crowd pushed me forward.

"You go home, bastards! Jewish traitors!" I heard someone shout back at the police.

"No! Don't provoke them!" I saw an alleyway. It was within reach. I want to go home to Miriam! "Let me by! Let me by!"

The Commander raised his club. "Go home! If you do not obey, we will disperse you!" A barrage of curses was hurled at the slowly advancing police. Several young men and women locked their arms together. Some demonstrators slipped through the opening the police deliberately left and slunk back to their homes. But most of the throng was steadfast, refusing to make way for the club-wielding officers.

"This is your last warning," the Commander shouted. "This street must be cleared immediately by order of the Chairman!"

People near me now linked arms. I snaked through, avoiding anyone reaching for me. "Go home. Go home," I wanted to shout, pushing my way to the alley, anything to get away.

A scream reached me. Suddenly, there were more screams. I looked in the direction they came from and saw the police swinging their clubs down on the backs, shoulders, and heads of the first rows of protestors. "No," I screamed, "they were hurting nobody!" The arms of the police, now turned into black clubs, swung down hard, and people screamed and fell to the ground, blood splattering. The truncheons kept striking them until the battered victims became unconscious or managed to slink away. I could only save myself. I had to for Miriam, for my child.

There were more screams, agonized wails. The crowd stampeded, many running over each other and their fallen comrades. The smell of urine was in my nostrils as I fled from their touch, pushed back and forth by the rushing people, as the line of police caps advanced, arms swinging and swinging, non-stop pummeling of the crowd.

"Stop! Stop!" Nobody listened. They were shoving me this way and that, children fell beneath feet. Blood streamed on faces and clubs.

"Clear the street!" The shout was closer, the pained cries louder.

"I'm not with them," I shouted, the police within yards of where I was trapped. I knew it was dangerous but waved my government identification card. The people near me were too busy escaping from the rain of blows, bloodied hands reaching for wounds. Men, women, even children, were reeling, falling to the cobblestones, blood shooting in the air. "For God's sake, I'm with the Chairman!" Someone reached to grab my identification. I pushed his bloody face to the ground and kicked him in the stomach with my shoe. I waved the card furiously.

"Let him pass," a policeman ordered. "What are you doing with them?" He demanded, his club, stained red, pounding his black-gloved palm.

"Oh God, thank you." I caught my breath. "These rabble-rousers show no respect for the Elders. They hate law and order," I said, recoiling when he abruptly swung hard, his club smashing in the side of a woman's face. I averted my eyes, but could not silence the animal scream as she fled, her hand holding her jaw together.

"Follow me," the officer said.

I wanted to protest the need for such violence, but not now. I had to focus on escaping this unreal scene. I had to get to Miriam, to live for my wife and child. I followed closely as he plowed through the stragglers. I held the pass in front of me, resisting the urge to run, walking upright among a sea of human beings, many knocked nearly senseless, zombies meandering away from the blood-soaked street. Anyone who came too close, he shoved out of our way. If they resisted...

I turned away from that sight but still followed the body-strewn trail.

I did not look back. I did not want to see the carnage. I crushed the flyers into my pocket. The line of police parted for my identification card. I was past the violence. I was safe. "Thank you, officer," I said, fearing he'd see through me and pound my brain into pulp in his rage.

"Steer clear of these bastards," he shouted and headed back into the stampeding crowd.

I hid in a doorway, bent over, catching my breath. I was panting like some dog after a long chase. The screams were fading. When I emerged again, the street was empty. The police had taken less than fifteen minutes to deal with the crowd.

When my legs felt steady enough to walk home, I avoided any street where I might encounter the beating victims. Police were checking alleyways, their red-stained clubs at the ready. I showed my identification, and they let me pass, some warning me to beware of the criminals who might still be lurking in the shadows.

I reached our building and stopped for breath again. I pulled my shirt tails into my trousers and dusted myself off. I'd made up my mind not to alarm Miriam by letting her know how close I'd been to getting caught up in the riot. I climbed the stairs, feeling dizzy, afraid she'd notice something different about me.

Miriam was asleep on our bed.

Relieved, I sat on a chair and a wave of nausea struck. I fought to keep it down. I did not want to wake Miriam. I felt as if at any instant I would burst into tears, but resisted that too. I don't know how long I sat in that chair contemplating what I'd witnessed, hating this shithole apartment, the whole damn ghetto, my life. Only Miriam and our unborn child kept me from wishing for death.

Miriam stirred.

I moved to the bed. "Hello, sleepyhead," I said, leaning down and kissing her forehead.

She groaned as she helped herself off the mattress. She gave me a cursory look and walked to the door.

I knew she was going to the outhouse to relieve herself.

I was exhausted. Without wanting to, I lay down on the mattress. By the time Miriam returned I was asleep. When I awoke hours later, she never asked me about anything. I think she had learned that I wasn't going to answer her questions anyway. I made an effort at small talk but how successful could I be when I was struggling to keep yet another secret from her?

That night, lying on my back, I couldn't sleep. I'd seen the protestors and heard their chants. It had almost been a party atmosphere, friends associating. Yes, it was a prohibited gathering, but harmless. I saw no weapons. Then the Jewish police arrived and Jew struck Jew. It was unthinkable…Jew clubbing Jew. The street was cleared in fifteen minutes except for those who could not walk. These wretches, young and old, were left in the blood and piss. Did Rumkowski authorize this? Is this what we had come to? I turned toward Miriam's back, praying she would sense my pain and take me in her arms. I never felt so alone.

Not able to sleep, I snuck from the flat before Miriam awoke. I was shaking but determined to revisit the scene of last night's horrors.

The square was cleared of all evidence that anything had happened. Where was the blood? Where were the bodies? Someone had to tell this story.

It was dark in our conference room. I turned on the ceiling lamp and settled in my chair. It was not easy to report what I'd witnessed. It was the most soul-searching assignment I faced since Rumkowski hired me.

"You're here earlier than usual," Cukier said. "Rough night?"

I handed him my report.

"You were there?" Cukier asked, after reading the first half.

"It was on my way home."

He looked at me and said, "I don't like this sentence: "Dozens of the civilians were badly roughed up."

"It's the truth."

He gave me a curious look. "How about making it: several of the civilians were badly roughed up." He penned the change. "Were any police hurt as well? You must tell their side."

Was he kidding? "I saw two with minor wounds. Nothing compared to the bashing they gave the protesters." Was I really saying this? I sounded like Singer or Miriam.

Cukier added a few words and handed the sheet back to me. "Type it with the changes."

It hurt as I typed his amendment: "Several of the civilians were badly roughed up and two members of the Order Service received wounds. Peace had been entirely restored by seven P.M. There have been numerous arrests of agitators in connection with the demonstrations."

I wanted to tell my friend, Julian, that I wasn't happy with the changes, but Rosenfeld returned from his further investigation of the kitchens. I could barely look at Cukier that day. I was grateful when it was time to go home.

Cukier saw I was leaving. "You had a close call. Be careful on your way home. There are not enough police on the streets to protect law-abiding citizens from the immigrants and criminals waiting to pounce on us. Desperate people do—"

I closed the door before he could finish.

CHAPTER 34

S **UNDAY, MARCH 9, 1941:** *A SEARCH*
Yesterday, officials of the German criminal police conducted a
search at 14 Brzezinska Street that resulted in the confiscation of
pelts and furs worth approximately thirty thousand marks.

I had an early morning visit from Neftalin. I again offered my condolence for the loss of his father.

"Cukier speaks very highly of your support of our objectives," he said.

"Thank you, sir."

"Call me Henryk, please?" He smiled and then sat down on the edge of the table. "The Chairman had an interesting visitor yesterday, the Eldest of the Jews from Aleksandrow Kujawski. It is a small community of about eight thousand people, with about one thousand Jews." He gave me a slip of paper. "The Chairman noticed that the Eldest, and his wife, Stars of David at least twice the size of our stars on their garments."

"Twice the size? Is this a tradition of some kind?" I hated wearing the damn things.

"No, my friend. These Jews are being punished for failing to observe the obligation of wearing their stars, by being forced to wear stars double the original size. Do you understand my point?"

Had Cukier informed the Deputy of my questioning the behavior of Rumkowski's Order Service during what started as a peaceful protest?

Neftalin aimed his eyes at me. "I think this example bears out the wisdom of our Chairman. He wants only what is best for our people, but many are too selfish to work for the better good."

I nodded.

"As you know, in his speech of February 1, the Chairman made it clear that malefactors and notorious criminals, and thieves of public property, will be ousted from the ghetto and sent to do manual labor in Germany."

Was he sending me to do manual labor in Germany? Miriam! What would happen to her and my child? "I remember his speech. It was a well-chosen scare tactic."

Neftalin shook his head. "Scare tactic? No, my friend. On instructions from the Chairman, a special squad of the Order Service has in the last three nights carried out mass arrests of thieves, habitual criminals, and disturbers of the present order in the ghetto."

My mouth was dry. The Deputy was threatening me. "Sir, I did not know this."

Neftalin nodded. "Yes, eighty-six prisoners were given medical examinations—"

"Medical? May I ask for what purpose?"

"The Chairman himself attended, to be certain the prisoners were well enough to perform manual labor outside our walls."

"I see." I tried to remain calm, but this was terrifying. Our Chairman was punishing Jews by sending them outside the ghetto to work for the Germans. I was at risk if Cukier had informed on my critical report of the demonstration. Why did I risk that? I'm not Singer, my brain shouted.

Neftalin seemed oblivious to the change in my demeanor. "Of those examined, seventy-five were found to be fit to be sent to work outside the ghetto."

I was struggling to digest this new development. "Sir, I want to be clear on this for my report, of course. These prisoners are now in the custody of the German authorities?" Say no.

Neftalin stood. "They were the worst offenders: malcontents, thieves, illegal aliens, and habitual criminals." He dropped a hand on my shoulder. "You understand. They destroy the fabric of our lives and threaten our very existence under this occupation."

Neftalin was waiting for me to agree. "Yes, Henryk, I fully agree."

He scanned my face. "Do you remember the story of the double-sized stars? Do you think the Jews of Aleksandrow put these on of free choice? Do not be naïve, my friend. Nobody here can afford to be naïve."

I nodded, unable to express my fear of the Chairperson acting as judge and jury, sending Jews, even if criminals, to work for the Germans.

Neftalin lifted his hand from my shoulder. I felt relieved. He said, "The Chairman has tried everything in his power to get these disrupters to embrace law and order. The recent demonstrations were incited by the underworld, to undermine our community. They prove that we must make a statement that none can ignore."

I felt he was staring at me. "Yes, I understand."

"Good. If we fail, the Chairman fears he will not be able to keep closed the floodgates. The Kripo, Gestapo, and the SS are the last ones we want to believe that we can't control our own population. Only someone who is foolish, or a criminal, can disagree with this. And you, are not either of those." He aimed his eyes into my eyes for what seemed a long duration.

I felt as if he was probing my soul. "We are doing what we can to support our esteemed Chairman," I said, swallowing any doubts I might have harbored about Rumkowski's efforts to maintain law and order in these difficult times.

Neftalin did not return my statement with a smile. His face remained stern. "And he knows this very well. He shows great appreciation to all who promote the smooth functioning of the ghetto. The special dining rooms, the increased rations, even the wonderful concerts, are all his way to thank those loyal workers who are keeping our ghetto autonomous. None of us want to wear even larger stars. Do we?"

I shook my head. "No. Of course not. Thank you, sir."

"Call me Henryk, please? You are one of us now. There is a concert tonight at the House of Culture. I hope you will be there with your charming wife. Thank you again for all your efforts. We appreciate it."

"Thank you...Henryk."

He finally smiled and left the room.

I sagged back into my chair. Why did I feel I had survived another close call? Was it my imagination? I closed my eyes, and in the swirl of my troubled thoughts about Jews being discarded into the hands of the enemy, I had a vision of my beautiful wife. Miriam was floating down a golden staircase, dressed in her black sheath, hair smartly coiffed atop her head, a string of blazing diamonds accentuating her lovely cleavage. I took her arm and with the crowd admiring us, led her to our seats in the ornate auditorium. Her petite hand resting on my arm, her eyes closed, as the lush music of the tuxedoed orchestra transported us over the dirty streets of the ghetto. Violins sang melodiously of verdant fields and enchanted forests, of blue skies and azure waterfalls. The ghetto was far away...far, far away. A low drumming heartbeat...louder, louder, louder...snare drums, kettle drums, guns, cannon, marching soldiers, tanks, airplanes, drums thundering, and cymbals crashing and crashing again... the ancient Semitic music of the Jews being ruthlessly crushed by the triumphant marching songs of the Nazis. A hand dropped and seized Miriam from her seat. I reached for her, but she was lifted toward a sky black with smoke.

Cukier said, "You were talking in your dreams."

I wanted to ask if he had informed on me to Neftalin but couldn't bring myself to confront him. "It was a nightmare," I said, wondering if I could ever trust him or anyone in the ghetto again. Then I thought of Miriam. I saw her sweet face, her passionate hazel eyes. I could trust her.

CHAPTER 35

MARCH 24, 1941: *Deaths and Births*
Between March 10-24, 529 people died in the Ghetto.
Twenty-nine births.

"It gets worse," I said, staring at a newly hung portrait of our benefactor on the wall. I wondered how long it would be before his visage was beaming down on us.

"So, Numbers Man, how much worse can it get?" Rosenfeld asked.

I handed him the entry I was working on, which I entitled, "SHOOTINGS."

"I don't like your title," Rosenfeld muttered, reading aloud. "March 12, 8:30, Wolf Finkelstein, 14 Masarska Street, was shot dead by a sentry. He was thirteen years old and shot in the heart and lungs. Oh, God." Rosenfeld licked his chapped lips with his tongue. "March 19, Rafal Krzepicki, 31, from Praszka, was shot dead around midnight. On the 23rd of March, at nine in the evening, Awigdor Lichtenstein was shot dead near the latrine at the end of the street near the barbed wire."

"Look at the last sentence in the report," I said.

Rosenfeld adjusted his glasses. "The victims were allegedly smugglers."

I waited for him to say something else, but nothing came. There was no point in asking if a thirteen-year-old deserved to be shot by a sentry, a euphemism for a German border guard, even if he was a smuggler.

194

The door opened.

It was Singer. He had not been here since after the riot. None of us knew where he was. I assumed he was on a binge with some woman he'd met. Desperate men do desperate things, I thought. It was quiet without him. I wanted to rush up, hug him, ask him where he'd been, but something about his face, now bearded and reddened, held me back.

Cukier seemed to be wrestling with his emotions as well. "Are you okay?"

Singer nodded. "I'm sorry I upset you, Julian, the other day. I'd never want to do that."

Cukier shook his head. "I'm sorry too. I over-reacted."

Singer nodded to me and sat down. "I almost didn't come back," he said.

I made a motion as if to speak, but Singer continued, "I saw something that made me think about quitting. I was by the message board when a proclamation from the Chairman was posted. It called for the registration of women from ages 20 to 30—"

"Wait!" I felt my body grow cold. "All women?" I thought of Miriam. How could I protect her? What was this about?

Singer's hand was a tight fist. "It is allegedly for those women who are applying to leave the ghetto to work. I tore the handbill off the wall." Singer pulled the crumpled sheet from his pocket.

"Are you crazy? Have I not warned you to be careful?" Cukier began coughing. "Goddamn it! You know better. That's a punishable offense—"

"May I see it?" I asked. "We should get Neftalin to explain it to us."

Cukier, the handkerchief before his face, nodded.

I went to get the deputy. When he returned with me, he had a curious look on his face. "Do you need some help? Julian, are you okay? Is he okay?"

Cukier charged in, "This new proclamation for women to be registered—"

195

Neftalin looked relieved. "Ah that. It is for women who are volunteering for work outside our walls."

"So, the women are all volunteers for these jobs?" Singer asked.

Neftalin shifted his weight from one foot to the other. "The proclamation was issued on orders from the German authorities." He seemed to be searching for the right words. "They have stipulated that one of the next transports of workers leaving the ghetto to perform manual labor is to include up to one hundred women."

We were speechless.

I asked again, "Are all these women volunteers?" I was thinking of Miriam.

Neftalin sighed. "Yes. Of course." He unfolded a document. "One more item you should know. Proclamation 233, from the Eldest of the Jews, has created a "summary court" at 27 Franciszkanska Street."

"What does that mean?" Singer asked, taking notes on his pad.

Neftalin took a moment to think. "The Chairman will select a judge and two counselors. There will be no attorneys—"

"No lawyers?" Singer looked poised to attack.

"He's suspending the right to a lawyer?"

I was surprised it was Rosenfeld sounding shocked.

Neftalin wet his lips again. "You must understand. This will be an independent body precipitated by our rampant crime which threatens all of our welfare."

"It is the suspension of a defendant's rights," Rosenfeld said in a strained voice.

"That is not for us to judge," Neftalin said. "You know your duty." He stood and headed for the door. "Oh. I do have some good news."

We turned toward him, eager for something good.

"Chairman M.C. Rumkowski turned 64 on the 13th of this month. His closest co-workers offered him their congratulations at his private apartment. The Chairman was presented with many gifts from the workshops, followed up by several wonderful concerts, which the chairman attended as guest of honor. His favorite by

far was a performance of music and vocals for the school children."
Neftalin beamed, "He adores children. You remember, he opened an
orphanage several years ago."

Cukier stood. "Please convey our congratulations to the Chairman
on the occasion of his birthday. We will be honored to highlight this
auspicious event in our journal."

Neftalin smiled. "Thank you, Julian. I hope I've answered your
questions."

I nodded, but still had my mind centered on the fact that one
hundred of our women had been ordered by the Germans to leave
our ghetto and work for them somewhere unknown. What if it had
been Miriam? But Neftalin said they were all volunteers. So why
was I uneasy?

After Neftalin left, I turned to Singer, having to share my thoughts
with someone. "Thank God, Miriam is pregnant," I whispered.

Singer replied, "We have to protect her."

I was surprised by the earnest look on his face. "Thank you, Oscar."
He didn't reply.

CHAPTER 36

TUESDAY, MARCH 25, 1941

The Eldest of the Jews ordered a one-time additional bread allocation in the amount of half a kilogram, also 80 grams of margarine and 200 grams of rutabaga.

I never knew what mood my wife would be in when I safely made it home, but today she had a happy look on her face as she dragged me through our door.

"I have a job," Miriam exclaimed the second I entered the flat.

I removed my coat. "You're pregnant. You can't work."

"It isn't hard work. The manager said I can leave when I can't work anymore."

"No. I won't hear of it. One accident and...I don't want to think of it. End of discussion."

Her face told me my stubborn wife wasn't happy with my decision. I realized I was crushing her effort to do something to help us, but she was with child. Things were difficult enough, dangerous enough, without her working. "Do you want to hear my news?"

Miriam didn't reply.

I decided to ignore her sulking, attributing it to her condition. I wished I knew more about women and especially pregnancy. "We had visitors today. They were Italian officers. Rumkowski was showing them the workshops. They looked impressed, but I didn't understand what they were saying." I laughed. "It could have been Chinese for all I know."

Miriam was serious. "The Chairman was with them?"

"Of course. The Chairman appeared very proud of our accomplishments, but only stayed a second."

Miriam didn't say anything.

I could tell she was still angry. "Miri, my love, I'm only trying to protect our child and you."

Still no response.

I sighed. "I should not have come down so hard on you. I sometimes forget that you are an extremely competent young woman. I apologize."

"Thank you."

There were times she exhausted me. "Okay. What is the job? Please tell me?"

"Why? You already said no."

"I was wrong to say it that way."

Miriam glared at me. "I would never endanger my...our baby. You should know this."

"I know. It is just such a scary time. I worry about you. I know it is wrong, but I feel very protective. Forgive me?"

Miriam nodded. "I went to the new factory. They are making caps."

"The factory that the Chairman just opened? I heard it will employ a few hundred workers." I still didn't like the idea of her working. "Miriam, you will be making caps for the German military. With your conscience, can you do this?" She hated the Germans. Could she work for them?

"You work for the Chairman."

"It is not the same."

"It is the Chairman's factory, so how is it different?"

"It just is. I don't know why, but it is."

"We need the money." She stood up. "Everything is getting too expensive."

"I am working now. It isn't the money. It's the Germans restricting what we can get."

"I want to work."

I recognized her stubborn look. I was too tired to argue. I didn't think she would follow through, not with a baby coming. I decided to try a different tack. "Okay. I understand. All I ask is think about it. I will leave the decision to you."

"Oh, thank you. Thank you," Miriam said, giving me a smile.

I waited until she was calm again. "By the way, did you know a Chana Lewkowicz?"

"I don't think so."

"She's a little older, forty-something I would guess."

"She's even older than you, Papa," Miriam said.

I'd have laughed, but she looked serious when she called me, Papa. "This Chana was shot dead by a sentry at Marysinska Street by the barbed wire."

Miriam looked shocked.

I rarely shared this kind of alarming news with her, but it was a nail I had to hammer. "It is alleged she was smuggling."

Miriam plopped down onto a chair. "The Germans shot a woman?"

"She is not the first, and she won't be the last. Miri, the Nazis don't care who they kill. That is why I don't want you on the streets."

Miriam's eyes watered. "What is the world coming to?"

"I told you it is unsafe. The Germans are becoming more intrusive and vicious every day. The immigrants and criminals are not quelled by the Chairman's police. Every time a young woman, or a man, ventures from their home, there is lawlessness and brutal violence." I took her hand. It was trembling. "My dear girl, you are all I care about. That is why I am so protective over you…you and our child, our blessing. Even that crazy Singer says he will protect you." I laughed. "Imagine that young radical taking care of you? He's a hot-head, but a good man inside. At least, I think so."

Miriam didn't respond. Instead she said, "And with all the craziness and bad news, the Chairman is hosting another concert tonight."

"You, of all people, know how music makes things seem better," I replied, even though my mathematical brain did question the logic of concerts when we were starving. It seems in the ghetto, two and two didn't necessarily equal four.

"Better for who?"

"You sound like Singer," I said and gave her a warm smile. "Would you like to attend the concert? You have your black dress."

She burst out laughing. "Idiot! Do you think that will still fit me?" She rubbed her stomach, now a noticeable bump. "You really know very little about women."

She was right.

CHAPTER 37

THURSDAY, MARCH 27, 1941
I arrived at our conference room early. I was typing when I came across an unusual entry. I read it aloud:

A CINERARY URN

Today, the ghetto received an urn with the ashes of Abram Wajsberg who had been in the concentration camp at Buchenwald. He was thirty-four years old and had lived at 10 Franciszkanska Street. It is worth noting that this is the second such incident. Several weeks ago, an urn containing the ashes of Sarna, a lawyer was brought to the ghetto.

"That's it?" I stopped reading.

"What more can we say?" Rosenfeld, who had compiled the entry, asked. "We received the urn and will bury it in our cemetery."

Singer looked ready to have a seizure. "This is the second such incident! Didn't you think that strange?"

"We have more dying here every day. What are two more to bury here?"

Singer fell back in his chair. "I give up."

Cukier leaned forward. "I think we're missing the point: they both came from Buchenwald."

"So, it says," Rosenfeld replied. "It's a camp for manual labor."

"Apparently the Germans are building a number of these labor compounds across Europe," Cukier said. "Let's leave the memo as is but let me know if there are more such incidents. Any more news?"

Singer leaned toward me. "It is strange that in the middle of a war the Germans are constructing labor camps."

I looked at his face and replied, "We have enough problems here without having to speculate about German priorities."

Singer shook his head. "It just seems curious to me."

"You're like a dog with fleas. You scratch one itch and get another."

Singer didn't laugh.

Rosenfeld held up another memo. "The Chairman issued another proclamation that anything hidden, or left behind, in the city of Lodz, can be turned in for cash."

"He never stops trying," Singer remarked.

"There've been a series of raids by the Order Service with arrests of criminals," Rosenfeld continued.

"Are they all criminals? Is everyone who gets shot a smuggler?" Singer held up a stack of papers. "These are all people who have been shot. Here's the latest: Abraham Dab was talking to a sentry. This same sentry then shot him in the shoulder shortly after. Nobody knows what they talked about, but Dab died the next day of the rifle wound. Of course, we're not allowed to say it was a German soldier who did this."

Cukier said, "It is obvious. No Jews are allowed rifles, not even the police. Let's move on."

Rosenfeld held up another memorandum. "This is strange." He flipped through a stack of memos. "I thought so. Just in January, there was a count of non-Jews living in the ghetto."

"So?" Cukier asked.

"This memo says that on German orders, a strict registration of Christians was carried out again."

"There can't be many Christians among us," I said. "I'd estimate less than one hundred."

Rosenfeld raced through the memo. "It says that on January 5, there were sixty-one Christians, including German citizens of the Reich, 2 ethnic Germans from Lodz, and 57 Poles. As usual, you are right with your estimations. How do you do that?"

"I'm a mathematical genius," I replied.

Singer made a face. "I'm glad I'm not, but why would they do another count so soon?"

Rosenfeld read further. "Apparently this time they visited all Christians in person. This time they counted one hundred ten Christians."

"That's almost double," I remarked.

"Always the number man," Singer commented, shaking his head.

Rosenfeld looked puzzled. "They broke it down in detail: 32 were of Jewish parentage; 13 of mixed marriages. 4 German women stated they preferred to stay with their Jewish husbands."

"Admirable," Singer said. "Stupid, but admirable."

Cukier was losing patience. "Leave the numbers for the engineer. Just report the fact that the German authorities ordered this count. We can't speculate on everything we come across."

"You do know that to a Nazi, a Christian woman who marries a Jew is considered a Jew?" Singer said.

Rosenfeld sighed. "It's the old story, if you have a drop of Jewish blood, you will be forced to shed it for the bigots of this world."

"We're the "chosen people,"" Singer said. "We're chosen to suffer thousands of years of hate, discrimination, and, what would it be without persecution and genocide. Why couldn't the almighty have chosen someone else?"

"I wish you'd stop your sarcasm," Cukier said and broke into a trio of coughs.

"I didn't attend Hebrew school," I admitted. "Why do we call ourselves the "Chosen People?" Isn't that inviting trouble?"

Rosenfeld gazed at me with paternal kindness. "This term is so misunderstood. It is not that we Jews consider ourselves better than others, as some would have the world believe, but the very opposite. You remember the bible story where Abraham was to sacrifice his son because God commanded it?"

I nodded.

"Well, after Abraham proved his worthiness, God said, "Of all people, your children will be chosen to obey all the laws I give you.'"

"The Ten Commandments," I said.

Rosenfeld raised his hand. "You see, this is what almost nobody understands. God gave the Ten Commandments to everyone. To the Jew he gave six hundred and thirteen laws we must obey. That is what is meant by 'chosen.' We are chosen to obey all the laws and not just the Ten Commandments which everyone must adhere to."

"I remember when my old Rabbi taught me that," Singer said and laughed. "I probably broke every one of those rules, but because I'm a Jew, I'm still chosen to suffer."

Cukier coughed into his handkerchief. "We are born to suffer, but God will see us through. He always has in the past."

"God helps those who help themselves," Singer said.

"Don't start that again." Cukier wiped his lips with his handkerchief.

"You know it's true," Singer persisted. "They are arming in other places."

I didn't want to listen to this discussion anymore. The clatter of the keys against the paper drowned out the rest. As I focused on the tiny letters, I thought of our child. Would he, or she, be born to suffer, as we were doing now? Answer me that, God, and I might just believe in you again.

The only answer was the clattering of the typewriter keys on the hard rubber cylinder muted by multiple sheets of carbon paper.

CHAPTER 38

SATURDAY, APRIL 5, 1941
     Yesterday's entries were of a sixty-one-year-old being killed by rifle fire near the barbed wire; a twenty-nine-year-old opening his veins to commit suicide, and of a homeless woman dying of hunger. Today began with a 60-year-old throwing himself from the Zgierska Street bridge, crashing onto the street below.

"I'm tired of writing about dead people," Rosenfeld said, staring at the ugly yellowed slips of paper on which these deaths were reported.

"I am too," Cukier replied. "They're becoming a blur."

"What's the point?" Rosenfeld asked, "We know nothing about them or how they died."

"They're just numbers," Singer said, "But at least we are giving them some obituary, some honor."

"Do they deserve it?" Cukier asked. "They're all either suicides or get too close to the barbed wire. They're asking for it."

"When you live like this, that is understandable," Rosenfeld said, gazing at the bowl of his pipe. "What I wouldn't give for a bit of tobacco."

"Suicide is never acceptable," I said. "It's an act of cowardice. We're all suffering, so should we all kill ourselves and let the Germans have their dream of no Jews?"

"You're too hard on your fellow man," Singer said. "We, working for this regime, are becoming distant from those our government should be serving."

Rosenfeld waved his pipe. "The real question is, does man have the right to destroy what God almighty creates? Suicide is a sin. It is destroying a gift only God can give and only he should take away."

"So, you agree with me that these people do not deserve to be honored?" Cukier asked, examining his handkerchief.

"I'm not saying that," Rosenfeld replied, staring longingly at his pipe.

"So, what are you saying?" Singer asked.

Rosenfeld gave me a playful look and said, "I'm not saying."

"I'm saying, let's compromise." Cukier interrupted. "We will continue to list all such incidents for the time being. Perhaps they will be an indication to researchers in the future of what we lived through. Let us pray we don't see more of these tragedies." He broke into a fit of coughing. "Sometimes… suicide seems… the best answer." He examined his handkerchief again and stuffed it into his pocket.

I was about to reply when our door opened. I was used to visitors and no longer became paralyzed with fear. However, this time, a man in a leather coat entered the room. Immediately, I stiffened. What did he want here?

"I am ordered to report to you by the Eldest of the Jews," he said. "I am Leon Rosenblat. I am Chief of the Order Service."

Crap, I thought, my stomach clenching. What is Rosenblat, of all people, doing here? I backed my chair against the wall.

Cukier stood. "I know you, sir. I am Julian Cukier, head of the Archives. May I ask how we may serve you?"

"Please sit. I'm not here on an investigation." Rosenblat removed his cap and looked a little less threatening.

Cukier retook his seat.

I remained where I was. This was the second most feared Jewish official in the ghetto.

Rosenblat remained standing, his posture stiff. He cleared his throat. "The Chairman has asked me to personally describe a meeting. I, and adjutant engineer, Julian Grosbart, were summoned to at Precinct VI of the German police force. We were driven to the headquarters outside the ghetto." He wiped his forehead with a white handkerchief. "It is claustrophobic in here."

He was right about that. I was always complaining about how suffocating this room was.

Rosenblat looked at his notes and continued, "At the meeting with the authorities, we were told that there will be a different force serving as sentries around the ghetto, the Schupo." He made a wry face but regained his composure quickly. "We were required to provide a report on the organization of our own force, maps of the ghetto, a breakdown of the ghetto by precincts." He wiped his brow again. "We were also ordered to provide an itemized list of the powers of the Eldest of the Jews, addresses of the ghetto offices and institutions, and other materials." He handed Cukier a folder. "Here are copies of the reports I provided."

"Do you know why the Germans wanted this information?" Singer asked.

Rosenblat did not look the type to welcome questions. He looked disdainfully at Singer and directed himself to Cukier. "You understand we were ordered to submit these reports."

Singer asked again, "Why do you think the Germans wanted this now?"

Rosenblat scowled at our youngest member.

"It's for the Chairman's records," I interjected, hoping to help Singer who seemed eager to jump into every firestorm that came his way. Rumors had it that Rosenblat could arrange imprisonment, or worse, with a wink of his eye.

Cukier raised his hand. "Sir, you do not have to answer our questions, but we work directly for our esteemed Chairman."

Rosenblat stared at him and finally nodded. "The Chairman asked me to report all to you, so I will answer what I can. No, I do not know why they want all this material now. Their request came as a surprise, to all of us."

"Have they ever asked for something like this before?" I asked.

Rosenblat remained stern and official. "Bits and pieces, yes. Nothing like this. You should also know there were representatives from the Lodz police, as well as from other nearby locations. Why? I do not know."

"Why did the Chairman send you to us?" I asked.

Rosenblat smiled.

I didn't like his smile. It seemed to hide something behind it.

"I am speculating, and please do not include this in your records, but I believe the Chairman suspects the German authority is losing patience with our crime situation. He fears, and I concur, they may want all this information as a precursor to, shall we say, taking their own action."

"Bullshit," Singer said.

Cukier shot him a look of daggers.

Rosenblat let out a solitary chuckle. "No. The young man is right. The Chairman also feels this would be catastrophic. He is already attempting a preemptive assault on crime. We have been ordered to arrest habitual criminals and anyone who threatens order in the ghetto to prevent such intervention." There were beads of sweat on his forehead. "It really is stifling in here. The arrests have already begun."

"We're running out of jails," I said.

Rosenblat's eyes skewered me. "They are being transported out of the ghetto as the need for workers in Germany increases."

"You're sending more Jews to work for the Germans?" Singer asked.

Rosenblat replied, "This is how the problem of ridding ourselves of undesirables is being solved. Currently, only one hundred of these professional thieves, fences, pimps, and the like, have passed medical tests showing they are fit for manual labor." He let out a tiny snort. "They are no longer a problem for us. They are Germany's problems now."

I must have looked upset because Rosenblat looked at me and said, "The Germans left us no choice."

I glanced at Singer, grateful he didn't unleash one of his outbursts.

Cukier asked, "Do you have any more questions of the Chief?" He shot a warning look at Singer who was staring hard at Rosenblat. "Thank you, sir, for filling us in. You can be sure we will support the Chairman's effort. We understand the gravity of our situation."

Rosenblat came to attention and replace his cap on his head. "If we don't stop crime, the Germans will."

With the cap on his head, Rosenblat looked seven feet tall. I was relieved when the Commander left.

Even Singer was silent.

Rosenfeld sighed. "And so, my friends, it begins."

Singer hissed into my ear, "It began a long time ago. The question now is how it will end."

CHAPTER 39

THURSDAY, APRIL 10, 1941: *WORK DURING THE HOLIDAYS*
On order of the German authorities, the Passover holiday and Easter are not to be a cause for an interruption of work.

After Rosenblat's visit, there was a sense of gloom in our little club. Each piece of news added to our suspicion that things were changing, and not for the better. Of course, I didn't share these fears with Miriam. She was already incensed about the latest proclamation from the Chairman.

"I'm not surprised," I said after she read the proclamation declaring Passover and Easter as days of uninterrupted work. "What does surprise me is that there will be any matzoh for Passover at all," I said to Miriam, who was pacing the room holding her stomach.

"They're charging enough for it," Miriam rasped. "There are shortages all over. Coal deliveries have been cut off completely. Even the public kitchens can't get coal to heat the food. It's disgusting!"

"Singer says you can buy anything you want for a price." I chuckled. "Leave it to him. I only hope he doesn't get into trouble. They're sending suspected smugglers to the German police now. I would not want that to be me."

Miriam looked alarmed. "Rumkowski is sending Jews to the Germans?" She sat in her chair, her hand rubbing her stomach.

I'd let something out I shouldn't have. I was tired of keeping things to myself, but I didn't want to upset my pregnant wife. "It's only being done in extreme cases," I said, trying to calm her. "Don't worry. I'm not doing anything illegal."

She still looked worried but gave me a cup of ersatz coffee. "He owns everything, they say. I'll bet he's not suffering."

"Please, don't start again?" If it wasn't Singer, it was Miriam. I couldn't escape these armchair critics.

"You know every factory, every garden, even the hospitals and orphanages, all belong to him and his family." She got back out of the chair, pacing around the table, rubbing her stomach.

"Rumkowski does it for the benefit of the ghetto. Nobody else can do what he does."

"So, you say." She let out a sigh. "You don't hear what I hear."

"They're all yentas. They have nothing better to do than complain. They don't understand the precariousness, the pressure the Germans are applying to the Chairman."

Miriam came to me, her eyes imploring. "What is going to happen to us?"

I took her hand. "Sweetheart, the Chairman has a plan. If we all get behind it, we will become a protectorate of the German empire. That is why he must enforce the law."

"I'm so tired of all this shit." Miriam looked like she was going to cry. "They want us now to start working at sunrise every morning."

"I told you to quit."

"What would I do? Stay here in this dump? Stare at these barren walls all day?" She shivered. "I want to leave—"

"Leave?"

"There must be a way to get out of here." She patted her stomach. "For the sake of our child...please, ask Singer. He must know—"

"No. There is no way. The Germans are shooting everyone who ventures near the barbed wire. They have no respect for our lives. We must hold on a little longer." I took her in my arms, but she felt limp against me, and then I felt her tears, her body quivering. "What is it? What's wrong?"

Miriam whispered. "They found Mr. Klingbajl."

"Who is Mr. Kling...who is this?"

"He was a teacher. He hanged himself...a school teacher."

Not another suicide? Would I have to write about this teacher in the chronicles? It was something we had to do every day—more and more. "He was probably ill. Perhaps he was mentally disturbed. Most of these people who end their lives are mentally imbalanced." That was what we were writing on our entries about our early trickle of suicides. Now, it was impossible to label every victim of this suicide epidemic as mentally imbalanced or insane. Besides, we were all being driven insane to different degrees by all we witnessed.

Miriam's voice was muffled by my chest. "Benny, the schools are all shuttered by the Nazis. How will our child be educated?"

I burst into laughter. "That is your worry? You mustn't worry about that now. The war will be over soon, and either the Germans will be defeated, and all will be restored to normal, or the ghetto will be preserved by the Germans as the paramount center of industry, as our Chairman has planned. Either way, this is temporary and nothing for you to fear. School for our loved one is years away." I laughed again.

Miriam pulled away from me. "I hope you are right," she said.

I kissed her on her forehead. "You must stop worrying. It is not good for our child."

She gave me a half-smile.

I left our flat and headed for the office. When I arrived, I noticed the area around our building was not blocked by the usual crowds. There was nobody there. At first, I felt a sense of relief. I hated having to plow my way through the unemployed masses to reach the front doors. But then, I felt uneasy with the sudden emptiness of the square.

I saw a black carriage, a plaque declaring it the coach of the Eldest of the Jews. It was the only horse-drawn vehicle remaining to us. It was surrounded by two bodyguards.

"Stay back," a bodyguard ordered a rubber club in his black-gloved hand.

Rumkowski hobbled from the building. He supported himself with a walking stick, a female secretary at his side. Two bodyguards scanned the area as he walked toward the coach. A guard helped him up into the rear seat. I did not see him thank the guard, but he gave the secretary, who I'd heard was named, Dora Fuchs, a slight smile as she climbed aboard. He then raised his coat collar and settled back in the coach. A bodyguard dropped a blanket over his legs. Smoke wafted up from his seat. I'd heard many complaints that while everyone was starving, the Eldest of the Jews, was able to get endless cigarettes and ride in his fancy coach, a king, an Emperor. Now I saw it for myself.

I was still blocked by a guard when the Chairman turned his eyes toward me.

Did he recognize me? I thought he might signal me to approach, perhaps give me a knowing nod. Instead, he stared into my eyes, and I felt chilled to the bone. I was grateful when he settled back into the leather seat, and the coach pulled away.

Safely ensconced in our barren work chamber, I searched the usual pile of papers. Finding what I was seeking, I began to write the one sentence announcement that a teacher had killed himself. I did not add the usual statement that he was insane. Miriam would never forgive me if she found out.

CHAPTER 40

F RIDAY, APRIL 11, 1941
Today, 169 men left the ghetto to do manual labor in Germany.

"There is more?" Singer asked, reading the report I had written.

"It gets worse?" Rosenfeld asked, shaking his head sadly. "How much worse can it be?"

Cukier had not arrived yet. We had grown used to him being late the last few weeks, his coughing fits slowing him down.

Singer sighed. "These figures are accurate?"

I nodded.

"You know him with his numbers," Rosenfeld remarked, not smiling.

Singer put down his pen and read aloud. "400 men will leave on the 15th. 130 women will be the first women's transport on the 18th. 300 men and 100 women on the 21st." He shook his pen at me. "So, you see, the women are going."

"Look down further. There will be 400 men each, on the 25th, 28th, and the 30th."

Rosenfeld looked frightened. "Engineer, how many is that together?"

"They say 2,700. 230 will be women."

The silence was a thick fog in the claustrophobic room, broken up by the entrance of Cukier. One look at our faces and he asked, "What is it now?" He placed his coat on the back of his chair.

I handed him my report. "Are you aware of the deportations the Chairman has approved?"

"Is that all?" Cukier looked surprisingly unconcerned.

"They're shipping out women too. How many did you say, Engineer?" Rosenfeld asked. "I'm getting forgetful in my old age."

"You're not getting old," Singer said.

"With all that is going on, I may not," Rosenfeld quipped. "None of us may."

"Nonsense," Cukier said. "I was aware of this news and have just come back from Neftalin's office. He assures me these workers are all volunteers."

"Volunteers again?" Singer asked, clearly incredulous.

Cukier smiled. "Yes. In fact, Neftalin said they have over 7,000 volunteer applications for manual labor outside of the ghetto. They will all be paid. Even their families remaining in the ghetto will receive compensation until their loved ones return."

"Neftalin assures you of all this?" Singer looked doubtful.

"My dear, Oscar, the Chairman set up medical examinations of all the candidates, and 40 percent were rejected. The Germans then rejected 7 percent more. Here are the documents." He handed me several pages describing the volunteer program. "If they were forced, would the Germans reject some for medical reasons? Would they bother with examinations?"

"That makes sense. But why so many at once?" Singer asked.

Cukier replied, "I've heard from Neftalin the Germans are working on the construction of the Frankfurt-Poznan highway. They know Jewish workers are the best, so they made this opportunity available. Now we have 2,418 of our people no longer unemployed. This also leaves more food and fuel for the rest of us. Any more questions?"

Singer looked skeptical but kept quiet.

Cukier handed the reports to Rosenfeld. "Please write this up?"

I was relieved to find out this was not a compulsory deportation as rumors had alleged. The news of the women especially had been disturbing. I thought of Miriam and once again thanked God for her current condition. Knowing my increasingly moody and stubborn young wife, she would be the first to volunteer in the hope she might find a way to free herself from Lodz. She often spoke of how she wished we could bribe our way to America. She could be so irritating at times, but I loved her. I could not imagine life without her. I turned to Singer, with whom I felt a growing fondness, and said, "I was worried about Miriam when I first saw this memo."

Singer looked up from the page he was writing. "I was too."

"It was bad enough to know we had deported men to Germany, but women?"

"Cukier says they are all volunteers."

"You don't believe him?" I had felt reassured until he sounded doubtful.

Singer leaned closer. "I don't trust anyone anymore. You should not either."

"Not even you?" I was about to laugh when he surprised me by saying, "Not even me."

For the next few days, I kept thinking about Singer's warning as I worked on typing up entries with less and less enthusiasm. We were now working on the Sabbath too. Nobody was exempt from the German authorities' orders that work had to continue unabated, without any of the previous disruptions. Rumkowski's summary court punishments hammered home his intention to stop all deviation from the law. There was much anger over some of the sentences. Ghetto law was strict and unwavering. It had to be.

Despite the harsh laws and stringent enforcement, there were still sporadic shootings of residents by the sentries. We could not write about them all. It was frustrating not being able to add comments, opinions, or explanations as well. The reports we received consistently blamed the victims, calling them all smugglers or mental patients. We rubber-stamped those labels. Rumkowski was reading every entry.

At least the reassurance that the workers sent to work in Germany were all volunteers was a relief to me. Once again, the terrifying rumors that were poisoning the climate of the ghetto were proven false. There wasn't any reason to alarm Miriam. Everyone leaving the ghetto was a volunteer.

CHAPTER 41

MONDAY APRIL 21, 1941

I was returning from lunch at the dining room for the intelligentsia when I spotted a woman, maybe in her forties, weaving unsteadily in the street.

I moved closer. The woman appeared to be dancing. She sang as she waved her arms and waltzed, then walked a few yards and began dancing again.

I followed at a short distance.

Without warning, she turned to me and lifted her skirt over her knees.

I froze.

She lifted her soiled skirt higher.

I'd had a terrible argument with Miriam. I was exhausted. I don't know what insanity came over me, but I followed her, more curious than tempted. But I followed.

"Don't go there," a voice warned. "This lunatic comes here every day. Walks right up to the barbed wire."

I turned, and a boy was smirking at me a few feet away.

Another adolescent, face disfigured with pockmarks, hissed, "Let him go. Let him be entertained."

The first boy came closer. "You don't want to be here."

I didn't want to be anywhere, so why not here?

The woman dropped her skirt and walked away, stopping here and there to resume her wild gyrations.

At the end of the street, a sentry stood on our side of the barbed wire. The German raised his rifle and aimed at the woman.

"He's going to shoot her," I rasped to the boy.

The woman walked right up to the sentry booth.

I didn't want to see what the sentry was about to do but couldn't leave. Was I suicidal too?

The sentry lowered his rifle.

I backed away behind a post in front of a boarded-up shop. "What is that strange woman doing?" I asked aloud.

The woman pointed at her chest.

The soldier shook his head.

She kept pointing at her body.

I heard a noise. My whole body tensed. The Germans shoot first and ask questions later. I let out a gasp of relief when I saw it was the first boy. "You scared the hell out of me," I said.

"I told you not to follow her," He replied, ducking behind me.

"Do you know what she's doing?" I asked. "You said you've seen her before."

The boy sniggered. "Do you see how she's pointing between her tits?"

I wasn't going to correct him at this point about his language. "Yes."

"She wants him to shoot her."

"How do you know?" I turned back to the surreal scene.

"She asks him every day." The boy grinned, revealing several missing teeth. "Everyone knows she's crazy."

I'd seen enough. It was like watching a woman dancing before a cobra, the sentry coiled and ready to strike. I backed away, the boy prancing around me.

Abruptly, he stopped and said, "Give me ten pfennigs, and I'll tell you a secret."

"I have no money," I said.

"Yes, you do. You have a coat and leather shoes." He grinned again. "Any Jew with those can afford ten pfennigs to help a hungry child."

I gritted my teeth and gave him five pfennigs. "Not all who have coats are rich. My coat has seen better days. Now, what is your secret?"

The boy chanted, "I am the son of the Eldest of the Jews."

"You are not." I burst into laughter that a child in such rags could claim he was the child of the Chairman. "He has no children. I know this for a fact."

The boy looked angry. "How can you laugh? I am telling you the truth. I am the Chairman's son."

"Hah! If you can prove you are our Chairman's son, I will give you five more pfennigs." I felt like swatting him, but he looked like he'd been beaten many times before. "Now, hurry, I must get to my office."

"Where do you work? Do they need a hard-working boy?"

I shook my head. "Don't change the subject. Prove to me you are the Chairman's child. I have no time for such nonsense."

"The Chairman himself told me I am his child."

"Now I know you're lying. You've never heard the Eldest of the Jews speak. You're just a liar. Keep your 5 pfennigs." I turned to walk away.

The urchin waved something in front of me. "This proves I'm an orphan. I live in his orphanage on the end of this street."

I turned and faced him, an angry look on my face. "I knew it! As an orphan, you have no mother or father," I said. "Now, leave me alone. The Chairman is not your father."

The boy jumped in front of me. "You are wrong. The Chairman always says he is the father of all orphans in the ghetto. Does he not? Then he is my father." The boy held out his palm.

"Damn." I dug out five pfennigs, and reluctantly placed them in the boy's palm. "The Chairman loves his children, especially his orphans. You win."

The boy laughed and ran off.

This orphan made me think of the child Miriam was carrying. At least my son, or daughter, would not be an orphan, I promised, reminded that Rumkowski had established several orphanages. I'd

221

forgotten about this generosity. The boy had given me something I could use to lessen Miriam's hostility toward our leader: He loved children, even if he had none of his own.

Several days later, Singer was reading police reports. "Listen to this. I think we're all getting crazier every day."

I put down my work and leaned back against my chair. I hoped it would be humorous. We needed a good laugh.

Singer read: "At two o'clock, Cwajga Blum, age 41, was shot to death at the end of Brzezinska Street on the ghetto side of the barbed wire. According to witnesses, the unfortunate woman had walked up to the barbed wire several times and requested that the sentry shoot her."

I froze. It couldn't be the same woman.

Singer kept reading: "After several days of this, the sentry asked the mentally ill woman to dance for him."

"Oh my God," escaped from my lips.

"Engineer, are you okay?" Singer asked.

"Please, read on."

Singer gave me a concerned look and read, "Witnesses said, after she had performed a little dance, she begged the sentry to kill her. The soldier shot her dead at nearly point-blank range." He dropped the paper on the table. "She must have been insane. They all are."

I took the paper from his hand. "Cwajga Blum, age 41. That was her name."

Cukier, who had been busy writing something up about a new park for children, said, "You look like you saw a ghost."

"No. It is nothing."

I turned to type up the brief article, aware Singer was staring at me. I hadn't thought of that poor woman since that day. Could I have saved her? Why hadn't I tried? What was happening to us? What was happening to me? Now, she was dead. I visualized her body, thin, filthy, lying bloody on the cobblestones. She should only have been another number on our long list, just another suicide, nameless. But

I saw her face. I remembered her dance. I had seen her point to her chest and knew she was begging, "Kill me. Please kill me?"

That night, I wanted to hold Miriam. I wanted to feel my body pressed against her. I crawled in behind her back and gently dropped my arm over her. I was about to tell her I loved her. I was desperate to convince her that nothing else mattered.

Miriam turned over and spoke before I could. "I'm uncomfortable. I'm sick and tired of being exhausted. I need to sleep, but who can sleep with all this?" She sat up on the edge of the bed. "You snore. You snore like a horse. I can't sleep. I can't breathe in here."

I leaped from the bed. "Go to sleep! I'll sleep on the chair, or on the floor, with the roaches!" I hoped she would reach for me, stop me. Not a word. "Good night," I said.

Miriam rolled onto her side, taking up most of our bed.

What is wrong with her? What is wrong with everyone? I hated the thoughts swirling in my brain. I was relieved not to be in bed. I had not been able to close my eyes. When I did, I saw a woman dancing near a wall of barbed wire, a bizarre, macabre, skeleton dance. A shadow was watching her, rifle pointed at her heart. When I saw her face, it was Miriam.

CHAPTER 42

SUNDAY, APRIL 27, 1941: MARKET STALLS DEMOL-ISHED

In view of the increasing shortage of lumber and fuel, all wooden market stalls and booths on squares and markets have been ordered demolished.

It really wasn't much of a market anyway, I thought as I passed the square where the rickety sheds had stood just yesterday. Wagons pulled by boys in prison garb were carrying the scraps away to the Chairman's warehouses. It was better than thieves tearing down the booths and selling the wood on the black market. The debris-strewn field was sad looking.

"They tore down the market stalls," I said when I entered our cell. I stared at the photograph of the Eldest of the Jews and wondered if his eyes staring into the distance could ever have foretold all we were experiencing.

"Where will they put their goods?" Dr. Rosenfeld asked.

"What goods? They were selling rags and anything they could get from desperate people," Singer said.

"The proclamation on the poster board states street peddlers will place their wares on the ground or on chairs and tables from their homes," I said, knowing where Singer got his goods.

"And soon the greedy bastard will take their tables and chairs and own them too." Singer poked at his reports from department heads.

Cukier had learned to ignore Singer's jibes at the Chairman. "What

224

is the latest population figure," he asked.

"150,436. Of these, 68,193 are men and 82,243 women." I was reading from the census of March 31.

Rosenfeld chewed thoughtfully on his pipe. "Our population is dropping rapidly."

Cukier said. "We have more food and fuel for the rest."

Singer threw down the report from the Order Service. "Do you realize that 1,011 arrests were made just in March?"

"It proves our police are doing a good job," Cukier replied.

"Does the fact that 1,023 died in the ghetto also prove something?" Singer asked.

Cukier looked annoyed but contained himself. "Ostrowski, do you think this number of deaths is unusual for this size population? Kindly explain to our young friend that people do die."

Singer charged in before I could say a word. "When people are starving, while others are chain-smoking cigarettes, and riding in ornate coaches, people do die."

Cukier's hands gripped the edge of the table. "Singer, I have warned you."

I was afraid he was going to have another coughing fit. "You're both right," I said quickly, although I believed Singer was closer to the truth in this instance. "The real test is the cause of death. In our situation, deaths by hunger and suicide would be considered by most statisticians high, given our diminished population." I saw Cukier wasn't happy with my response, but numbers can only lie for so long.

Rosenfeld got into the act. "The truth is our mortality figures would be far worse if our esteemed Eldest of the Jews were not protecting us from the wolves that want to destroy us. Is that not so?"

Cukier smiled. "That is indisputable. The threat is always there, but he stands in the path of the tanks and SS and miraculously keeps us from being devoured."

Singer stared incredulously at Cukier. "You say his policies are indisputable, but how then do you explain that we have lost one hundred thousand Jews from this ghetto? Our people are starving, but Princess Helena, and our King, our devil—"

"Don't call him that!" Cukier was on his feet.

I pressed Cukier's shoulders to get him to sit down before he had another attack. "Calm yourself, Julian. He's a youngster. He's entitled to be rash."

"Singer, name-calling doesn't win debates," Rosenfeld said in a tone he might use to educate a child. "Whether you like our officials or not, we must show respect for the office. If we do not show respect, how can we expect others to do so?"

"Respect must be earned," Singer said. "I owe no respect to leaders when they do not practice what they preach."

Cukier looked like he wanted to reply but was coughing into his handkerchief.

We were used to his coughing and no longer paid it much mind.

"You must weigh the positives against the negatives," Rosenfeld instructed his difficult student. "I admit our Chairman may have some flaws. However, In my humble opinion, all the good he does far outweigh the negative."

Cukier managed to speak. "Dr. Singer, if all you hold against our leader is that he smokes, and possesses a carriage, then grant these as small compensation for responsibilities you would not wish to bear. Be grateful they are not German demands, which would be far worse."

"I agree," Rosenfeld said. "The carriage is necessary for his rounds. A supervisor must be able to tour his factories, to assure all is running smoothly, or the German tanks will be doing the job with far more gusto."

"We are all sheep," Singer muttered and went back to work.

Cukier glanced at me. "Tell me, Engineer, some good news?"

I smiled. "55 births were registered in March."

Rosenfeld said, "And soon one additional shall be added. Eh, my friend?"

I felt a rare surge of optimism. People were still having babies. Despite all we had been through, the ghetto was springing new life. God had commanded us to multiply and be fruitful. I had questioned that commandment in this time of despair. And then I remembered it was Miriam, who, after we made love, had asked, "How can we bring a child into a world like this?" She would never know how that question tormented me. I finally had an answer: even in these darkest hours, a child is a light God gives us to rekindle hope. A child would bring us back together. For a few seconds, I was lost in the dreams of a future father. I saw myself playing on the grass, under a brilliant blue sky, with my child. I heard lilting childish laughter. Miriam was there too, looking down at us, her sensual lips smiling.

Singer whispered, "Are you alright?"

"Yes. My friend, I am fine." I leaned closer.

Singer looked alarmed. "Is something wrong?"

I cupped my hand over his ear. "Oscar, will you be my child's godfather?"

Singer looked surprised. He didn't reply.

I'd deliberated this long and hard and ultimately chose Singer. He had the street smarts to protect my child. I sensed that buried beneath his playboy facade, there was strength and integrity that would compel him to help Miriam, and our blessed baby, if something happened to me. Why was he not responding? "Oscar, please, will you be my child's godfather?"

"You're serious?"

"I've never been more serious in my life. I know you will take care of my child and Miriam. Please?"

Singer nodded his head. "You need not fear. I will take care of your child and Miriam, but nothing will happen to you."

"God willing." I felt a huge load had been lifted from me. I could trust him. "Thank you, Oscar." I gave him a warm smile.

He didn't reply.

CHAPTER 43

MAY 21-26, 1941
In this six-day period, 200 people died in the ghetto. One girl was born.

It was good to feel sunshine as I walked to what had become my second home. My shoes had thin soles but, at least they had soles. Leather was hard to come by since the Germans had ordered our leather shop to only make boots and belts for the military.

I had taken to walking, when feasible, before the curfew. Sometimes I would walk to the beet fields. Other times, I would venture near the vegetable allotments, their area shrinking, cordoned off by barbed wire. Last evening, I had meandered over to what had been the western quarter of our ghetto. A new barbed wire fence had appeared overnight. A crowd of people was lined up, belongings in improvised bags and a few weary-looking suitcases.

"What is happening?" I asked an old man staring with hollow eyes at one of the shabbier buildings on Lutomierska Street.

The old-timer acted as if he didn't hear me, but then replied in a creaky voice, "They are removing our homes from the ghetto." His bony finger pointed. "More barbed wire. More fences."

"Who is doing this?" I asked, and then saw a cadre of Order Service men chasing people out of the buildings. Some residents were crying, but most looked dazed, barely alive. I sought out an officer, overcoming my innate fear of the brutish police, to learn first-hand what was happening. I held up my government identification card. "Officer, what is happening here?"

The officer glanced past me at the growing line of mostly elderly people, and then back at my identification. "This section is being severed from the ghetto."

"Who ordered this?"

He looked uneasy. "All of our orders come from the Eldest of the Jews." He leaned closer. "I suspect it was under command from the German authorities."

"Can you tell me approximately how many people are involved?" There was my obsession with numbers again. These poor souls were losing their residences, shabby as they were, and what few possessions they still had. Some had never known other homes than these rickety tenements with their cockroaches and rotting wood floors.

The officer shrugged. "Not many. We have registered 1,130 inhabitants to be evacuated from 64 buildings."

"What will happen to the people now?" I stared at the line of sad and lost faces. Was this a harbinger of what was to come for the rest of us?

The officer looked past me again. "I have to go."

"Where will you take them?" I repeated.

The officer looked at me with what I took to be contempt. "It does not matter. I have my orders." He walked away.

In the hot sun, a long line of men and women stood by what little they had been able to gather as the Order Service men checked the dilapidated buildings and alleyways for anyone who might be hiding. It brought back memories I'd forgotten now that I was in the inner circle. I remembered our anguish as Miriam, and I were given five minutes to gather our things and get the hell out of what had been our flat in the city. I heard screaming, curses, as we scurried like frightened rats, cowering from fists and sticks, rushing toward the ghetto. "It's happening again," I said, as I turned away from the lines.

I'd seen enough. I would read the report, and it would become another entry in a chronicle that was longer than I ever anticipated.

I had hoped that the war would be over and all would be reset to normal before our child was born. As I walked away, I realized the only predictable thing about our lives was that the sun still rose, but in the ghetto, it was often hidden by the smoke of factory chimneys churning out uniforms and other supplies for our oppressors. Singer argued we should not be helping them. Was he right?

When I got to our workroom, the sun blocked by our boarded-up window, I reported to the others what I'd seen. "Where will they put these unfortunates?" I asked. "Has anyone gotten notice of their disposition?"

Cukier dug into his pile of Order Service reports. "Not to worry. They're being re-housed in Precinct II. They'll all be given homes."

Rosenfeld looked up. "This is encouraging. The Germans are remodeling a building outside the ghetto for their administration. They're moving from here."

My heart sank. "A new building could mean permanence. I hoped with the war raging the Nazis would lose interest in our community, but a new headquarters is evidence they are planning to stay."

Rosenfeld looked stunned, the document still in his hand.

Cukier held up a sheet of paper. "We have some good news! Our Chairman has just returned from a trip to Warsaw and guess what?"

I hadn't seen Cukier so excited in weeks.

"He was in Warsaw?" Singer asked, leaning forward.

I knew little about our friend but recalled he claimed to have come from Poland's largest city.

"Singer, listen to the news," Cukier said. "Gentlemen, our Eldest of the Jews, Chairman Rumkowski reports he will be bringing us...are you ready for this?"

I was eager for any good news. "What is it already?"

"Our great leader is bringing thirteen new doctors to the ghetto!"

"New doctors?" Rosenfeld asked. "This is marvelous news. This will be an enormous help."

Singer was silent.

"Is this not welcome news?" I asked.

"I hope it happens," Singer replied.

I shook my head. "You are a hopeless pessimist."

He hissed, "I was hoping for different news."

"Like what?"

"You will know soon enough, my friend. Not all Jews are sheep."

I had no idea what he meant. So much about him was a mystery. He had leaked that he had come from Warsaw, but always clammed up when we tried to probe him for more. I'd learned to accept him as he was. I read the memo in my hand, "May 21-26, 1941: 200 people died in the ghetto in six days. One girl was born." I looked at Singer who was staring at me. "You have a way of bringing me down," I said.

Singer smiled sadly. "I'm a realist," he said.

"That is a good quality in a godfather," I whispered.

He returned to reading more reports.

I was pleased. Singer had not rejected becoming my child's godfather. If anyone could protect my family, it was my friend, Oscar Singer.

CHAPTER 44

J UNE 5, 1941

Singer was in a rare good mood when he rushed into our room. I was glad because Miriam, now in her last weeks of carrying our child, had become impossible. She acted as if I were the enemy. I actually shouted at her that she sounded crazier than Singer.

"Go to hell," she said, her eyes taunting me.

I would have slapped her, but she burst into tears. I had to leave. I felt trapped in that disgusting flat. I felt trapped everywhere these days. When would all this end? It will get better after the baby is born, I reminded myself, as I escaped to work, the warm sun making me feel better.

"Listen to this," Singer said a smile on his face. "Bronowski was arrested!"

"Another arrest is no big news."

Singer laughed. "Bronowski is the judge our wonderful leader appointed to run the Summary Court. He's been arrested, the bastard."

"I remember him. He was made solely in charge of dishing out all sentences," Rosenfeld said, looking up from his work. "You're right. He is a bastard."

"The Chairman put all his faith in this corrupt character," Singer exclaimed. "Ah yes! Apparently, they found 1000 German Marks in his apartment. Now he's screwed."

"That's a lot of money." I thought of what I would do with that kind of money. Would that buy happiness for Miriam?

"You just can't trust anyone these days." Singer laughed.

"What's going to happen to him?" Rosenfeld asked.

"The Chairman says he will decide his judge's fate and will personally decide sentences in all cases of corruption, fraud, and theft committed against the community." Singer shook his head. "Rumkowski has what he wanted. He is now judge and jury. Oh, yes, we are in good hands."

"No comments. Just write it up." Cukier ordered.

I wondered if he had finally learned to tolerate Singer's cynicism.

"Who went to the show last night?" Cukier asked.

"What show?" I asked, wondering if a performance might have been soothing for Miriam. She would have been wild that she could not fit in her dress though. I saw her again, as she had looked in that lovely black gown. If only she could wear that again someday.

Rosenfeld looked up from his paper. "I was writing it up. "I enjoyed it, although it lacked professional performers."

Cukier nodded. "I agree. It far surpassed my expectations."

"Agreed," Rosenfeld said. "I wrote, "This show can, without reservation, be ranked with those of pre-war theaters.""

"Yes. I can always trust you to properly present our cultural events."

"It is a rare pleasure these days." Rosenfeld looked wistfully at his pipe.

"Was the Chairman there?" Singer asked.

"Not only was he there, but he gave a speech," Cukier said.

Singer said, "Naturally."

"I thought it was a bit lengthy." Rosenfeld said, looking apologetically at Cukier.

"I don't know. I found the Chairman's comments about his Warsaw visit interesting. He described the huge disparity between the impoverished masses and the very few who remain wealthy and still "enjoy pastry shops, restaurants, and stores," where prices are "dizzyingly high." It was illuminating," Cukier said.

"As if things are so different here?" Singer spat.

Here we go again, I thought.

Rosenfeld ignored him. "He went on about how the rich were dressed in fine clothes while he saw masses of unemployed people whose appearance was frightening." He glanced at Cukier. "I'll add that in," he said, grabbing a pen.

Cukier nodded. "Also add, "Complete disorganization and chaos." I found those words to be a powerful summary of what he says is wrong in Warsaw." He glanced at Singer. "Didn't you say that is where you are from?"

I looked at Singer.

"And what did our incorruptible egalitarian say about corruption right here?" Singer asked, ignoring the question. "Did he say it does not exist? Did he take credit for wiping it out?"

Rosenfeld shot Singer a disapproving look.

Cukier smiled. "On the contrary, young Singer, the conclusion of his speech was dedicated to the latest phase of his relentless struggle against what he called the "rampant hydra" of crime and corruption that is keeping work from being performed in harmony here."

"Rampant hydra." I like that." Rosenfeld jotted it down for his entry.

"You can't kill a hydra without chopping off its heads," Singer said.

Cukier was about to speak when the door blew open, and Henryk Neftalin stormed into our room shouting, "They threatened to shoot one hundred people."

CHAPTER 45

J UNE 6, 1941

I stared at my report, still not accepting it was true. When we first heard Neftalin, I think we all went into shock. It was unimaginable. How could any sane person believe, that even the Germans, vicious as they were, would threaten to execute one hundred innocent people?

Henryk was blabbering. "They were going to execute one hundred of us. He saved us! He performed a miracle."

"Calm down, Henryk," Cukier said. "Please, tell us what happened?"

"Yes. Yes. You must write it all down. Our Chairman was magnificent. He was heroic."

Even Singer peered anxiously at the deputy.

"It began around 5 o'clock in the afternoon. A tramcar was passing by on Limanowski Street when a brick shattered a window."

"I know that tram," I said. "Was anyone hurt?"

Neftalin shook his head. "An important representative of the German authorities was on board. The Kripo suspected it was an assassination attempt."

"Oh my God!" Rosenfeld exclaimed.

Singer smiled.

I knew he welcomed any actions against our occupiers. He was young and didn't understand the consequences.

Neftalin nodded. "We were given orders to hand over the perpetrator within fifteen minutes, or the Commander threatened that 100 people would be shot. Imagine! They were going to shoot 100 Jews!"

"Oh my God," Rosenfeld repeated.

"What happened?" Cukier asked.

"Our Chairman, without wasting a second, ordered a full investigation by every available unit of our police. Everyone was tense. The lives of 100 innocent people were at stake."

Would the Germans carry out such a threat? I doubted any civilized people could be this inhuman.

"What happened?" Cukier repeated.

"It was a miracle. Thanks to the fast action of the Chairman, we learned it was a ten-year-old boy who had thrown the brick at the tram."

"A boy?" Singer echoed our surprise.

"Ten years old?" Cukier asked.

"Yes. It seems this child had been amusing himself throwing rocks and bricks at passing trams. He had no idea it would break a window."

"Of course not! He's just a child." Singer said. "So, what did the Germans do to him?"

"The Chairman raced to the Gestapo's office. He risked his own safety, as he has done thousands of times."

"Yes. Yes," Singer said.

Cukier glared at him.

Neftalin didn't catch the sarcasm in Singer's tone. He proceeded, "Our leader told the Commandant the culprit had been found, but he needed fifteen more minutes. He begged and pleaded for just fifteen minutes more. He swore he was telling the truth. In the end, after his impassioned plea, the Commandant extended the ultimatum by another fifteen minutes."

"That was good of them," Singer said.

Neftalin nodded, again not catching Singer's sarcasm. "The Chairman took charge of interrogating the boy himself. After ten minutes, by the use of his subtle questions, he established that the brick had been thrown by this youngster who had not realized what he was doing."

"A ten-year-old should know better," Singer said, glancing at me.

I felt like telling him this was no time for his attitude, but this was also not the right time to chastise him. This crisis was unprecedented. I was on the edge of my chair waiting for Neftalin to continue.

Neftalin sighed. "The poor lad is sick and retarded."

We all are, I thought, hearing the familiar excuse.

Neftalin sighed again. "The Chairman dictated a report in record time and handed over the boy in person to the German police seconds before the deadline elapsed."

"He turned the boy over to the German police?" I asked before Singer could.

"Yes. Barely in the nick of time."

"But he handed the boy to the Germans," Singer said.

Cukier glared at Singer. "It was the boy or 100 innocent citizens."

Neftalin nodded in agreement.

"What did the Germans do to him?" I couldn't imagine the tension everyone must have experienced, the fear for the boy.

"Of course, we were all worried for this poor child. There were long, torturous hours as we waited. When the Chairman returned, nearly three hours later, drained of all energy, looking haggard and worn, he gasped that after they evaluated all the facts, the Gestapo released the child into the Chairman's custody."

"Thank God," Rosenfeld said. "That poor child."

Sweat was dripping from my face just from the story. "He must have been terrified."

Neftalin fell back in the chair. "It was a happy ending to what could have been a tragedy. Our brave Eldest of the Jews saved us."

I think we all breathed a sigh of relief, but after the initial relief wore off, the reality sank in: The Germans could, at any whim, any perceived provocation, threaten to kill us. One hundred Jewish souls were nothing to them. Only Rumkowski might be able to prevent it.

"It was a happy ending to what could have been a tragedy," echoed in my exhausted brain. I wondered if this episode was a precursor to greater tragedies under German rule. One thing was evident, we had no choice but to support the Eldest of the Jews. He had proven again our only hope for survival was to keep the Germans convinced that we did not need their interference. Despite Singer and Miriam's criticisms, Rumkowski was the only flimsy barrier between one hundred and fifty thousand weak and defenseless Jews, and the wolves circling us. "I'll write this entry," I said. "Please convey our congratulations to the Chairman for his success in saving us from this terrible mass punishment."

"Thank you," Neftalin replied and stood. "I admit to you, I've never been more frightened. I am convinced they would have carried out their threat. We would have lost one hundred of our souls at random due to the act of a child." He let out a sigh. "By the way, tomorrow, we are expecting an important visitor. Heinrich Himmler will be meeting with the Chairman, who will guide him around and highlight our well-run factories." He glanced at Singer. "We must pray that everyone is on their best behavior."

"Himmler is coming here?" Rosenfeld looked frightened. "What does he want?"

Singer whispered, "The noose is tightening. We must try to get Miriam out."

"It is too dangerous. You must never let Miriam hear this," I hissed. Singer did not reply.

CHAPTER 46

J UNE 9, 1941
    On Saturday, June 7, Himmler visited the ghetto.

I was depressed. The news of our near escape from having 100 of our people shot had made a deep impression on all of us. I was struggling to record what was happening to our people without making some comment about the cause, which of course, was the tightening Nazi noose. It was also making it more difficult to talk to Miriam, who was more despondent with each passing day. The baby was near, and she complained of feeling trapped within our tiny apartment in the stifling heat. She was not putting on weight. All food was so severely rationed that milk was only given to children to the age of three, and to expectant women, when available. The lines at the soup kitchens had grown to be miles long. Tempers flared, but people were too weak to get into fights.

As if things were not bad enough, Rumkowski announced to his administrators and workshop managers that Himmler was going to visit. He ordered all shops to make their work progress even more smoothly, to impress the Germans with our efficiency. Unfortunately, someone took shots at a sentry booth the day before Himmler's announced visit.

The Germans were incensed, and the Gestapo ordered the Chairman to select twenty- five people, of his choosing, to be flogged in public for the shots allegedly fired at the sentry. The Chairman, risking the ire of the German authorities again, negotiated a different punishment, one that he argued would better make the point.

Neftalin informed Cukier, who relayed to us, that as punishment, the Germans had accepted a twenty-four-hour house arrest of everyone in the ghetto.

"I'm surprised Rumkowski even questioned their orders," Singer said. "He usually does exactly what they want."

"Perhaps now you see our Chairman differently," Cukier replied.

"A public flogging would have been a terrible precedent," I said. "It seems odd that this alleged shooting takes place a day before Himmler's arrival. Don't you think it's a bit coincidental?"

"I thought that as well," Singer said. "But of course, I'm skeptical about everything." He aimed his eyes at Cukier.

"Do you think it's some sort of demonstration for Himmler?" I asked.

"By the German ghetto authorities?" Singer said. "Yes, that would make sense. They would not want to appear too lax before one of the big-shot Berlin Nazis."

"Speculation is useless. Here are today's death reports," Cukier said, handing them out as if he were dealing cards in a game.

"I see we have more suicides. It's becoming an epidemic."

"Just count them up and elaborate about any if they are unique in some way," Cukier replied.

"Now who is the numbers man?" I asked, thinking it a friendly joke.

Cukier looked annoyed. "There are just too many of these suicides now. Every day someone else jumps from a window or a rooftop. I'm more interested in the ones who get shot, especially by the sentry booths and the barbed wire." He coughed several times, very hard.

We had learned to ignore it, regarding his coughing fits as emotionally triggered. Cukier got nervous, he coughed. He got angry, he coughed. "Singer, you handle reporting the shootings. You do it well. What else is happening?"

"Where is Dr. Rosenfeld?" Singer asked, "It is rare that he is late."

Just then the door opened. Neftalin walked in. He looked pale, his usually shiny hair, disheveled. "The Germans accepted the Chairman's deal," he announced without his usual ebullience. "There will be a one-day universal house arrest. Everyone is prohibited from leaving their residence."

"Did they find the culprit who supposedly shot at the booth?" Singer asked.

"No. What is important to us is that the Chairman was able to use his influence with the German authorities to avoid this hideous public flogging." Neftalin wiped his brow. "You must make it clear that he risked his own safety to win this concession, this victory, from the occupying force, especially with Himmler due to arrive. Terrible timing."

"May I ask what the precise conditions for this house arrest are?" I was concerned since Miriam was close to delivering our child.

Neftalin pulled out the proclamation which would be posted all around the ghetto. "Nobody may leave their house from nine P.M. Friday to eight P.M. Saturday."

"The Sabbath?" Cukier asked.

"We are fortunate they even accepted this, so we can't push it. We were able to get permission to give special passes to the ghetto administration and essential workers, but nobody else can set foot out of their premises, not even into their courtyards."

"How will this be enforced?" I asked.

"Good question. The Chairman has authorized all Order Service men to strictly enforce this ban."

"So, our police will once again be doing the dirty work," Singer mumbled.

Neftalin exploded. "Young man, you don't realize how damn close we came to have our people humiliated in front of the German high command! Flogging! People don't know the dangerous tightrope the Chairman walks in protecting us."

"You're right," Cukier said, glaring at Singer. "You must forgive my naive friend, who is representative of the young in the ghetto, which is why he is so valuable to us. Sometimes he is an irritant, but it is important for us to obtain his views, and address them in our work. You might say he is our gadfly."

That would be an appropriate word to describe Miriam lately too. It struck me how much she echoed Singer's thoughts. Perhaps they attended the same club of angry, cynical, radical, young Jews. Maybe they were listening to one of the young prophets who railed against our Chairman in the ratholes of the ghetto. The Chairman wanted to root them out, but they moved from one location to another.

Neftalin stood and gazed down at Singer. "You may speak your mind freely within these walls, Gadfly, but be aware that once you are free of this chamber, you will espouse the party line. This incident, like so many others, bears out the need to show unity behind our Chairman. The Germans are eagerly waiting for any disruption. The consequences will be terrible if they sense any weakness. God forbid it."

Once the Deputy left, Singer delivered his usual diatribe about the Order Service and Chairman doing the work of the Germans, but I think even he realized there was little choice.

As it turned out, the house arrest took place with relatively few incidents. We reported two fracases involving residents wanting to pray in one of the make-shift synagogues scattered around the ghetto. They struck Jewish police who obstructed them, and they were arrested. But while Himmler was here, no residents appeared on the streets other than those few given special passes to keep the factory machinery going. Only the best workers were visible as the production lines ran smoothly for the big day.

There was one aspect of Himmler's visit not known by the public. Neftalin gave us the low-down of what happened. He was sweating, exhausted, and drinking water as if he'd come from the Negev, the Israeli desert.

"Damn the Germans," he uncharacteristically cursed, and then, as if realizing we were all staring at him, said, "I'm tired. You must forgive me."

"What is wrong, Henryk? Are you ill?" Cukier asked.

Neftalin drank more water and lowered his tie. "We just got back. It was a long, terrible day." He sipped again. "Our esteemed Chairman deserves better. He, and his entourage, I included, were ready to greet the German leader at his announced time of arrival, nine this morning. All was ready as if for a royal visit. The Chairman waited in his best suit outside his office. We were all on the road watching for the cars carrying Himmler and his staff. The bastards kept the Chairman waiting all day."

"What do you mean?" Cukier asked.

"They didn't arrive. Our Chairman refused to let anyone leave. All of us were waiting in the street until the black car bearing Himmler and his high command finally pulled up at four P.M.! The bastard deliberately kept us waiting."

Singer contained his thoughts until Neftalin, clearly frustrated and exhausted, left. "The Chairman never left the spot where his master, Herr Himmler, was to arrive. Do you think the egotist is finally getting the message?"

"Singer!" Cukier exclaimed. "Will you stop! Don't you realize what this means to all of us?"

"Yes. Reality is finally setting in. Perhaps now our esteemed leader, as you call him, will recognize how the Nazis truly regard him. He, like the rest of us, is only a Jewish dog to these wolves. Perhaps now he will see how he is lowering himself, prostituting the ghetto—"

"This is something to celebrate?" Cukier interrupted. "If you are right, this is disastrous for all of us—"

"No. Now maybe we can focus on what we should have done since the beginning, fighting the bastards in every way we can. We shouldn't be producing supplies for Hitler! We should be sabotaging them at every turn. We should bomb the shit out of them—"

"And all die? Wonderful plan!" Cukier slammed his fist on the table. "You and the other radicals will get us all killed. You're irresponsible!

You will get the ghetto destroyed." He burst into a frightening fit of coughing. "Damn you! Damn the Germans!" He could barely speak in between hacking and spewing phlegm into his nose rag.

I jumped out of my seat and helped Cukier leave the room. "Calm down, Julian," I urged, supporting him as he groped along the wall, blinded by his incessant coughing.

Cukier sagged against the wall outside the door. "I'm afraid of dying," he whispered.

I held my friend quivering against me. I did not realize he was so ill. I prayed nobody else knew either.

CHAPTER 47

J **UNE 16-22, 1941**
Two hundred and six people died in the ghetto. Three boys and four girls were born.

And I was still waiting.

The anxiety was intolerable. Miriam was irritated by everything, especially everything I did. "You snore. You fart. You hog the bed." I was tired of it. "I'll sleep on the chair," I shouted, and slept on the floor, which thankfully still had a piece of tattered rug covering its hard surface. I assumed her moodiness to be a result of being cooped up in the dark room, and of course, the pregnancy, with all its bodily changes. It was not what I expected. Where was the joy? Where was the happy wife about to give life to my child?

Every day, there was another battle, many begun by her incessant needling about the rumors she heard at her job. The Chairman was valiantly trying to stop these alarming rumors, but nothing stemmed the flow of lies and gossip. The horror stories were like the flies feeding on the dead. The officials would swat and swat, but still, they buzzed all around us, picking at our bones.

I'd barely closed the door and removed my coat when Miriam started in on me. "Did you hear the latest?"

"What now?" I was exhausted after a day of counting suicides and shootings.

Her smile was evil. "The Emperor's own men defied his royal decrees."

"What are you talking about? What new tall tales are you listening to?"

"Eyewitnesses saw this." She shifted her chair toward me. "It was at a restaurant... the... the... Adriatic."

"The Adria?" I tensed. "I know nothing about this."

She peered at me. "You remember that house arrest bullshit?"

"It was not bullshit. It was to save twenty-five people, chosen at random, from a public flogging, to be staged before Himmler. We should be grateful to the Chairman for risking his own safety—"

"Stop giving me his propaganda. I've heard it all before." She got up from her seat, holding her stomach. "Why doesn't it move?"

"What do you mean?" I felt a chill race through me. "Are you alright, Miriam?"

She looked frightened. "My baby isn't moving. By now I should have felt something." She rubbed her stomach. "Benny, what's wrong?"

I got up from the chair. "Do you want to see the doctor?" I was ready to use my influence to get her in. The lines at the doctor's offices were incredible. It was almost impossible to see any of the few doctors the Germans had not conscripted for their own use.

"No. I don't want to see those butchers. They don't want us to have babies; too many damn mouths to feed." She backed away from me.

"More nonsense. I can get us in, ahead of the line."

"Of course! You're one of his special people!"

"What the hell are you talking about?"

"You and your friends have fancy dining rooms while the lines at the soup kitchens stretch around the block!"

"What does this have to do with getting you medical help? I was only trying to help you and my son."

"Your son? God has spoken to you? Have you already picked out a name too?"

"I was thinking Oscar. After my friend, Singer—"

Miriam burst into laughter.

She sounded insane. "What's so funny? He's a good friend. I've asked him to be our child's godfather. I was going to talk to you about it, but you've been—"

"Crazy? Irrational? Is that what you think?" She laughed again. "I'm not the one crazy. You are. You're blind. You don't see anything going on around you!" She was screaming at me. "You and that sonofabitch, Rumkowski, are both blind and deaf."

"Don't talk about him that way. He's doing everything he can to protect us—"

"He's protecting his kingdom! He's selling us out to the Nazis so he can own everything. He wants only to save himself and his greedy family."

I wanted to calm her, but she was storming around our flat, looking as if she wanted something to throw, something to smash. "Miriam, stop!"

She stormed toward me. "He rides around in his coach like a king. His whole family is getting rich while we're starving in these shitholes."

"Enough! I have seen close up—"

"You don't even know what happened during the so-called house arrest."

"Are you back on that again? You mustn't listen to every lie. Only the Chairman has the ear of the Germans. They respect him."

She stared incredulously at me. "You actually believe the Nazis respect a Jew? Not even his own people respect him. His officials, the men he most trusts, were at the Adria restaurant gambling when they were supposed to be under house arrest like the rest of us. That's how they respect your precious Chairman."

"Nonsense! More malicious rumors!"

Miriam pointed her finger at me. "You know shit about what is happening. His precious highest officers were caught gambling at the Adria. Some other 'rat' must have informed his majesty. I can imagine the scene when he found his friends drinking and gambling.

On Shabbat yet!" She let out a hideous cackle. "So much for respect!"

I had the image of a red-faced Rumkowski roaring at his officers. "Who were they?"

"I don't know. I just heard that the devil went crazy. He arrested everyone. He is judge and jury. Next, he'll be executioner! It's a madhouse."

I was worried about her sanity. I tried to hold her, but she pulled away. Her face did not look like that of the child I'd seen only a few weeks ago. "Miriam," I said, "My beloved."

She looked at me and shook her head. "I have to get out of here. I have to." She wiped her eyes as if she was fighting tears.

"Do you want to go for a little walk? It is past curfew, but tomorrow I'll come home early and—"

"Are you crazy? A walk? Look at me! I can hardly stand! A walk?" She was in my face. "I don't want a damn walk. I want to get out of this awful ghetto! I told you months ago! I begged you. I begged you."

Again, I tried to reach for her hand. She yanked it away.

"Why didn't you listen? Why are we still here?" She walked around the table again, her lips moving but no sound coming from them.

"It's not so bad. I have a job now."

"What good is your job if we live like rats trapped in this damn cage?" She twisted her apron. "Please, before something terrible happens, get us out of here? I beg you again. Remember when they deported us from Lublin? You said it would be better. Remember?" She pointed her hand around the room. "Is this better? We are at the mercy of the Nazis. Singer says-—"

I woke up at the pest's name. "Singer says? How do you know what that upstart says?" I rose over her. "I asked, how do you know what that radical says?"

Miriam fired back, her eyes blazing, "You told me. You complain about him all the time."

That was true. What was I thinking? I glared at the walls of our tiny room and felt them closing in on me again. "It's stifling in here." My heart beat erratically. I had to calm myself, calm her. "I'm sorry. You're right. We need to get out of here." I sat on the chair, hoping she'd sit as well.

Miriam moved toward me, dropped to the floor and gazed into my eyes. "You're going to get us out of the ghetto? Oh, thank God! Thank you, dear husband." She lowered her head onto my lap.

I stroked her hair. It felt moist and matted...her beautiful hair. I let out a deep sigh. "I will ask my friends in the housing department if we can be moved to someplace nearer my office." I kept stroking her hair. "Yes, that will work. You'll see, in a new apartment, a larger one, two bedrooms... one for our child... you'll feel better." I felt her trembling in my lap. "My darling, Miriam, there is no way out of Lodz. The barbed wire is everywhere. The sentries shoot anyone who even approaches. One after the other they shoot Jews dead." I felt she might be falling asleep. In the old days, her head on my lap would have been enough to arouse me. That had not happened for weeks. Why? I don't know. Was it the pregnancy? Was it the nagging? I just didn't feel she was Miriam anymore. I didn't know who she had become...who we had become. "You mustn't listen to rumors. The only thing you need to know is that God, for some reason, has chosen we Jews to face annihilation at every turn of history's wheel. But Miriam, we have always survived. We have overcome every sword and flame aimed at us. The war will be over, soon, and our beautiful child will be out in the glorious sun, long after Hitler is rotting in hell, where he, and all the damn Nazis, belong."

Miriam let out a deep sigh and pulled her head from my lap.

I bent to kiss the top of her head, but she was gone. Sitting in the darkness, I heard her settle onto our bed. Was she weeping? I waited for her to call me.

It was a dark night. Blackout dark. I pulled off my shirt and pants, placing them neatly folded on a chair. I would need them again tomorrow. I'd have loved to go for a walk, to see the stars, feel the cooling breezes one could still catch sporadically in the hot June night. I hadn't seen stars in nearly a year. The Jewish police, the Order Service, patrolled the streets to ensure the curfew was strictly observed. Of course, they couldn't be everywhere, so thievery still occurred, as in the case of the missing stairway. I laughed, remembering that incident, where the people, some after making love, woke and found their staircase had been stolen while they slept. I tried not to laugh out loud. Miriam needed her sleep. But it was a funny image, all those people staring with stunned faces. "We're naked. How do we get down?"

I heard Miriam's soft breathing. How I used to look forward to curling up behind her, pressing against her, my arm holding her, touching her. The longing was still there, but I remained in the chair. It was peaceful without her.

Sometimes, in all the commotion, in the clutching tightness of the two rooms that were prison cells to me, the conference room in the Archives, and this room with Miriam, my trapped animal, I welcomed being alone. Tonight, I felt too lonely. I was shell-shocked and desperate. "Desperate people do desperate things," Rosenfeld often said.

Without any logic, still not believing in God, but so desperate I could cry, I closed my eyes and prayed. I remembered bits of prayers I'd learned as a child, a few ancient melodies and Hebrew words whose meaning I did not know: "Baruch atah adonei elohenu melech haolom… shehechianu vkiemanu, vhigeanu..lazman hazeh." How did I remember this? Well, most of it. Some words were missing. Some mispronounced. Every Hanukkah, the joyous festival celebrating freedom, this was the blessing Jews said on the first night of lighting the candles. Even though I couldn't recall all of it, I thought it was the appropriate prayer. It was one of the few this atheist remembered. "Blessed art thou, O Lord, our God, who has allowed me to live to this day."

I looked at the shape in our bed that was Miriam and asked God to please protect her and my child. Irrational, illogical, but from that moment on, I prayed every night. I promised God that whatever sacrifice he required I'd make if Miriam and our child would be safe. I begged him to help me. I never let Miriam, nor anyone else, know about my praying. Maybe that's why I never heard God's reply.

CHAPTER 48

J UNE 25, 1941

"You look like you didn't sleep last night," Singer said, letting out a loud yawn.

"I'm alright. Thank you."

He smiled. "When a bachelor doesn't sleep, it is different than when a married man doesn't sleep." He gave me a sly wink.

Why was it whenever it seemed as if he was a caring person, a human with a soul, he would wreck it with innuendos about his sexual exploits. Even in this ghetto, with all the hardships we were enduring, young men like Singer could sow their oats. "You have no morality, my young friend," I replied, a bit envious.

"Life is too short. We must take pleasure while we can. Even a married man must enjoy himself once-in-a-while."

Why did I feel he was probing? "Not when his wife is about to give birth," I hissed, hoping that would shut him up.

"And how is the mother-to-be? As godfather, I'm entitled to ask."

"To be honest, I'm a little worried about her."

"Is Miriam not well?"

"How well can she be with all that is going on?"

He nodded. "It must be hard for her. I don't know if I would want to have a child under these conditions."

"I was hoping the war would be over by the time our baby was born. What do you think? Will it be over soon?"

Singer brushed back his thick hair, making me feel self-conscious at my baldness. Even in this awful place, though thinner than he

252

had been when we first met, he still looked handsome, boyish. He was more muscular than I and smiled more readily. I could see why young women liked him. If I were not her husband, Miriam might have fallen for his bad-boy charm. "I also hoped it would be over by now. Such a waste of life."

"Thanks for adding to my depression."

"It is the most common illness here." He held up a small stack of papers. "Another woman shot by the barbed wire. This one, I knew. She was thirty-six. It says she was "mentally ill," and so we'll write that. But I know her. She was as mentally ill as you or I." He flipped his finger through the pile. "They can't all be mentally ill."

"I sometimes think we're all going insane." I gave him a bitter laugh.

"Even you, Engineer?"

I nodded. "Miriam wants to get out of here." I gave him an inquisitive look.

He leaned forward, his voice low. "It's impossible. Don't mention it again." He shifted his chair away from me.

"You asked me what was wrong." I shifted my chair closer to him. Nobody else had arrived yet. As crazy as I knew it was, I had to be sure he couldn't work a miracle. "You always brag about your connections."

"It's impossible. I just told you the Germans are shooting to kill anyone who even gets close to the barbed wire." He gave me a hard look. "Don't ask me again."

The door opened.

I quickly moved back to my position. I was a trained seal, returning automatically to where I had been since we began this tedious task last November. In less than a year, everything had changed. It had all turned to shit.

Cukier entered, holding more papers in his arms. "Did you hear what happened?" He asked, placing the stack in a large box crudely marked "In." We had not needed such boxes in the beginning, but now the news was coming in buckets. "The Chairman shows no favoritism."

Singer's face revealed his incredulity.

"Even his closest associates, the highest echelon, are not shielded from his impartial justice," Cukier announced, beginning to sort through the memos.

Singer couldn't resist. "What are you talking about?"

Cukier handed him a report from the Chairperson. "Even you, our resident skeptic, will have to admit that nobody is above the law in the eyes of our Eldest of the Jews. God bless him and keep him."

Now I was curious. "Singer, would you please tell me what our fearless leader is rambling on about?"

Singer was reading the note. "I don't believe it. It says that on Saturday, June 7th, when Himmler was here, and we were all under house arrest. Remember that? I couldn't even get laid on a Friday night!"

"Will you please stop talking about your sex life and tell me what happened?"

Singer laughed. "My sex stories are more credible than this stuff."

"Singer!" Cukier shot him an angry look.

Singer began to read again, "The Chairman arrested several members of his high command for violating his ban on leaving their homes."

The gossip Miriam had thrown at me was true. "Was this at the Adria?"

Singer looked surprised. "You knew about this?" he asked.

"Yes. Partly. There are rumors. Who was arrested?"

"Oh God! They were gambling in the back room of the restaurant!" Singer burst into laughter. "Can you imagine their faces when the Chairman stormed in on them?"

"Who was arrested?" I held my pen in the air.

"Oh my God! It was Commandant Dancyger, the chief of the Sonnerkommando!"

"The commander of Rumkowski's special police unit? He's one of the Chairman's most trusted men. Who else?"

"Oh, this is great! His deputy, Marek Kligier, and some unemployed character, and get this; Librach!"

"The head of the bread department?" I remembered Miriam complaining about the endless lines and this administrator was playing cards?

Singer nodded. "Every one of these bastards is corrupt. The whole damn government is a mess of greedy pigs. I told you so. Nobody listens—"

"Singer!" Cukier was livid. "Just because a few men are corrupt, does not call for you to malign the entire government. By arresting these criminals– that is what they are—these rotten apples, the Eldest of the Jews proves he favors no one, not even those closest to him."

I didn't understand. How could men with so much at stake show such contempt, not just for our leader, but for all of us, who depended on them? "What did the Chairman do with them? Whatever it is will not be enough."

Cukier replied. "First, from what Neftalin tells me, he personally reprimanded them sharply."

Singer laughed. "A reprimand is a fit punishment while we all sweat in our cramped quarters and stand on endless lines for a few crumbs of bread and I can't even get—"

"Singer!" Cukier shot him a warning. "You didn't let me finish. The Chairman suspended all three gamblers, and replaced Dancyger with Julian Grosbard."

Singer whispered in my ear, "He replaces a rat with a snake. Well done."

Cukier didn't hear Singer's comment. "You see, this should even satisfy you."

"Yes, Julian, it does," Singer said, avoiding another quarrel.

I wasn't sure what it proved. "I'll write it up," I said, reaching for the paper.

"I'm glad you're doing it," Singer said. "You can put a positive stamp on everything."

And you always put a negative stamp on everything, I thought as I focused on my typing. Even the clatter of the keys did not drown out Cukier's damn coughing.

CHAPTER 49

J UNE 30, 1941
From June 26-30, one hundred and sixty-one people died. Three boys were born.

I was writing about a 73-year-old man who had hung himself in a lavatory at 18 Lagiewnicka Street, the building where he resided, when I noticed that another man, 42-year-old Jakub Mordcah Joskowicz had taken poison to end his life, also in a lavatory. "No bathroom is safe."

"What do you mean?" Singer asked.

"It seems that every time you need to pee or shit, you have to watch out for a corpse. Bathrooms are becoming the favored site for suicides." I laughed at the bizarre situation.

"Nowhere is safe," Singer said. "I almost got hit by a body falling out of a window the other day." He gave me a teasing look. "You wouldn't miss me at all if a corpse landed on top of me and crushed me to death?"

Cukier, who had been ignoring our idiotic conversation couldn't resist. "I'd miss you. Like my bottom misses the bite of a gadfly." He laughed but immediately broke into a coughing fit.

Singer looked concerned. "You shouldn't laugh. It makes you hack like an old horse."

"You...never...heard...of...dying...from laughter?" Cukier said from behind his handkerchief.

That was when the door opened, and Doctor Rosenfeld staggered in. "Oh God," he cried and leaned against the wall, his back to us.

Singer jumped from his chair as did I. He was closer and offered the doctor his support, but the elderly man pushed him off, slumping against the wall, shivering, face turned away.

Cukier, still coughing, made his way toward us. "Close the door," he said. "My friend, are you, all right?"

Rosenfeld was leaning against the wall, still trembling.

"Doc, what is it? What happened?" Singer was stroking the old man's back.

"It was terrible. I was scared shitless. I don't like admitting that." Rosenfeld pulled his hat down over his face.

I shrugged my shoulders at Singer.

Cukier, calm, as he was at most times, asked gently, "Please, Oskar, tell us what happened? We want to help."

"There is no help for us," Rosenfeld said in a voice that sounded as if he'd been crying. "Look. Look what they did." He turned toward us.

At first, I didn't notice anything different about him. From the way he was carrying on, I expected a bullet hole, a gash from a bayonet, a stream of blood. There was nothing.

It was Singer who said in a reverential voice, "Your beard. What happened to your beard?"

How did I not notice that? His beard was no longer on his face. "What happened to your beard?"

Rosenfeld's hand ran over his face. There were splotches of drying blood on his flesh. "I was nearly here. I suspected nothing." He turned back to the wall.

"Do you want to sit down?" Singer asked, still stroking the old man's back through his coat. "Please, let me help you to your chair?"

Rosenfeld nodded his head and Singer guided him gently toward his chair. "Do you want help to remove your coat?" he asked.

Rosenfeld shook his head and pulled the coat tighter around him. "No. I'm cold, very cold."

Singer glanced at me, and we helped Rosenfeld sit down. He remained by his side, his eyes glued to the man I now regarded as his father figure.

Rosenfeld pulled his coat around him even more. He kept on his hat, a wide-brimmed fedora that had seen better days. And, of course, his gloves, which I'd taken from a corpse lying in the street.

"Can you talk now?" Cukier asked, smiling approvingly at Singer.

Rosenfeld's eyes stared down at the table surface. "I was on this very street, eager to come to work...to be with all of you, my dearest friends. A sentry stopped me."

"One of ours?" I asked.

He shook his head. "I was surprised. The Germans never appear on our street in daylight. It is an agreement. So I thought. I reached for my identification card, but he ordered, "Halt." I had nothing to fear. I had broken no laws. I held my card for him. He pulled me toward him—"

"He put hands on you?" Singer asked.

"He grabbed my beard." Rosenfeld's hand slid up his jaw. "He grabbed my beard."

I was shocked. A German policeman grabbing an elderly Jewish man by the beard was unheard of.

"He dragged me by my beard. I was struggling to keep my footing. He was huge, a giant in black shining uniform. I was helpless. He pulled me by my beard. He reached for a table, and I heard a strange noise. Scissors. He was chopping up my beard. I couldn't pull away. I tried and tried. I screamed. I cried. I kicked." Tears rolled down his face.

"Shit!" Singer said, balling his fists.

For once, Cukier didn't glare at Singer. He looked shocked. We all were.

Rosenfeld was still talking, his voice quaking. "The brute kept cutting and cutting. Then he grabbed a razor, and without any balm, he scraped the blade across my face and cut into my flesh. See. See the blood. It was dripping down my face. I was too frightened. He was holding me so tight by the throat. I could not breathe, could not think. The razor kept going up and into my skin, but I was too shocked to fight. He was so strong."

"Sonofabitch!"

It wasn't Singer cursing. It was me.

Rosenfeld gazed up at me. The glossiness of his eyes broke my heart.

He spoke again, his words halting, tears flowing. "When the bastard finished, he squeezed my throat hard. I thought I was dead, but then he let go his grip around my neck. He released me suddenly, without warning, so I collapsed to the muddy ground, unable to breathe. He kicked his boot and mud splattered onto my face." He wiped his face with his hand and stared at the glove.

"My god," escaped from my lips. "Are you all right?" I couldn't stop trembling. I envisioned my old friend lying in the mud. How could this be? It had to be an aberration, one rogue sentry who would be punished by the German ghetto administration once the Chairman informed them of his transgression. No civilized beings would accept this humiliating behavior, this unprovoked abuse of a harmless, old, Jewish doctor, my dignified friend.

Rosenfeld's hand gripped the table. "I got up from the mud. My legs would not hold me. I heard screaming behind me. Another man was in the grip of the monster, being dragged to where my beard lay in the muddy street waiting for the wind to blow it free from this hell hole." He shrugged his shoulders, voice quaking. "I thought he was going to slice my throat with that razor." He looked at Cukier. "The thing is, my friends, I wanted it."

"No, you don't! Goddammit!" Singer shouted into his mentor's tortured face. "Every day we report about someone giving up. And what do we say? We say they are mentally ill, disturbed, off-balance. We know it isn't true, but we still say it. You are not going to make me put those words with your name. We are going to survive this.

The Soviets are now in the war. The English are not capitulating despite all of Hitler's efforts. We hear this from our hidden radios. We must keep on hoping. Nothing is impossible unless we give up hope."

I was shocked. Singer, the eternal skeptic, was giving a pep talk to Rosenfeld, the most logical and reasonable man I'd ever met.

Cukier nodded and then smiled sympathetically at our old friend. "For once, I agree with our gadfly. Oskar, dear friend, we can't let this one bastard's behavior defeat us. In the end, we will win."

Rosenfeld smiled sadly. "You are right. A beard is nothing now that your fellow Leninists are coming for us." He laughed. "Singer, you are a good boy."

We all agreed a beard wasn't that critical, but in the back of my mind, I saw it as an omen of what the Germans were capable of unleashing upon us. I thought of Miriam and wished there was some way I could make the impossible happen for her, for her and my child. I vowed to approach Singer again. He was our only hope. We had to escape the tightening noose.

CHAPTER 50

J ULY 1-5, 1941: DEATHS AND BIRTHS
One hundred and twenty-two people died in this period. Four
births: three boys and one girl.

The summer heat in our small room was like thorns on a cactus
prickling at me. Miriam, about to give birth at any instant, was still
working. She always came home before the curfew and seemed less
despondent than only a few weeks earlier. "Where do you go when
you leave work?" I asked.

"It is like an oven in here." She fanned herself with a piece of paper.

My pleas for a better apartment had thus far gotten the usual
bureaucratic response: "Yes, we understand. Yes, we will try to help
you. Yes, we know your wife is due any day now." It was frustrating.
I told Miriam I was trying. Perhaps that helped calm her down. "So,
tell me, my mother-to-be, did you have a nice day?"

Miriam looked at me as if I was crazy, but then answered, "It was a
good day."

"What did you do?"

She gave me a curious look and then said. "My days are dull. What
did you do at work today?"

"Working at the archives is like working in a library. Nothing much
ever happens." I told her nothing and she told me very little.

"No news is good news." Miriam sat on the chair, her hand rubbing
her stomach.

"You're right. Oh. One thing did happen. A 14-year-old boy walked from the ghetto of Warsaw all the way to Lodz."

Miriam sat up. "He walked all the way? How is this possible?"

"I don't know how he did it, but he didn't have one cent in his pocket. His mother died and his father, from what I heard, disappeared during one of the roundups in Warsaw."

"What roundups?"

I hadn't meant to let out that bit of the story. "The Germans were rounding up able-bodied men in Warsaw, volunteers, like they do here sporadically, for work details."

"Oh."

I thought she bought my explanation, but with Miriam, I was never quite sure. "Would you believe he was on the road for three weeks?"

Miriam moved her chair closer. "Where did he sleep? How could he manage this by himself?"

"He said he stayed at peoples' houses along the road, both in cities and in the country."

"People helped him?"

"I suppose. Even the German sentry, who he first encountered when he arrived here, was fascinated by his story. He could have shot him as he approached the booth, but thankfully this German was a father himself. He interrogated the lad and then handed him over to a Jewish Order Service worker who brought him to the Chairman's attention. You know how much the Eldest of the Jews loves children."

For once, Miriam didn't say something sarcastic. Apparently, like everyone else, she found the boy's feat amazing. "Where is the boy now? Is he being sent back? Did they imprison him?"

I chuckled. "No. Far from it. The Chairman ordered that the lad is taken care of and made a permanent resident."

"The boy is here still? He doesn't want to go back to Warsaw?"

"Miriam, my love, it's as I've been telling you. Mendel, that's the boy's name, says it is much worse in Warsaw. In fact, he told everyone he likes it here. I tell you, that is the work of our great Chairman. Even a boy from Warsaw, our largest city, would rather stay here than go back."

"It's a remarkable story." Miriam looked thoughtful. "I think it would be nice to send him some kind of welcome note." She gave me a warm smile.

"That would be nice. Yes, very nice."

"Do you know where he is staying…the address? Do you know his last name?"

"No, but I can find it out for you. Would you like that?"

Miriam smiled. "Yes, please?"

How could I resist her?

That night, I slept in our bed. It was oppressively warm, but I didn't care. I was back where I belonged. Everything was back to where it had been weeks ago. Love-making was impossible. I was grateful for that, unable to be aroused by a wife who had been distant, unreachable, for days. After many nights of straddling the kitchen chair, or huddling on the rug, I was nestled next to her. My fear was I'd fall asleep, roll over and somehow hurt the child now growing in her stomach.

When I awoke, Miriam was still asleep. I stood over her. My need to protect her, which I had nearly lost, swelled inside me. Asleep, curled under the thin coverlet, she had that look of vulnerability which made me want to keep her safe…her and our child. Whatever I did right last night, I wanted to do again and again. I asked God to give me the wisdom to know what to do to protect our future.

CHAPTER 51

JULY 20, 1941
I hated leaving Miriam was alone in the hot flat when our baby could arrive at any time. I was edgy, but she seemed more relaxed. I was walking down Dworska Street, feeling good for a change, reflecting on the miracle that had happened earlier this morning.

"I felt it move at last," Miriam said, holding her stomach. "I was so terrified I lost our blessing."

I reached tentatively for her. "It moved? Really?"

She grabbed my hand.

I was afraid she would not let me feel, but no, she placed my palm gently on her stomach.

"I feel nothing," I said, disappointed, not wanting to press down too hard.

And then something moved. Barely felt, but something moved. "It kicked. Was that him?" I asked, unexpected emotion swelling inside me. "I felt a kick again."

She nodded. "Yes. But you know it might be a girl."

"I don't care what it is, as long as it's happy…and healthy." I was enjoying the feel of my hand on my wife's stomach. "You should be fatter by now. Shouldn't you?"

"You know there is rationing."

"I'll ask for more on our card, now that we're near the end."

"Yes, we're near the end," Miriam said. "Go. You must go to your job."

"Are you in a hurry to get rid of me? Do you have some young suiter coming to woo you?" I was enjoying the tease.

Miriam looked shocked. "Look at me! Who would want a woman so fat and miserable?"

I kissed her forehead. "I can think of one."

"You always had bad eyesight," she said with a laugh.

She was right. I did have bad vision, but to me, seeing her laugh was a sight to treasure. I was thinking about that when I heard a loud sound coming from behind me.

I jumped to the side just as a black car rumbled down the street. "What are the Germans doing here?"

A military truck raced after the car.

The car stopped at the hospital for the mentally ill on Wesolo Street.

I made myself invisible, hiding around a building across the street, as officials in dark business suits, escorted by German officers, pushed their way into the building. A group of soldiers leaped from the truck and stationed themselves at the hospital entrance.

It was not safe to be here. There was something ominous about so many Germans rushing into the mental hospital under such a heavy guard. I backed away and rushed to the Jewish Ghetto Administration offices.

When I got to our sweatbox of a room, I searched the piles of papers for any announcement of a visit to the mental hospital by Germans. There was none. I wondered if Rumkowski was aware of this visit. Something about it was boring into my brain.

"Good morning, Engineer," Cukier said. "How is Miriam?"

"Better, Julian, thank you." I wondered if he knew about the hospital. "We're both getting antsy. Any day now."

Cukier smiled and then became his official self again. "Write up the new suicides. One was 23 years old. He jumped from the fourth floor of a stairwell. We also have an unidentified female shot by a sentry as she tried to leave the ghetto." He sifted through his files as he spoke, "My friend came home the other day from the primary school at Franciszkanska Street. He is the principal there. He told me a German commission showed up unexpectedly."

In my head, the alarm went off again.

Cukier looked up. "I asked my friend what the Germans wanted. He said they examined the curriculum and demanded to know the number of teachers and children."

"It's probably nothing to be concerned about," I said but was worried. The Germans were taking an increased interest in our daily goings-on. But our schools? "Have you told Neftalin?"

"He didn't seem concerned." He frowned. "I'd like you to do me a favor. Keep your eye on any more such unexpected visits, especially when it concerns children."

There was such concern in his demeanor I didn't think it was the right time to add to his worries by reporting what I'd witnessed at the hospital. Besides, I had found another bit of news that might distract him. "Have you seen that no mail is allowed to go to the United States and Western Europe as of July 17th?"

Cukier groaned. "I have an uncle in New York. He wanted us to join him, but of course, it was too late. We should have left."

I nodded. "Who knew?"

"We should have guessed. Hitler telegraphed his hatred of Jews in *Mein Kampf* and in his rabid speeches." He sighed. "Nobody believed so many would blindly follow such a lunatic. Hate is a forest of dried, dead, wood, just waiting for one match." He let out a deep sigh. "I'm so damn tired. Why doesn't America get into this war?"

"Nobody cares about Jews in a Polish ghetto," I replied. "I tell Miriam every day, I tell myself, that this war can't last much longer. The Soviets are fighting Hitler. They destroyed Napoleon. Soon it will be over." I prayed, a non-believer, I prayed in silence, that someday soon I would see my child playing in a sandbox in a free land. I prayed that Hitler would get his ass beaten by the Communists. I prayed Roosevelt would finally hear our entreaties. But most of all, I prayed Miriam would forgive me for not getting her out of here when she had begged.

CHAPTER 52

J ULY 22, 1941: *IT WAS RECENTLY DISCOVERED IN THE GHETTO*
    That the leaves of radishes and young carrots are edible if cooked.
Trade in these items has assumed considerable proportions.

"This is bullshit," Singer said, storming in late, a habit he'd acquired in the last few weeks.

"What is?" I asked, exhausted from the heat and from the moodiness of everyone around me. Miriam made it clear with each passing day that she couldn't wait until the baby finally came. Everything irritated her. Yet, she dressed every morning, as if awaiting a special event or an expected visitor. "I'm sorry, what did you say?"

"Are you alright, Engineer?" There were black circles under Singer's eyes, most likely from a late night with his disreputable friends. I almost envied his bachelor lifestyle, no involvements, just fool around and then go on to the next willing female. Morality didn't exist for young men. It's war. Who knows what is right? "I'm fine. You were reading your report about school books."

Cukier looked up.

Singer continued reading: "The Chairman convened a special commission of teachers to examine all the books we use in our schools." He laughed bitterly. "You know whose idea that was."

"Go ahead. What did this 'commission' do?" Cukier asked, standing near.

Singer read from his notes, "They removed all passages and pages related to Poland." He looked amused. "It's as if Poland never existed and we were always part of Germany."

Cukier nodded. "That's why they changed our street names too. The Chairman believes they are doing this to assert their claim over the entire territory, especially the ghetto, as a kind of protectorate. He hopes the Germans will protect us."

"Yes, but who will protect us from the Germans?" Singer asked.

For once, Cukier didn't argue. "I must admit the new interferences by the Germans are worrisome. They are taking a far more intense interest in our daily goings-on than I would like."

"You're coming over to my side?" Singer asked.

Cukier coughed. "Never that. At least I hope not." He gave Singer a smile.

Singer brushed back his hair. "We should expect more intrusions as they assert their power. He's allowing it."

"I think the Germans are choking off our supplies," I said. "Have you seen the bread lines? Miriam says they are miles long."

Singer replied, "A girl I know—"

I couldn't resist. "Which of the many?"

Cukier laughed. "How do you know he even likes girls? We've never seen one of his dates."

Singer looked flustered. "Of course, I like girls."

Rosenfeld jumped in. "So why is a great catch like you not married? By your age, I was married ten years to my beautiful Rosalie."

Rosenfeld always got sad when he spoke of his wife. Just as Hitler was marching into Poland, he'd sent her to England. It had been many months since he'd heard from her. He always said, "At least she is safe."

"Why haven't you married?" Cukier asked. "Any girl would want a handsome, articulate, and most important, well-employed, husband."

I laughed. I thought Cukier was going to say, "well-endowed."

Singer looked as if he'd been backed into a corner.

"Come on, Oscar," I joined in. "Why aren't you married? Then you can be miserable like the rest of us."

Singer looked at me. "Are you miserable?"

"Of course. All married men are. Especially married men with wives who are about to pop out babies. Oy! You playboy bachelors have no idea. You really have to love someone to survive a pregnancy." I laughed again.

Cukier joined in the laughter. "Hey, Singer, haven't you ever been in love?"

Rosenfeld looked upset. "Don't make fun of the poor boy. He only wants to get laid. How can he know what love is?"

"I know what love is."

"You do?" I was enjoying this. "You, the fun-loving bachelor, who can get any woman he wants, you know what love is? So, tell me, what is love?"

Singer looked at his friend, Rosenfeld, and said, "Love is when you are willing to sacrifice your happiness, your life, for someone you care about more than yourself. Oskar loved when he sent his Rosa away."

Rosenfeld turned away from us. He was quivering.

I was silent. Singer did know.

"But you've never felt that, have you?" Cukier said, sounding as if he was angry at Singer. "You've never felt that unselfishness that is love. Have you?" He shook his head. "I feel sorry for you. I feel sorry for all you, young people, who will never know this kind of love."

Rosenfeld raised his hand. "Stop it, Julian. That's not fair. He's a young man in a dysfunctional time. Who can blame him for wanting to grab what little fun there is in this damn world? If I could, I would want to get laid, drunk, die...yes, die, too."

We were all silent because we knew it was true. Each, in our own way, was thinking about grabbing a little fun in the throes of a war that was dragging on interminably.

"You're all wrong," Singer said softly.

I looked up.

"You don't know what the hell you're talking about," he said in that same soft voice. "I do know what love is. I know what sacrificing for love is." He stood up, grabbed his jacket, and walked out the door.

Rosenfeld broke the silence. "We were too hard on the boy."

Cukier looked angry. "He dishes it out to us. Let's get to work."

I stared at the door. I would never have guessed that Singer had been in love. He had never shown any sign of being able to care that much about any woman. I owed him an apology. I hoped someday he would tell me who the girl was.

Rosenfeld startled us by shouting, "Damn them! No wonder we can't get bread! The kitchen reports that all the flour they deliver is old! It's got labels for England. The shit is hard as a rock, and some bags are empty! The Germans are trying to starve us."

"Let me see that?" Cukier said. "The Chairman won't let the Nazis get away with this."

Could anyone stop the Nazis from getting away with their shit? Rosenfeld sent his Rosa away because he loved her. I stared at the door praying Singer would come charging back. I'd made up my mind that I loved Miriam enough to risk everything to get her out of this ghetto. If Singer couldn't help her, I'd find someone who could.

CHAPTER 53

J ULY 25-29, 1941
We were all feeling the stress of the German wolves biting at
life here with increasing ferocity.

It was Singer who brought us information about what was happening beyond the barbed wire. We never asked how he got it. We
had learned not to question how Singer managed to do some of the
things he did. Even Cukier had given up threatening him for being
habitually late and leaving early. Some days, he was an hour late
returning from lunch.

"Why don't you eat with us?" I asked one day. "The food and service
in Kitchen 2 are excellent. I only wish I could bring Miriam."

"She wouldn't eat with those elitists. She's like me. Everyone else
starves, and they eat on gold-rimmed plates and drink from crystal
goblets? No, that is not for me."

Rosenfeld put his hand on Singer's shoulder. "When I was young, I
was like you. Old age eats at idealism like a capitalistic rat."

Cukier snickered, "Our young Casanova probably has a fresh tart,
if you know what I mean."

Singer jumped from his chair. "It's none of your business what I do
with my private time."

"Ho ho! You think you have private time, now, do you? There is no
such thing anymore."

Rosenfeld interceded, as he usually did when Cukier or I went after
Singer. "Leave the boy alone. We were all young once."

"I'd like to know where he goes," Cukier said.

"I told you it's my business. Now, let's move on. I do have some news that is significant."

"I'm sure it's bad, as usual," Cukier said, rolling his eyes.

"It's kind of strange." Singer pulled up his notes.

"What isn't strange these days?" Rosenfeld remarked, sucking at his empty pipe.

"No. This is really weird. The other day, I was walking by the barbed wire when a Pole shouted at me from the other side, "Jew bastard, you will not only have nothing to eat but soon we won't give you water to drink."

"So, what's unusual? The Poles hate us as much as the Germans." Cukier said.

"I agree," Singer said. "What's strange is that when I went back a day later, the street was deserted. All the houses had been emptied."

"That doesn't seem possible," I said, "All in one night?"

"There was not one man, woman, child anywhere."

"The whole area was vacated in one night?" I thought of the logistics of such an action and doubted it was possible.

Singer nodded. "I know. It's strange, but here's more. An informant told me that all Poles who don't have working papers have been expelled from Lodz."

"What are the Nazis up to?" I asked.

"I don't know," Cukier muttered. "I can tell you that Jewish males, age 17-60, from countries that are at war with Germany, have been placed in Radogoszcz prison by order of the authorities."

"Shit!" Singer said. "They say that's a torture chamber."

Rosenfeld nodded. "It used to be a factory owned by Jews."

"Well, it's ironic that it now is a prison and a place to torture Jews." Singer said. "German resourcefulness strikes again."

I was deep in thought. "It sounds like the Germans are 'purifying' Lodz. They got rid of the Poles surrounding the ghetto and now foreign-born Jewish males."

"Why would they suddenly be doing that?" Cukier asked.

"That, I don't know," I replied. "The logistics involved are incredible."

Singer blew up, "Logistics? Ostrowski, they're moving hundreds, perhaps thousands, of Jews and Poles, and you're focused on the mechanics? Germans don't do things without damn good reasons, and our Leader is aware of everything those bastards are up to."

Cukier stood. "Enough."

"But—"

"I said, enough."

Singer nodded, perhaps not wanting to send Cukier into another coughing fit.

"Any more wonderful news?" Cukier asked. "We'll watch the other as it develops, but no more futile speculation."

Rosenfeld pulled up a report he had been working on. "Do you remember the German commission that inspected the hospital for the mentally ill, about a month ago?"

"Yes, I remember," I replied, an alarm ringing again in my head. So much had happened since that day I'd almost forgotten about that incident.

"Was that the one on Wesolo Street?" Cukier asked.

Rosenfeld nodded. "Yesterday, Chairman Rumkowski arrived at the hospital with two German doctors."

"How many patients are there?" I asked.

"Always with the numbers. Sixty were there." Rosenfeld said.

"What do you mean were?" Singer asked.

Rosenfeld sighed. "The Germans demanded records—"

"The doctors gave confidential records to the Germans?" Singer asked.

"Yes. All of the patients were included."

Singer said, "I saw a lot of people gathered in front of the hospital. They told me they were family members waiting for their relatives. Many were worried."

"Oh, God. I forgot to tell you about a few weeks ago. I saw a group of German officers and men in suits, possibly doctors—I didn't think about that then—enter the hospital with armed guards. I'm sorry. With so much going on…I forgot."

Cukier looked sympathetic. "Don't worry about it. There would have been nothing we could have done."

"The Chairman could have been told," I said, feeling terrible.

"He knows," Singer said.

"What do you mean?" Cukier asked, coughing into his sleeve.

"It was his police that were supervising."

"Supervising what?" Cukier asked.

Rosenfeld sighed. "The removal of the patients. I thought you knew."

Cukier looked stunned. "The Germans took them?"

Rosenfeld nodded slowly. "The doctors gave the patients special injections to keep them tranquil." He grunted. "I wish I could get such a tranquilizer."

Cukier searched his files frantically. "They did this last March as well. Nobody ever heard from those patients again."

"None of them?" Singer asked.

Cukier looked up from his files. "One shouldn't assume the worst. Perhaps the Germans have placed them in a better hospital? Lord knows, we have no medicine and everything from bedclothes to bandages, are in short supply." He coughed again. "Yes. I'm sure that's it."

Singer stared at Cukier. "You don't really believe that. Do you?"

Cukier glared at him. "What the hell do you want? Do you want me to admit that our Chairman is complicit in murdering mental defectives who do nothing for us but eat up our limited rations? I can't believe that! I won't believe it! But you keep pushing and pushing. If you're so damn sure, why don't you get off your ass and find out for yourself what happens to these sad souls, most of whom only want to shirk work." He broke into a terrible round of coughing, his face hidden by his handkerchief. "God damn you! I'm leaving.

I've had enough of you for one day!" Cukier grabbed his jacket and stormed out of the room.

"What was that about?" Singer asked.

"Look what you did again, Oscar," I scolded him. "You're not a gadfly, you're a damn vulture, picking the flesh off all of our bones with your constant sniping at our leaders."

"Listen, Ostrowski, you and the others are blind. I've said it before. You don't know what is happening. You think we're doing something under the Germans' noses? Bullshit! They're doing it to us! And that smug bastard, Rumkowski, is helping them. I don't know where he's taking our people, but mentally ill, or not, our leader should be protecting them, not helping ship them out to God knows where."

"You're as bad as Miriam," I shouted. "If you're so convinced, then why the hell are you working here? Just quit already. I'm sick of your constant questioning. I'm sick of all this shit."

Rosenfeld burst out laughing.

"What the hell are you laughing about?" I was shouting at an old man who did not deserve such disrespect.

Rosenfeld shook his head. "There's to be a special holiday weekend in Marysin."

"What?" Singer looked at me, and I looked at him, and we both burst into laughter. "Let me see that?" I demanded. "I'll do this one." I grabbed my pen and almost tore the paper writing, "GHETTO HIGH-LIFE SPENDS WEEKEND IN MARYSIN."

"You bolded the entire headline," Singer said.

I read the rest of the entry, anger seething. "Any able-bodied person, and especially people with pull, make every effort to be in Marysin on Saturday or otherwise, God forbid, they might not be considered part of the elite." That, my friend, is an exact quote."

"Holy shit! They finally got to you, Engineer," Singer said.

He was right. I was steaming mad. I was also feeling guilty. Could I have saved the patients from whatever fate they were now facing? Probably not. But I should have tried. I should have told Neftalin and demanded to see the Chairman. Face to face, I would have finally known if he really gave a damn for the poor souls struggling for survival in the ghetto or if it was all an act. Seeing his eyes and his face, I would have known if he'd sacrificed our weakest brothers and sisters to satisfy the German appetite for Jews and his own interests or was suffering as we all were. God, what the hell do you want from us?

CHAPTER 54

J ULY 31, 1941: QUITE TYPICAL
Of conditions in the ghetto is an event that took place in Precinct III of the Order Service. A woman leaving a distribution point with two long rolls of white bread had them torn away from her by a man who appeared to be starving. He swallowed both rolls so quickly that no one had time to stop him...

"I'm tired of writing these things. Where's Singer?" I asked. "Why don't you chastise him for being so disrespectful of time regulations?"

"Why bother? You're only young once. Here, you're not even that." Cukier coughed. "Besides, he always adds a unique slant to everything when he gets here."

"He's unique alright," Rosenfeld said. "But you know, if I had a son, I would want him to be like young Oscar, questioning everything, resourceful."

"A pain in the ass?" I said.

"Just so," Rosenfeld replied. "He brings humor to these old ears."

"Humor? Singer? An oxymoron," I said. "Shhh. What's that?" I raised my finger to my lips. I'd heard someone turning the knob. Whenever we heard that sound, we expected Germans SS officers to enter and discover what we were doing. "Singer, why are you hanging outside?" He always just charged in, mumbled some excuse about being late, and then acted as if he'd been here all along.

"What is wrong with you, son? You look white?" Rosenfeld asked, looking alarmed.

"I have something to tell you." He fell to his chair. "I know what happened to them. I know." His eyes looked wild, and he was trembling.

"What are you talking about?" Cukier asked, already impatient.

"I heard rumors. Everyone was talking about the patients, the mentally ill patients."

Cukier rose from his chair. "Are you starting that again?"

"You don't understand." Singer said.

"No, you don't understand. Okay, I wasn't going to bring this up again, but since you've done so, I will tell you what Neftalin told me. He said that when the German doctors refused to release more than five of the patients, the Eldest of the Jews, and I quote, "used every argument to gain the doctor's approval for releasing all of the 12 who had been deemed cured by the institution." He used all of his influence. That is a direct quote."

"I don't understand," I said. "Why would the Chairman do that?"

Singer broke in. "Because he knew what was in store for these helpless people."

"What is he talking about?" I demanded.

Singer shouted. "You don't know? Why do you think the damn Nazi doctors gave them tranquilizer shots?"

I shook my head.

"Even the mental patients knew what was in store for them. They understood why they had been injected with tranquilizers during the night." Singer said.

"How do you know that?" Cukier shouted. "Let's move on. These are all rumors."

"Is it a rumor that under orders of the German authorities, the patients were given scopolamine?" Singer threw a paper at Cukier.

"It's just a rumor. It's all rumors," Cukier said, refusing to pick up the page from the table.

Rosenfeld picked up the paper. "Scopolamine? Are you certain?"

"My informant was a nurse. She said some of the patients resisted, but in the end, they were all injected." Singer pointed at Cukier. "My friend, your Chairman, allowed this."

Just then there was a knock on the door. The Germans don't knock. It was Neftalin. He looked even older than when I'd seen him last, his eyes deeply set. "I have a notice from the Chairman. You will record it exactly as he dictated this to his secretary, Dora Fuchs, with myself as a witness. Thank you." He looked like he wanted to add something but left.

It was the Chairman's report about the removal of mentally ill patients from the hospital. As he read the memorandum, Cukier's face turned pale. "Here, Engineer, I would appreciate you reading it to the others." He coughed into his handkerchief. "Damn this cough."

I took the paper as if it was the hot coal Moses clutched centuries ago. I saw Cukier slumped in his chair, struggling to contain his painful hacking coughs as I read the Chairman's note aloud. Near the end of the short report, I found myself struggling to continue. *"The Eldest of the Jews used every argument to gain the doctor's approval for releasing all of the 12 who had been deemed cured. Specifically, the chairman spared no efforts in regard to a Mar Illsberg, whose mental condition was on the good side."*

"Illsberg is a friend of his. I've seen them at the dining room," Rosenfeld said.

"That figures," Singer shot in. "There's no favoritism in Lodz."

Cukier shot him a warning glance.

I continued, "Unfortunately while being examined, this patient became extremely nervous because he was fully aware of the horror of what was happening." I looked at Cukier. He was silent, his eyes closed. Did he know something I did not? "His test proved unsatisfactory. Monday night, a night of tragic expectations—"

"Did you hear that?" Singer interrupted. "Cukier, "tragic expectations." They knew what was happening. Even mental patients knew what you refuse to accept."

"May I continue? We must not judge until all the evidence is in."

Cukier was frozen.

Rosenfeld's hands were spread flat on the table.

I felt my throat tighten as I read more of the Chairman's memo. "Monday night, a night of tragic expectations, left the hospital staff in a state of shock. In spite of their mental confusion, the patients realized what fate was in store for them. They understood, for example, why they had been injected with tranquilizers during the night. Injections of scopolamine."

Singer looked at Cukier. "Exactly what my informant told me."

Cukier barked, "Finish it."

I glanced at him and continued, "Injections of scopolamine were used on orders from the German authorities." I stopped. "Our people did that on orders of the Chairman?" I was shaking but had to read on. "The patients resisted in many cases..."

Singer gulped hard. "I was told, a covered pickup truck with a squad of uniformed escorts came for the patients." He took the paper from me. "The nurse told me some jumped out of the windows trying to escape. The guards threw them to the ground and then dragged them screaming and kicking to the trucks." He read the rest of the report silently. "Oh no! I'm not writing this. Not this last sentence." He threw the paper on the table.

Rosenfeld beat me to it. I wasn't that eager anyway. He read the last sentence. "Thanks to the selfless work done by the hospital staff, the loading of the tragic transport took place with exemplary order." He put the paper on my pile without saying another word.

Cukier was staring at his handkerchief. "Type it as is."

Singer picked up his jacket and walked to the door. He didn't say good-bye.

I typed the Chairman's report, the vision of hospital clothed patients jumping from the windows adding to my guilt.

That night I walked out of my way to Wesolo Street. The building was still there, but it was vacant, a shell, no heart, no soul. I wondered how many Jews had jumped from its windows. I imagined the scene of the Jewish police dragging patients in their hospital gowns from the building. Despite being tranquilized, Singer's witness said several had jumped from the windows in a mad dash to escape. They were rounded up and thrown like sacks of garbage into the trucks.

Singer said the Chairman had allowed this to happen. Rumkowski's report said he had tried his best to save them but failed. Had he really been powerless to stop it? The sight of that building remained with me. It was as if it was haunted by ghosts. Was it a warning of what we could all expect?

CHAPTER 55

AUGUST 1, 1941: *TANNERS,*
Tanners, the last Jews working in Lodz proper, were sent back
to the ghetto yesterday. The reason: an alleged fear of espionage
by Jews.

Sirens blared outside the ghetto. Cars raced through the streets. A tank pulled up in front of a house. The sentries, guns aimed at chest level, ordered everyone away from the perimeter fence.

Rosenfeld slammed his hand on the table. "The Nazi sonofabitches!"

"Now what?" I asked, feeling as if I was the last to know everything.

Rosenfeld snarled, "Didn't you hear the racket? The Germans discovered a large cache of hidden weapons."

"In the ghetto?" That would be too much to hope for. Shit! I sounded like Singer.

Rosenfeld laughed bitterly. "Seriously? We're sealed tighter than a drum. No, in Lodz itself. They found machine guns and explosives."

"I'll bet the Nazis were mad about that," Cukier said.

Rosenfeld nodded. "They arrested hundreds of Poles. Two hundred and fifty are to be shot. Others were taken to Radogoszcz prison. I don't envy them. It's the Nazi torture chamber."

Cukier sighed. "Did they really think they could defeat the German force with a handful of guns and machine guns?"

"Maybe we should have tried?" I said in a low voice.

"Are you crazy? Don't you see how the Germans treat anyone who lifts a finger against them?" Cukier coughed. "You sound like Singer."

"Is it worse than how they treated our mentally ill?" Rosenfeld asked.

"I see the price of cabbages is up again," Cukier said as if he hadn't heard us. "I remember when we used them only to feed our cattle because people would not eat them. Remember?"

"People will eat their own children if allowed," Rosenfeld said and burst into laughter that made him sound as if he were insane. He saw the shocked look on my face and quickly said, "I'm sorry, Engineer, I shouldn't have said that. Please forgive me? How is your wife these days?"

"We're both anxious. Miriam is due at any time now." I thought of the argument I'd had with her last night, and my stomach churned.

"If there was a way out of here, would you go with me?" Miriam had asked, holding her stomach, which still looked too small, given how close she was to deliver.

"This is foolish talk," I said. "I've told you time and time again that the Germans shoot anyone who even goes near the wire. I can't tell you how many tragic stories I've written. End of discussion."

Her eyes became hard. "What do you mean you've written?"

Oh shit! "I meant heard. Gossip we've heard even in the Archives."

She gave me a suspicious look. "You never talk about what you do."

"It's dull as shit."

"That's fine. I'm still interested in what my husband does for work while everyone else sweats in factories and warehouses."

"I've told you. We sort old books in the Archives. We are trying to preserve German culture—"

"You're preserving the culture of our enemy?"

"Not just them. Our own books...the ones they allow. We try to protect them as well."

"Books, you protect, but the mentally ill are sent away by your holier-than-thou Chairperson, the Eldest of the Jews, to die in some damn forest."

"Die? What are you talking about? They were sent to a specialty hospital where they could get treatment."

Miriam burst out laughing, an insane, terrifying laugh. "Is that what you really think? You're a bigger fool than I thought."

I held my hand in check. Miriam was expecting any moment. I could not hit the mother of my future child. "I'm not a fool," I said through gritted teeth.

Miriam cried, "Oh my God! I'm sorry. I'm sorry. I didn't mean that." She reached for my hand, but I pulled it away. "I'm so tired. I hate carrying this child. No, I'm sorry. Don't look at me like that."

I headed for the door. "I'll see you tonight."

"Wait! Don't go. Not like this."

I stopped by the door waiting for a few seconds for her apology.

"Don't you see what is happening to me?" She trembled, tears flowing down her face. "Benny, we have to get out of here. First, it's the criminals, so-called criminals. He sends out his enemies and anyone who won't adhere to his demands. Then it's the mentally disturbed. Out they go. Who's next?"

I could barely stand looking at her. I was enraged. "It's not Rumkowski. It's the Germans. I keep telling you they're the ones doing this to us, not him."

"Germans? Him? Who cares anymore? We're starving and living in a shithole. Your uncle is safe and comfortable in America. We should have gone when he left—"

"You think I don't know that? Yes, we should have seen in our crystal ball and all left. But we didn't. It's my damn fault."

Miriam grabbed my hand. "Let's go now?"

"We can't. We're closed in here. You know that. Stop asking."

"What if there is a way?"

"There isn't. We can't take a chance with our child."

"If we stay here, what will our child's life be like?"

I ended the argument as I always did: "Miriam, please be patient? The war will be over soon. I know it will be, and then, with our beautiful child, we will be able to live anywhere we want, even in America. All I beg of you is a little time. For God's sake, please, a little more time?"

Miriam shivered. "Don't you see? There is no time. Those patients…those poor people."

"I told you. They were moved to a better facility," I said, wishing I could reveal to her my sources.

Miriam stared at me and said, "Benny, they were taken into the forest and shot."

"Ridiculous! There's no proof of that!"

"Everyone knows but you," she screamed then the pains started, and Miriam ended the argument as she now always did, rushing to our bed and crying into her pillow.

"It isn't true," I said, glaring down at her, but inside I knew it was. The Germans would never waste their resources on mentally ill people, especially not if they were Jews."

Miriam writhed on the threadbare mattress. "Oh God," she moaned. "When will this end?"

I left for work, grateful to be away from her, but feeling guilty for wanting to leave.

My reflections of the terrible morning were interrupted when Singer rushed into the room. "Did you hear they caught Zawadski?"

"The smuggler?" Rosenfeld asked, his eyebrows raised high on his wrinkled forehead.

"They finally caught him. He'd escaped from a hospital while under guard by an Order Service detachment."

"He is a legend, smuggling medicines into the ghetto." Rosenfeld remarked.

If I could learn how he managed that, it might help me get Miriam out. "How did he escape them?" I asked.

Singer laughed. "Do you know anything at all about him?"

I nodded no.

"He's fourteen years old."

"What? The legendary smuggler is just a boy?" I almost burst out laughing.

"Just a boy? No. A genius." Singer exclaimed. "He's been a thorn in the side of the Germans and Jewish authorities for months. The last time he escaped he paid a Jewish policeman 500 marks to help him."

"The policeman took the bribe?" There was hope. If I could get enough money, I could bribe our way out of the ghetto. I listened attentively as Singer praised the boy's exploits.

"The policeman claimed the boy framed him. His excuse didn't save him. He was detained by the Kripo for several days and is now getting "medical treatment." We know what that means."

"So how did the boy escape again?" I was itching to know.

Singer laughed. "The legendary 'smuggler' convinced the guards to let him go to the bathroom, where the stalls showed only the feet. When, after a long time, he didn't come out, and did not respond to knocks, the guards forced the door open. Zawadski had left his shoes to deceive the guard while he escaped through the window. All the guard saw were shoes. The kid was gone. Good for him!"

I wasn't laughing. I wondered how a fourteen-year-old kid had managed to get in and out of the ghetto so many times without getting caught. Escape was possible. I was ready to talk to Singer. He could find out how this boy did it so many times. All we had to do was accomplish it once. Surely God would let us manage that.

CHAPTER 56

AUGUST 7, 1941

I was up all night. Miriam had not been easy to get to sleep. Hunger and anxiety had taken its toll. Nothing I could say cut through her gloom. I sat in my chair until morning and then, with her still sleeping in our bed, trudged to my second 'torture chamber' barely awake. The sight of our leader staring down at me from his portrait on the wall did not reassure me about our future. I gave him a half-hearted salute and plopped down on my hard seat hoping some bit of news in the stack of reports would make me feel more optimistic.

Rosenfeld arrived next. He too had become morose, but asked as he did each morning, "And how is your sweet wife today?"

I merely shook my head.

He let out a good-natured chuckle. "Soon, my friend."

Cukier entered the room and grunted a hello and, "Not yet?"

Again, I shook my head.

He shook his head right back at me and sat at his post, sorting through his baskets of mail.

None of us bothered asking about Singer. He was a phantom who came and went as he pleased. No discipline whatsoever, I thought, but secretly envied him.

"I can't write this," I said to Cukier. "Perhaps the good Doctor would be so kind?"

Cukier looked up. "Your mind is not here today, Engineer."

"It's understandable," Rosenfeld said and picked up the report. It was from Neftalin. He read silently and then looked up. "Death sentences?" He shook his head. "The Germans are crafty. They want the Jewish courts to do their work."

"Look at the last sentence. It says it all," I said, fed up with the whole thing.

Rosenfeld read the last sentence aloud, "In cases concerning murder and the spreading of information that could be injurious to the Reich, a motion for a death sentence by the German authorities is to be binding on the court." I don't believe I am reading this. You're right, absolutely, the crafty bastards want our judges, our Chairman, to do their executions."

"Murders," I corrected, surprised how much I sounded like Singer.

Rosenfeld crushed the paper. "I never thought I'd live to see the day Jews would kill Jews to enforce German decrees."

"The Chairman will never go along with this," Cukier said. "Our Eldest of the Jews will not be a rubber stamp for German death sentences on our people."

"He's gone along with everything else," I snapped. "I know he has perhaps no real choice in most matters, but this?"

"You're right. Our leader has no real choice," Cukier said testily, "Neither do we. Doctor, please write it up without comment, as we have done all along."

"But Julian, surely we can voice some protest—" I must have been tired.

Cukier interrupted. His voice, raspy and rough, was evidence of his exhaustion, or frustration, both of which we all shared. "Doctor, from the start we knew what we wrote would be scrutinized by the Chairman. Knowing him as I do, voicing our contempt for this new German ruling would be preaching to the choir. He most likely hates this more than we do."

"But he will do it anyway," I argued. "Just as he acceded to the emptying of the mental hospital."

"What? Are we back to that?" Cukier barked.

"Do you know what happened to them?" I asked.

Rosenfeld spoke calmly, "The report said they were taken to a specialty facility," he said, pipe in his mouth.

"Were they?" I asked.

Cukier began coughing so hard he couldn't speak.

Rosenfeld looked curiously at me. "The reports we received—"

I shivered. Should I reveal what Miriam said?

Cukier held up his hand and said, "Rumkowski will find a way to avoid this. I trust him. I must trust him. The alternative is unthinkable. Just write it up and know he will never allow our courts to be the tool of German executioners." Cukier choked and then began his incessant coughing again, his eyes bulging and his face red.

I was about to argue with him when the door swung open, and Singer raced in. "You must go home. Miriam—"

I was out the door before he could finish the sentence. I didn't even ask how he knew.

"Good luck," Cukier gasped.

Rosenfeld waved feebly. "May God be with you," he muttered.

I wanted to run. I wanted desperately to run. There were Order Service men along the route, all watching for illegal acts, for suspicious characters. A running man was someone who had to be stopped. I did not want to waste time showing papers and seeing the sneers of fellow Jews when they saw I was part of the ghetto administration, one of the hated bureaucrats.

I averted my eyes from the mental hospital which held patients again. Even though most had heard the gossip of the tragic fate of the last occupants, desperate, hungry, men and women had willingly placed themselves inside the hospital to receive food or medical care. I didn't want to see their faces. Miriam had said that all the previous patients had been taken into the forest and executed by firing squad. I'd denied it to her, "Rumors! More wild rumors!" Who could believe even Germans were capable of such atrocities? Me. I believed it.

I passed a meat distribution point. It was deserted. Because much of our meat had come from the Soviet Union—Singer had seen the labels—and now Russia was at war with Germany, the Nazis had cut off all meat deliveries to us. Instead, we were promised that workers would get a little extra bread, and maybe some margarine. Big help! Just the other day, a dead horse—one of the last in the ghetto—had been flayed and brought to the rubbish area. Because of the lateness of the hour, the burial of the steed was postponed until the next day. The carcass was doused with chloride for safekeeping. The next day it was discovered that flesh had been cut off from the horse's hindquarters in the night! The poor starving culprits were caught and sentenced to four weeks in prison each. As Rosenfeld says, desperate people do desperate things."

As I walked quickly through our sewage-laden streets, I saw others roaming aimlessly, the zombies of our barbed wire world. Many had lost twenty, thirty kilograms of weight and more. Men's collars were far too large for their thin necks. Dr. Rosenfeld said the weight losses had resulted in muscular atrophy, giving these starving people their zombie-like appearance and gait. Only the intelligentsia and trade workers were able to maintain some ability to function, thanks to the Chairman's dining halls, each of which served three meals per day to a thousand or more patrons. I eyed each of the zombies with a challenging glare. They had to believe I could defend myself or they would have stolen the clothes from my body. Even daylight was no longer safe. I was grateful the Jewish police were highly visible, their truncheons ready to protect the law-abiding from the criminals, most of whom, I thought, the Eldest of the Jews rightfully asserted, were transported here from other villages and Jewish ghettos throughout Poland.

I was on our street. I heard a series of loud screams.

A small crowd, many zombies, were peering up at our window. A Jewish policeman, his cap and armband distinguishing him from the rest, was glaring at the shiftless rabble but didn't move them. Even the police feared a wrong action, when they were isolated, might provoke a cannibalistic attack. His club was ready, but these bony people were merely staring at a window behind which some poor woman was screaming, about to bring another mouth to feed at the nearly empty trough.

I held up my identification card and, the officer shot me the usual sneer. "I'm the husband," I said, hurrying the card back into my coat pocket.

"Let me see that again," he demanded.

I fished it out with trembling fingers. "Please? My wife is giving birth."

He examined the paper with indifference to my plea for urgency. "You are in the Archives Department? I've never heard of it. What do you do there?"

"Officer, my wife. Please, I must go to her."

He returned my papers. "Go then. We'll talk another time."

I gave him my fake smile, forced thank you, and raced up the stairs. The stench when I opened the door, was overwhelming. It smelled like vinegar, sour and potent. The room was dimly lit by a candle. An enormous white blob of a human back is all I saw at first. Terror raced through me. It looked like a ghost was bent over our bed.

A closer look and I saw Miriam's face writhing back and forth, eyes opening and closing as she screamed in pain.

"She should be in a hospital," I barely managed to say, stunned by the sight, smells, and sounds.

The ghost turned. "You're the husband? Where the hell have you been?"

Who was she to question me? "Do I know you? Who the hell are you?"

"I'm the midwife. Call me Bronka. Your wife is in distress." She turned back and shouted, "Hold her legs so she can't kick."

I walked to the bed, dazed, unsure of what I was capable of, faced by all this. "Shouldn't I get help?"

"Hold her damn legs. I wish I had a pain killer."

"I can run to the apothecary." I did not want to look at Miriam. Her face was unrecognizable, contorted in agony. "She's too small. You must give her something."

The woman gave a hideous laugh. "There are no painkillers. Hardly any drugs at all. You need to pay a king's ransom—"

"I'm with the Council," I shouted over Miriam's screams, still unable to force myself to grip her ankles.

"Just hold her, dammit! Men are useless. Right sweetheart?" She cooed to Miriam. "Hold her tight."

Another scream. Why was Miriam being tortured? I saw the vision of my wife's beautiful face before this war; the woman on this bed was a demonic version of that child's innocent face. I didn't recognize her. I was staring in disbelief. This wasn't my wife.

Miriam's eyes cleared, and she looked at me…it was as if she hated me.

"Talk to her. Calm her," the midwife ordered. "Grab her ankles! Wake up!"

"You'll be alright," I said hoping I sounded confident. I struggled to grab the top of her ankles, which were kicking my hands away. I averted my eyes, daring not to look at the part of her that was about to be stretched to its limits to give life to our child.

"Push, darling. Push now." The midwife reached for a piece of cloth. "I wish it was cleaner. No such thing anymore."

Miriam's legs thrashed against my hands. I tightened my grasp.

"She kicks like my old horse. God rest her soul. Hold tight. Push darling. Push." The midwife's sweat was dripping on Miriam's nightgown.

Miriam compressed her strength into the push but then sagged against the bed.

"Shit!" The woman turned to the table. I saw for the first time several metal instruments. They looked rusty.

I was going to lose her. I was going to lose them both. "God, please help her?"

The woman shouted, "The umbilical cord is wrapped around the fetus's throat." She held up an ominous-looking tool. "I wish I had a tranquilizer, but there's not even a drop of liquor in your flat." She lowered the tool. "Please God, at least save one?"

Miriam stared up, open-eyed, at me as if she knew this would be the last time our eyes would meet. I closed my eyes. I couldn't bear to see her. I prayed to God.

"Got her?" The woman asked. "Hold her legs tighter."

Eyes still closed, I clamped down hard on Miriam's ankles. She kicked and tried to pull free, but, I held her down, my eyes locked shut. She kicked and kicked again. Then her legs were still. There was no more screaming. I kept my eyes closed, praying, praying, praying. There was no sound…no movement. Oh, God, you hate me. I lost them both.

And then I heard the slap of a hand on flesh.

Silence.

Another slap.

The wailing cry of a baby.

"Is she alright? My wife?"

"You have a beautiful, little girl," the ghost said, cradling a small package nearly hidden in a blood-stained rag.

"My wife?" I didn't dare look.

"She'll be fine. Thank God, she's stronger than she looks." She laughed, my child held tenderly against her blood-soaked smock. "We all are, I guess. Would you like to hold your baby?"

I was staring at Miriam. She was sleeping, the sleep of someone who had endured great pain and was now exhausted, perhaps barely alive. "Will she be alright?" There was blood. I felt that protective instinct rising powerfully inside me. I hadn't felt it for her for a long time. "Please, Bronka, is she alright?"

The midwife smiled. "Yes. Let her rest. She will be fine. Do you want to hold your daughter?"

I was so nervous. I'd never held a baby before. I felt as if I'd drop her as the midwife placed the tiny package in my arms. "Are they always so small?"

"Now, with so little food, yes. But, God bless her, this one is healthy. You can tell by her cries. What will you call her?"

"Regina," I said. "After my mother."

"That's a lovely name. May Regina live in happiness and health with God's blessing." The midwife smiled and then packed her odd-looking tools after wiping them free of blood with her apron. "I will be back tomorrow to check on your wife and the baby."

"My wife. She'll be okay?" I looked at the baby in my arms. "I'm not going to lose her?"

The midwife smiled. "God would not want to separate a child from its mother. No, you will enjoy them both for many happy years."

I squeezed some Rumkowski bills into her hand. "You are a miracle worker. Thank you. Thank you so much."

"What kind of man puts his face on every bill?" She shook her head. "Thank you."

I watched the ghost leave our flat. It was quiet and dark. The only sounds I heard were the little beating of my daughter's heart and her gentle breathing. Sitting on a chair, I remained awake all night, holding my child against my chest, a feeling I can't describe. I wanted it never to end, but exhausted, I ultimately had to place the little bundle into the box-like crib which I never took my eyes off for the entire night.

In the middle of all our misery, God had given me a gift, a miracle, but now I had to protect her. When she had been resting upon my chest, her tiny heart beating against me, I felt as if she was part of me. I felt as if she had stolen my heart and brought light to my tormented soul. I knew I would never be the same. "I'm a father," I said to the ghosts of my parents. "God, I'm a father."

I was frightened that I was unfit for the job.

CHAPTER 57

*A*UGUST 8, 1941
A freight car of meat arrived in the ghetto after traveling three days. The meat was covered with worms. After eating the sausages allocated to their factories, many workers fell ill from food poisoning and ran high fevers.

When daylight awoke me, the smell hit and I saw the same dark and dingy room. Miriam was sleeping in our bed, a thin lump covered by a threadbare sheet. I thought it had been just a wishful dream. Then I saw the small crib, almost hidden in the shadows. I rushed off the chair. It was not a dream. Under a small square of linen, little toes peeking pink at my fascinated eyes, lay our little miracle.

I leaned closer, peering down at her. Yes, she was breathing. Her eyes were closed. What color would they be? Would they be brown like mine, or hazel, like her mother's? I studied her nose. It was so small. How could she breathe? I laughed. The Germans thought every Jew was recognizable by a large nose, often depicted as a hooked nose, in their offensive caricatures. Mine was prominent, but hardly hooked, and Miriam's was dainty. Regina's nose—Regina? I couldn't believe we had a Regina. Her nose looked too small to be functional. She was beautiful. I wanted to tell the world, "my daughter is beautiful." But did I want the world to know about her?

"The baby?" It was Miriam's voice. "Is it okay?" She sounded strained, each phrase halting, questioning.

I approached the bed. "Yes, God bless her, she's beautiful." I kneeled next to the bed, about to kiss Miriam's forehead.

"She? A girl?"

"Yes, a beautiful Regina." I took Miriam's hand. It felt clammy. "Are you feeling okay?" I felt her forehead. "Are you fevered?"

Her eyes stared into mine. "You are telling me the truth? We have a girl? She's okay?"

I didn't care that she was questioning me. I shared her disbelief. "Miriam, God has blessed us with a beautiful girl, and, you, my love, are here to enjoy many wonderful years with her."

Miriam sighed and sank back on the mattress. "You never believed in God, and now, in this cursed ghetto, you believe? You're a strange man." She closed her eyes and I heard her breath become regular in sleep.

I sat at her side for a few minutes, thinking of what she'd said. Perhaps it was strange to become a believer in God when it was clear he'd forgotten us, but it had snuck up on me. I found myself praying at odd times: bad news, good news, times of fear, times of sadness...times when Miriam made me feel as if I was alone. It was as if Miriam and I had reversed roles; she, becoming the pessimist, the skeptic, the Singer; while I had become the believer, the one with hope. Even my co-workers noticed that every so often, I would slip and say, "With God's help the war will end soon," or, "God will punish the Nazis for what they are doing."

Singer would confound me when he'd reply, "If God could punish the Nazis, why would he create a Hitler?"

I had no answers for that. I was learning I did not have the answers I'd always assumed I had for many questions.

Miriam and Singer, so much alike, could dance away from me without answers. Did they realize they left me forever searching? As irrational as I believed it was, I turned to the invisible and deaf God of the Jews and prayed he existed.

When the baby woke, I watered down the milk ration. I estimated her feedings, dividing and dividing again what little we had for her.

Miriam's eyes were open.

I lowered the baby to the bed. I had an odd premonition, a fear that Miriam wasn't going to accept her. "Here's your daughter, my love," I said softly as if afraid I'd frighten the new mother. I placed Regina between an arm and her right breast. "Look how beautiful your daughter is."

"I can't see her face," Miriam whispered.

I lowered the coverlet. "Our angel looks like you. Thank goodness."

Miriam's eyes examined each facet of the child's face, much as a jeweler examines a diamond. "My child?"

"Ours," I said. "Meet Regina. Regina, meet your mommy."

"Regina?" She looked at me. "I like that. Good morning, Regina."

"Welcome to our world," I said, my thumb inserted in my daughter's delicate fingers. "She seems so weak," I whispered.

"Place her on my breast?" Miriam lifted her arms, but they dropped back to the bed. "Open my shirt."

"You're still tired, my love." I lifted Regina to Miriam's chest and gently pulled her shirt open. "I don't know how to do this?"

Miriam lifted Regina's lips to her nipple. "Drink, sweetheart, drink."

I was standing in mute awe at the painting before me. I never dreamed a mother nursing her child could be so lovely a sight, but here it was, my little Miriam, giving of herself, to a tiny suckling mouth. Little hands were pulling at the source of her nourishment. Regina's eyes, barely open, explored the new mother, who was curiously examining the new child. I was grateful Miriam did not cover herself. I felt a warmth surge through me I had never felt before. All the anger I'd felt for Miriam these last awful weeks dissipated with every second my daughter was locked onto her mother's breast.

"I'm out of milk," Miriam said. "I hope it was enough."

Regina yawned and then her eyes closed.

"She's a bug. So tiny I'm amazed she took so much milk at all." I couldn't stop looking at her.

"She is small," Miriam said. "And fragile. I'm frightened for her,

Benny."

I smiled, my hand cradling Regina's pink foot. "Don't be. I won't let anything hurt our child."

"Nor will I," Miriam said, a determined look on her face.

CHAPTER 58

T HE MONTH OF SEPTEMBER 1941: TRAMCARS PUT
INTO SERVICE
*As a result of long-standing efforts by the Eldest of the Jews, the
ghetto was provided a tram system on September 13.*

Miriam's strength was improving daily. I needed to get back to work,
or we would not get our ration cards. I was hardly eating, giving
most of my allocation to Miriam, who was trying to nurse.

"I have no milk." She pulled Regina from her nipple. "The child is
too weak to even cry."

I took her hand. "She'll be fine. I'll eat all my meals at Kitchen 2.
That will mean more food for you and our miracle."

Miriam got out of bed, but her face grimaced in pain when she
walked and peed.

I wished there was more I could do, but there weren't any drugs in
the ghetto. Of course, Miriam said this was the fault of the Eldest of
the Jews. "I'm certain he and his family can get whatever they need."

I saw no use in arguing with her, not with her eyes so fierce. I
knew she would not do anything to hurt our baby. The truth was,
she would use any weapon she could find to protect our Regina from
anything that might threaten her. I kissed her on her forehead, threw
a kiss to my sleeping Regina, and left for work. To be honest, it was a
relief to get out of the flat after being stuck in that cramped space for
so many days.

There was a sulfur smell in the air. The factories never stop, I mused, as smoke trails rose over the brick chimneys. As usual, a few zombies were roaming the streets, several searching through the trash on the ground. A fecal gathering cart, pulled by two young men in prison garb, was moving haltingly down the muddy road. Behind the vehicle, I counted two young girls, also in prison garb, scooping up piles of human feces—there were no horses or dogs left in the ghetto to pull the cart—the boys pulled while the girls followed, heavy shovels hurling the stinking, steaming piles into the growing mess on the wagon.

The Chairman is still doing an efficient job of keeping the streets clean and stemming disease, I thought, walking as far away from the disgusting odor of the cart as I could. When one of the girls looked pitifully at me, I shivered. That girl could have been my Regina. "That will never happen," I vowed I would do everything possible to provide a better life for Regina than these poor girls had. I was curious to discover what crime they had committed, but the Order Service men supervising their work did not look as if they would allow any interference. So, the cart moved on, and I closed my eyes to the plight of these children as God closed his eyes to our suffering.

"Welcome back, Papa Engineer!" Rosenfeld exclaimed. "I would give you a cigar, but who has any?" He shook my hand.

Cukier rose from his seat. "Miriam is well? The baby is fine?" He choked back a fit of coughing and laughed. "Mazel tov, my friend! A boy or a girl?"

"You don't know? You usually know everything going on around here," I said with a laugh.

Cukier shook his head. "When I first started here, I thought I knew, but now, nobody knows."

"The Chairman does," Rosenfeld said. "He has his grasp on every tentacle of this apparatus he has designed."

"You sound like Singer," Cukier said, giving the old professor a smile.

Rosenfeld nodded. "Perhaps our young hot-head was the wisest of us all."

I frowned. "Gentlemen, is this the way to greet the father of a beautiful baby girl? God bless her, she is the image of Miriam."

"Thank God she doesn't look like you." Rosenfeld slapped me on the back.

His slap was so weak I barely felt it.

"Mazel tov! Mazel tov!" Cukier repeated. "Today, you shall have my ration card. It is the least I can do for the new arrival. What is her name?"

"Regina. She's a week old."

Rosenfeld sighed. "Rosalie and I wanted a child always. God knew better. He did not want this old professor to bring a child into this crazy world."

His words were like lightning bolts. I'd forgotten Miriam's words, but now they came back to me with the force of a bomb: "How can we bring a child into a world like this?"

"What's wrong, my friend?" Cukier asked, seeing the color had drained from my face.

Rosenfeld was studying me. He studied everything with the same scrupulous care. "I know what you are thinking. But don't. Your baby will be fine. God willing, this war will soon be over, and your child will grow to be old and accomplished, and logical, like her father."

"Amen," Cukier said.

"Amen." It came automatically from my mouth. "I'm ready for work," I said, settling down before the large piles of paper at my station. "You had nobody to type while I was away?"

Cukier laughed. "Who could replace our Engineer?"

"You could have hired a beautiful girl, someone who would not raise questions." I began to sift through their entries for September. There were the inevitable suicides. I barely noticed how old the victims were or how they did it. It was something to type and then erase from my memory. More interesting was that a 32-year-old Pole had been shot near the barbed wire. I looked for some explanation, but as always, there was none.

"What's this about three men brought to the ghetto?" I asked Cukier.

"Not much is known, but the German authorities turned over the remains of Abram Josek Grossman, Mendel Hannstein and Perec Blaz...something or other. Check my notes." Cukier said.

"I just read your final sentence. Do you want that included? It has a bit of an insinuation to it."

Cukier nodded. "I worded it very carefully."

I read it aloud: "There is a supposition, based in particular on the external appearance of one of the corpses, that they died violent deaths." Do you really want that in there?"

Cukier looked deep in thought. "The remains came from Rado-goszcz prison. Yes, I think I do want it written like that."

"Julian, my friend, everyone will know you're accusing the Germans," Rosenfeld said.

Cukier nodded. "I know. You can add one more case." He handed me a short entry entitled, "A Death at the Police Station." "This one is a real mystery. Apparently, this man, Arthur Berkowicz, 55 years old, was an informer for the criminal police."

"He was an informer for the Germans?"

"Apparently. The memo states this rat was an informer for them from the very inception of the ghetto. At any rate, on September 20, a hearse was summoned to take his body to the cemetery."

"But how did he die?" I found this incredible, a Jew spying for the enemy.

"The Germans only say he "died a sudden death." The strange thing is he was released from prison, in the city, only a few weeks ago, after serving a six-month sentence."

"That's all we know?"

"That's it. And we'll probably never find out from the Germans what really happened." Cukier said. "People disappear. The Germans don't have to answer to anyone."

"Is there any good news?" I asked. "I would just like one piece of good news to give my wife and daughter when I get home tonight."

Rosenfeld smiled. "The Chairman has his new tram line. I've seen it myself. There are two motorized cars, the old type naturally, and a few passenger and cargo cars."

Cukier nodded. "The Germans are training several drivers. The goal is to link the ghetto to an outside line. Everyone was excited when the first cars were tested. You, an engineer, realize the time, effort, and cost of such a system. It is all due to the long-standing efforts of our Chairperson."

I took this as very hopeful news. "A new line will enhance our productivity and make it possible to bring more food into the ghetto. It is quite an accomplishment. Such a tramline will bring us into the twentieth century."

Cukier said, "Everyone must now agree our Chairman was right after all. The Germans would not be investing in such an enterprise unless they recognized the strategic value of the ghetto. This is good news."

I thought that even Singer could not puncture this balloon with his cynicism.

Cukier was rattling on, "That's what our wise Eldest of the Jews has been saying all along. That's what I've been saying. This proves the Germans need our manpower, our smooth-running machine. They know without their Jewish labor force, they will lose the war."

Rosenfeld held up a flyer. "Perhaps things are looking up. On Saturday, September 6, a show entitled Summer Holiday was staged at the House of Culture."

I groaned. "Another show? We need food, not more shows."

"Wait. You didn't let me finish. Papa, the cast of the program was composed completely of children." Rosenfeld smiled, "Someday, your little girl will be in such a show."

"I was there," Cukier said. "The Chairman attended as well. In fact, he made a short speech."

"He always does," I said. I really did sound like Singer.

Cukier laughed. "Yes, he seeks every opportunity to reassure his flock, but in this case, he did much more. He stated that children would always be his primary concern. He then said, and I'm quoting this, "There is no sacrifice too great when it is a question of helping the ghetto's youngest inhabitants." The applause was deafening. Of course, who would not applaud helping children."

"May I continue?" Rosenfeld looked like a professor waiting for our attention. "Afterwards the children made a ring around him on the stage and danced joyously, accompanied by the sound of music and cheers for the ghetto's first citizen."

Regina was my first citizen now, I thought, picturing her in a ballet dress, dancing for the great Chairman.

"The Chairman gave a present of bread and candy to each of the show's young performers. It was a wonderful event." Rosenfeld added. "And someday, your Regina will be there too."

I remembered how Miriam loved to dance and saw my little Regina, a miniature of Miriam, dancing on the stage of the House of Culture. She would be the prettiest and daintiest dancer there. Miriam and I would be seated with the great Rumkowski proudly admiring her perfect skills and lustrous beauty. "Thank you, Doctor. Tonight, I shall go home full of the news about the children's performance. I will spend the night talking and dreaming of our child's future." Yes, things were looking up. If only we could hold out a little longer.

CHAPTER 59

SEPTEMBER 22 and 23, 1941: THE JEWISH NEW YEAR 5702

The ghetto synagogues had been burnt to the ground, but our populace found small niches in which to pray on New Year's. Regina was little more than a month old, but Miriam wanted her to be part of the festival, a symbol of renewed hope. She dressed her in a tiny white outfit, brushed her hair with her fingers, and then tied a little red bow on her honey-colored curls.

"She is adorable," I said, not caring any longer that I was dressed in a suit and leather shoes, which were severely worn. I felt the cobblestones as I pushed the carriage, a gift from Singer, Neftalin, Rosenfeld, and Cukier. As always, I didn't ask how Singer got this treasure but noted it had been used before. I didn't care. It was a Godsend.

Miriam had slimmed down and could walk longer distances without pain. "I would have preferred a smaller shul with our neighbors," she said. "I'm not comfortable in the House of Culture with all the 'mucky-mucks' and their wives."

"They'll love you and swoon over Regina. We may even get that new apartment if the housing director is there."

Miriam didn't reply.

As soon as we reached the House of Culture, people surrounded the carriage and peered down at our blessing. I never felt so proud as when I lifted my sweet Regina and carried her into the last great hall in the ghetto.

Dr. Rosenfeld approached with Singer at his side. The doctor was using a cane, and his hands were encased in the gloves I'd given him.

"I thought you said you'd never set foot in here," I teased Singer.

My friend looked dapper in a jacket and tie. "It is a special occasion," he said, looking at my little bundle with unconcealed affection. "She's gorgeous. Like the mother," he said and then backed away as Rosenfeld stepped forward.

The Doctor raised his hands over Regina's tiny head. "I'm a Cohen, a descendant of Aaron, Moses's brother, the high priest. May I bless our delicious child?" He didn't wait. He parted his fingers as required by traditions, raised his hands over Regina's head, and chanted in the ancient Hebrew: "May the Lord bless you and keep you. May he show his countenance upon you. May he grant you long life and peace. Shalom and amen."

Singer and several others nearby added their "amen," and then entered the auditorium with its rows of velvet seating. It was an ornate last vestige of Jewish culture and elegance whose survival was an enigma.

"There's Rumkowksi," I said, pointing to the front row.

Miriam turned to look but remained silent as the Eldest of the Jews, in his famous tweed coat entered the hall and was guided to the front row. Using a cane, he climbed to the stage, Neftalin assisting him.

Singer poked me. "If speech were action, the Hun would have been defeated ages ago."

I held my fingers before my lips. "Shaa. My daughter's godfather mustn't get in trouble."

Regina's godfather laughed.

I sat back as Rumkowski delivered a short speech expressing his joy at being able to pray along with everyone else after an illness that had kept him home on several recent holidays. Then he looked sternly at the faces tilted up toward him and said in his sonorous voice, magnified by the microphone, "menacing clouds are hanging over the ghetto as the New Year begins."

I searched around me, wondering if I was the only one taking his warning seriously. He had made similar speeches, so many times it had become routine.

Oblivious to the lack of reaction from the audience, the Eldest of the Jews asked people to "pray to God that He spare the Jews of the ghetto from any new affliction." He assured everyone that he would continue to "stand guard over the fate of the Community and that he trusted that the Community would successfully extricate itself from all the difficulties."

"He sounds different, older and less sure of himself," Miriam whispered.

I noticed Rumkowski looked more stoop-shouldered as if he literally was carrying the ghetto on his back.

Singer, on the other side of Miriam, his finger playing with Regina's twitching toe, said, "He sounds worried."

"He always does," someone behind us remarked. "It's always the same lately."

Rosenfeld was silent.

I studied my friend, Rosenfeld's face. He looked lost in his own world. He had been fading away from ours for several months. "Clouds bring storms," he muttered, and ducked back into his prayer book, his lips mouthing silently the incantations passed down for hundreds of generations.

Regina was squirming and making little squealing noises.

"It's time to feed her." Miriam rose from the chair.

"Aren't you going with her?" Singer asked, rising to let her by.

I thought about leaving but decided to try and pray to this God who never listened to me when I was alone. Perhaps he would hear me if I was surrounded by holier people, people who believed. "She'll be fine out there. There are police protecting the building."

"I have to pee," Singer said and moved into the aisle.

I shook my head and laughed. Who was I to try and domesticate our savage?

Rosenfeld slid over. "You know, when I first met that young man, I didn't like him. I thought he was a sneak, a thief, and a playboy."

"I thought so too. But he isn't any of these, is he?"

Rosenfeld laughed. "No. He is all of those things, which is how he survives. But I will tell you something. Our Singer is also a good, caring man. Just don't tell him I said so." He slid back in his seat, nose deep into the prayer book.

I saw an empty seat in the front row, not far from Neftalin. I scanned the audience. There was no sign of Cukier. "Have you seen Julian?" I asked Rosenfeld.

The professor searched the auditorium. "He usually sits near his friend, Henryk. I don't see him."

Several minutes later, Singer returned. Shortly after Miriam slid back into her seat.

"Is everything okay?" I asked Miriam while playing with Regina's fingers. "You were gone quite a while."

"I was talking to a friend," Miriam said and dove into her prayer book. She knew all the prayers, far more religious than me.

It never occurred to me to ask her who this friend was.

The service was unending. Regina was letting out whimpers and cries that some of her earlier admirers were now finding annoying. I could hear their muttering.

Miriam stood. "I think it's enough for one day. Let's go home now." I rose from my seat.

Singer reached forward. "Would you like me to take her, so you can pray longer? You know I don't believe in all this crap."

Rosenfeld looked shocked. "Shaa, Singer! You will bring down even worse upon us."

Singer shook his head and smiled. "I think I've worn out my welcome here."

I replied, "No. That's fine. I'll escort them home. Thank you for your kind offer."

Singer shrugged. "I'm leaving anyway. I can walk you part of the way."

"Thank you. We'd welcome your company."

Singer smiled and said, "As Regina's godfather, it is the least I can do."

Miriam held Regina in her arms. "Thank you," she said.

It was a surprisingly joyous way to start the New Year. Even the zombies shouted out, "L'shana tova! L'shana tova! Have a good New Year!" As we walked, Singer accompanying us, I felt safe. It reminded me of walking home from shul when I was younger with my mother and father holding hands.

Through the barbed wire, I saw a line of black cars.

CHAPTER 60

SEPTEMBER 24, 1941

Yesterday, the Chairman's New Year Celebration was interrupted by the arrival of a delegation from the German administration. He was summoned to the German Ghetto Administration offices sometime after 4 P.M.

SEPTEMBER 27, 1941

Rumors were flying. They always were, but this time, the narratives were about something that none of us could wish away. There were too many witnesses.

It was on the same day as the Chairman had celebrated the Jewish New Year with us at the House of Culture. He was at his apartment on Lagiewnicka Street when a group of Jewish officials arrived with New Year greetings. Children from the schools, orphanages, summer camps swarmed the apartment and presented him with a hand made album with more than 14,000 signatures. The Chairman made a short speech thanking the children for coming. Everything was going well.

There was a loud knock on the double doors. Then there was another, more forceful.

The German authorities had summoned the Chairman to their headquarters.

This interruption of festivities was unique enough, but to take him to their office on the holidays was an especially alarming event. I wanted to get to the truth, so I was waiting eagerly for the others to arrive.

Cukier rushed in, dropped his jacket on the chair. "Did you hear what happened to the Chairman?"

"Just lots of rumors. Everyone is worried about what it means. There are many versions."

Cukier nodded. "I heard, and this is a rumor, more than 20,000 Jews expelled from other parts of Poland are to be resettled here, and that is why the Eldest of the Jews was summoned so precipitously."

"That is better than what Miriam heard through her grapevine. How they learn these things is beyond me. According to her spies, the Germans have directed the forcible evacuation of a large part of our ghetto's population and the conscription of all males for manual labor in German territories." I studied his face for any reaction that would reveal the truth of Miriam's rumors.

"I've heard nothing like that," Cukier said and promptly began to cough.

The door opened.

Rosenfeld rushed in. "You're discussing the German meeting with Rumkowski? Is it true the Germans have ordered the division of the ghetto into two parts; one inhabited by workers and artisans and the other by everyone else?"

"Each of the stories are different," Cukier said. "We have no evidence any are true."

"Where there's smoke, there's fire," Rosenfeld countered. "Did the Chairman have his holiday celebration interrupted? That much we should know."

Cukier nodded. "Yes. That part is true."

"Was he summoned to German headquarters?" I asked, hoping his answer would be negative.

Cukier sighed. "Yes. That is also true. But it doesn't mean these other rumors are true."

Rosenfeld shook his head sadly. "Where there's smoke..."

"I know. There's fire." Cukier sank back into his chair.

The door opened and Neftalin entered with a stack of memos in his hand.

I took the papers and asked, "Do you know the truth of what happened yesterday at German headquarters?"

"You've heard the rumors, I take it? Very well, the Chairman has addressed the situation with the following. He read one of the memos: "All of these rumors merely increase the sense of depression and are the result of stupidity and ill will." Neftalin shook his head. "The Chairman is urging the ghetto population to ignore these trouble-making rumor-mongers who seek to disturb the peace." He looked at me. "You may quote this in your entry."

"I've heard the Eldest of the Jews speak against the rumor-mongers many times," Rosenfeld said.

Neftalin looked angry. "As the Chairman says, we must do everything to remain calm."

The door opened, and Singer walked in, a surprised look on his face upon seeing Neftalin. "What's going on?"

Rosenfeld replied, "We were discussing the rumors circulating about the meeting our esteemed Chairman had with the Germans."

Singer remained standing, directing his comments to Neftalin. "That is why I'm late today." He looked at Cukier, perhaps to assure himself that Julian would not inform Neftalin that he'd been late many times recently, all without offering an excuse. "I heard that a commotion was taking place at the Radogoszcz rail track in Marysin. I walked to the nearest safe point and was shocked to see what looked like a huge crowd of people climbing off the rail cars."

"When you say huge, about how many would you say?" I asked.

Neftalin looked anxious. "The number isn't important. On the orders of the Chairman„ I have been working tirelessly to arrange for the arrival—"

Cukier shouted, "You knew? You didn't tell me? About how many, Singer?"

"I'd say about one thousand," Singer replied. "Almost all are women and children."

Neftalin sighed. "Julian, the Germans have ordered the resettlement of large numbers of Jews into the ghetto, and the Chairman appointed me to direct this campaign. We are already in full swing, working to accommodate the arrivals with rooms, documents, etc. The point is we don't want to panic our population."

I was trying to visualize how our ghetto, already starving, could feed a thousand more women and children. "This news is less disturbing than the rumor of liquidating the entire ghetto," I said, feeling a little less worried.

Cukier, clearly annoyed he had not been included in the inner circle on this news, asked, "So you want us to do what?"

Neftalin approached Cukier. "As always, we require you to present our efforts in the best possible light. I apologize for being unable to inform you earlier, but the Chairman is under great pressure and must scotch the rumors. I assure you that everything possible will be done so that the new arrivals have a roof over their heads with the least possible trouble to our residents."

"Where are you going to put all these unfortunate women and children?" Rosenfeld asked.

"They will be in houses in Marysin, and in the prison," Neftalin answered.

"The prison?" I imagined—God forbid— being forced to live in prison with Miriam and my little Regina.

"The prison is empty for the holidays," Neftalin said. "The new arrivals are all being given free food. They were bathed when they arrived from Wloclawek."

"I know that place. It had 4,000 Jews," I said. "What happened to the others? Where are the men?"

Neftalin frowned. "The women reported that the men had been separated from their families and taken away to perform manual labor. The Germans need large amounts of laborers these days."

I thought how I would feel if I had to leave Miriam and Regina to work on some public works project for the Reich.

Rosenfeld sighed. "I feel sorry for these women, with their husbands gone to work and being moved to a new locale. A thousand women and children are not so terrible for us to help. The rumors were much worse. I will write this entry. Trust me, I will show how diligently the Chairman, and his Deputy, strive to assure the least disruption for all concerned."

"Thank you," Neftalin said. It is a difficult time for all of us. Your support is appreciated." He stood to go.

Once the door closed, none of us spoke. Rosenfeld had said it best. We all felt sorry for these poor displaced women and children but were also grateful we only had one thousand more mouths to feed.

On September 29, 1941, a second transport arrived with over one thousand more women and children. Again, we did our best to house and feed them. We were sure this would be the end of the new arrivals. How could we possibly take in more? How could we feed them when we had so little food for ourselves?

The Chairman assured the people that the influx of Jews had stopped. Winter was approaching. Everyone was grateful that our food supplies would not be stretched even more.

From October 16 to November 4, 1941, 20,000 Jews from Germany, Austria, Bohemia, Moravia, and Luxembourg, were resettled into our ghetto.

"It's inhuman," Rosenfeld railed, rubbing his hands.

"I don't understand it," Cukier said. "The Chairman promised there would be no more. Why are the Germans doing this to us?"

I looked to Singer for some insider information. He had his connections. Someone in the black market surely would have news.

Our gadfly listened silently.

I'd noticed a change in him. He was still often late for work, and he vanished at lunchtime, but he was more restrained in his comments and demeanor. It was as if he'd aged or taken on some unknown responsibility. I put it down to this interminable war and our universal hunger. None of us were the same as when this incarceration started. "What do you think, Oscar?" I asked my daughter's godfather.

Singer aimed his eyes at Cukier. "Do you know?"

Cukier trembled. "No. What the hell are they doing to us?" He burst into a hacking fit.

Rosenfeld sighed. "Oscar, please don't upset him again."

Singer nodded. "I know I sound as if I told you so, but we should have been fighting them. We never should have let them control us like this."

Cukier sputtered, "We've heard all this before. Just answer the goddamn question."

"Please Oscar," I said, afraid Cukier was going to cough out his lungs.

Singer sighed. "I think we're some kind of holding tank for the Germans."

Rosenfeld looked at his pipe. "What do you mean?"

I looked at Singer. "That makes sense. They've already dumped more than 20,000 Jews on us."

"Always the number man," Rosenfeld said.

I looked at him and then at Singer. "Moving that many Jews here took a lot of resources and money. They wouldn't do all this without a damn good reason."

Singer nodded. "I think they want to corral all the Jews in one place."

"You mean like horses?" Rosenfeld asked.

Singer nodded.

Cukier's eyes were watering. He was holding his chest with one hand and his nose rag with the other. "The Chairman says he didn't know more would be dumped here. I believe him."

I shook my head. "This just doesn't make sense. In the middle of this terrible war, the Germans build a tram line in our ghetto to help move 20,000 Jewish women and children here. Why? Why would they do this now?"

Singer peered into my eyes. "Why? I wish I knew."

Rosenfeld rubbed his hands together and replied, "Only the Germans know."

CHAPTER 61

O CTOBER 15, 1941
From October 1-15, 277 people died in the ghetto. 89 persons were arrested for theft, 14 for resisting authorities and 216 for various other offenses.

Regina was two months old. I couldn't take my eyes off her. Miriam had given up on giving her breast milk. Her own malnutrition made that impossible. I traded in my ration card to Singer who managed to secure milk. I did not ask where. Watching my daughter, her hazel eyes looking so serious as she pushed and twisted to see me, filled me with the little joy I experienced. I feared the arrival of colder weather with its accompanying shortages of wood, coal, and food. I swore that somehow or other, Regina and Miriam would be protected, even if I had to risk my own survival.

Singer had become a more caring friend since Regina was born but was still too busy chasing skirts to be a regular visitor, even though he was our child's godfather. He also seemed unable to remain in our conference room for more than a few minutes, preferring to run around and bring us news first-hand. He claimed he was tired of writing about suicides and the growing litany of misery. I cautioned him against taking risks, but as with most young people, the warnings went in one ear and out the other.

Cukier was writing about the weather. The first snow had fallen on the night of the 12th and had been accompanied by furious gale force winds. "God does not give us much respite with this weather," he grumbled, "Hot summers and now snow in October. One wonders what else the good Lord is going to throw at us."

Rosenfeld was keeping his coat on, and lately, even his gloves. "Did you see what happened on Wolborska Street?" He shifted toward me.

I looked up. "That's near me."

"I know. The Germans are demolishing a building there."

"Yes, the dye works. People are living there."

"So, it seems. A boy was in the building when the chimney collapsed."

"Did he die?"

I was surprised at how matter-of-fact Cukier sounded when he asked that question.

"Yes. The next day. Poor child." Rosenfeld hated hearing of the suffering of children, always wishing he had a boy of his own.

Cukier waved a pile of papers. "Look at these reports, all suicides. One by swallowing pills, one drank iodine, one hung himself, one leaped from a window, and one swallowed cleaning fluid. The boy, if you ask me, was fortunate."

I was shocked. Cukier rattled them off as if these people were merely numbers to him now. Is that what I sounded like?

Rosenfeld looked surprised too. "Julian, what is wrong? Has something happened?"

Cukier laughed. "Do you see what we've become? We are bookkeepers of the dead and dying. This one died from pills; this one died hanging naked in his closet, and this one…" He let out a deep sigh.

Rosenfeld smiled sadly. "Julian, my friend, you're right. It weighs us down. It is endless misery. Since my Rosa left, I am more dead than alive. Someday, perhaps, you will write about your old friend too. I have thought of taking my own life…many times. But you know it is wrong. God creates, and it is a sin to destroy what he has given his hands, heart, and breath to form. We are in his image. Julian, you…we must not destroy—"

"Even the Nazis?" I asked, unable to believe in a God that would create such mal-formed beings. "Why would a God, a God worthy of belief, create such monsters?"

Rosenfeld gave me his paternal smile. "For the same reason he created your precious Regina."

"What the hell do you mean by that?"

"Just as we don't know why God places a lovely child in our arms, we can't know why God places a Hitler in his parents' arms. That is the eternal question."

"Bullshit! They're not the same at all!" I was angry the professor could even think there was any relationship.

"I never said they are the same in the result, but in origin. Both the good child and the evil child are made from the same clay. But what purpose there is to an evil child is for God to know."

I was about to answer when the door swung open, and Singer entered. "There's been a murder! Two brothers got into a fight over gambling money and one killed the other."

Rosenfeld sighed. "Jew is killing Jew, and for what?"

Cukier burst into an uncontrolled fit of laughter and then was overcome by a painful bout of coughing. "Don't you see, they both lost. One killed the other, but now he will be executed for murder. Isn't that humorous?"

I had always thought of Julian Cukier as the sanest and most congenial of the men in this strange enterprise. Now I worried about his mental health. I worried about all of us.

Walking home, I passed snow piles, yellow with human piss. Watching for Gestapo and Order Service men, I pulled my coat around me. As I tried to keep my footing on the treacherous ice, I heard Cukier's laughter again. I saw his handkerchief. He had tried to hide the red stains.

CHAPTER 62

NOVEMBER 29, 1941
During the month of November 914 people died.

I was playing with Regina's fingers. I loved how they wrapped around my thumb, but I barely could feel them. They were so delicate and light. I'd pull free, and she'd grab hold again. She'd try and lift my thumb to her mouth—was she hungry? We all were. The bread lines were endless. Miriam had gone to the market, and I was left with my little girl, both of us exploring each other with curiosity.

Miriam pushed open the door. She was shaking, tears streaming down her face.

I rose with Regina clutched against my shoulder. "What's wrong? Did someone do something to you?" I hated letting her go out on her own, but it was too cold for Regina and Miriam refused to let me shop for us in the little time I could spend with my daughter.

"I hate the Germans," she said. "They're all assholes!"

"Miriam, she'll start talking soon. She'll repeat—"

"Are you serious? She's four months old!" Miriam shook her head. "Okay, you're trying to be a good father. I understand, but the damn Germans. Life means nothing to them. Absolutely nothing."

I reached toward her, baby in one arm, my other hoping to bring Miriam into my embrace.

She pushed away. "I was on Brzezinska Street. I heard a motor sound, and suddenly a German car comes racing down the road."

"You weren't hurt?" I examined her with my eyes but saw nothing amiss.

"Would I be here?" She shook her head. "Another woman wasn't so lucky. The car ran her over. The driver just kept going. What kind of humans are these?"

"My God! And you saw this?"

"It was terrible. The woman was so bloody. How could they not stop to help?"

"Miriam, it could have been you and Regina. You must be more careful. The Germans care nothing about Jewish lives."

"Your Chairman was supposed to protect us, but the Nazis are more and more in our lives."

"It's not his fault. He's trying his best." A frightening thought, "Miriam, nobody took your name? Nobody saw that you witnessed this?" I gripped her shoulder. "You mustn't tell anyone else what you saw. Nobody."

"Why not? If they catch the pig, should I not tell them what he did?"

"No. You mustn't. It isn't safe. Think. If the Germans suspect that you can be a witness against one of them—a car means it might be someone of some importance—they would want to stop you. I don't want you to talk to anyone else about this. Please, Miriam? I know how much you care. I know you always want to do the right thing—"

"You used to as well."

I looked at my daughter's face, those sparkling, hopeful eyes. "I still do but look at Regina. Please, look at her. What would her life be like if something happened to you? The poor woman is dead. She is gone, but we are still here. God took her for a reason and left you here because he wants you to take care of our daughter. She must be your first responsibility, as she is mine."

"Her name? I don't even know the poor woman's name." Miriam wiped her eyes. "May I hold her?"

"Of course. She is your sweet baby." I reluctantly lifted Regina from my shoulder and placed her in Miriam's hands. "Look how she's looking at you. She trusts you. She loves you more than anyone else on Earth."

The baby gurgled, little bubbles on her lips.

"She trusts someone who must hide the truth," Miriam said. "For her sake, I will keep this to myself. You're right, she must come first." She placed Regina on her shoulder. "You should know I will do anything to keep her safe."

"I know." I stood silently as Miriam rocked Regina in her arms. "The war will be over soon, and God will punish the Nazis as he punished all of our enemies throughout history."

"You always say the same thing." Her eyes had a far-away look. I thought it was from the soothing action of rocking the baby.

The next morning when I went to work, I found the notice from the hospital that on November 6, 40-year-old Laja Breneskowska of 48 Brzezinska Street had died of wounds sustained by being run over by a car the day before. "I'll write this one up," I said. I knew it was a German driving the vehicle even if the report was not allowed to specify it, because Jews were not permitted automobiles. I didn't have to lay the blame. If God read my entry, he would know it was a damn German. We all did. There was nothing else we could do.

Cukier was in a foul mood. "They're reducing the bread ration again. It's those damn immigrants they've thrown in here. We hardly have enough food for ourselves, and now they shove more hungry souls into our sardine can."

Rosenfeld shrugged his shoulders. "Have you seen the prices in the markets? Everything is going up because of this new influx. I need new shoes." He raised his foot. "I have holes big enough for moon craters, but who can afford new shoes?"

"The problem is that with all the new arrivals, the prices of food and everything is skyrocketing," I said.

"We need to stop letting newcomers in. Or send them out," Cukier said. "The Germans put in an order for 1,000 men to be shipped to Germany for manual labor, but the problem is the terrible state of health among the immigrants. Less than 25 percent were judged by the health commission to be healthy enough for work."

"How can they be healthy if they can't eat?" Rosenfeld asked. "It's a vicious circle: no food, weak body, no work, no food. It's disgusting."

I burst out laughing.

"What's so funny?" Rosenfeld asked.

"I've never seen you get so angry before."

Rosenfeld held up his hands. "Some bastard stole my gloves. Do you think that is funny too?"

CHAPTER 63

NOVEMBER 30, 1941: A PUBLIC FLOGGING
On November 21, the janitor of a coal yard, caught stealing coal, was publicly flogged...

Can babies sense something is about to happen? Regina was turning her head this way and that as Miriam held her. "I don't know what's wrong with her tonight," she said, "Maybe the milk is spoiled?" She opened the bottle and inhaled. "Just as rotten as ever."

"Let me hold her?" I reached for Regina.

"No. I'll do it. She needs her mother at times like this."

I had to agree but lately had noticed a coldness in Miriam toward me. It could have been my imagination, or due to the severe weather and our hardships in the ghetto. I sat down on the chair and watched her rocking Regina, but the child still seemed ill at ease. "Why don't you get some rest and I'll sit with her?"

Miriam gazed at Regina and finally handed her to me.

"I'll take good care of her," I said, "Please, dear, go to bed and get some rest."

"I'm so tired," Miriam said. "I'm feeling old these days."

"You just gave birth." I gave her a loving smile. "That isn't easy in any circumstances, but in what we are living with? That is all. You are still my beautiful bride."

"This is some honeymoon." She settled down on the mattress. "I wish you had listened to me. Anywhere but here."

I don't know how much time passed. I was nodding off, Regina in her crib, asleep at last when the night was shattered by an unholy sound.

Regina burst into a terrified cry as air raid sirens blared seemingly from everywhere around us. All windows had been ordered blacked-out months ago, all street lamps unlit, so I could not see anything outside.

With Regina in her arms, Miriam was staring in terror at the ceiling, as the sirens blared again.

I rushed toward Miriam and held her and our baby in my arms, seeking anywhere we might hide. There was nowhere. Our table would be no protection from a bomb dropped from high in the night sky. I crushed her and Regina up against the wall farthest from the window, my body protecting them from any shards of glass or wood that might be propelled into our flat. The baby's body was aquiver as her screams were muted by Miriam's hand over her mouth, my wife whispering, "Shaa. Shaa, Regina. Shaa."

A third siren.

I wished I could see the planes in the sky. Were they the Luftwaffe or hopefully the French, the English, even the Russians? This is serious, I thought, three alarms. There had never been one alarm before. I wanted to tell Miriam, this is hopeful. This is the sign we've been waiting for. The war is ending. Germany is losing. I prayed to hear bombs falling. I didn't care if the bombs destroyed every factory. I didn't care if I'd wake up to cavernous empty holes where the factories had stood. It was the first air raid, and I prayed it was the end of the German occupation. These were my thoughts as I protected my wife and child with my body in the screaming of the alarms.

It was silent too soon. I'd heard no explosions. The sirens stopped.

I peered through a thin opening in the boarded-up window. Almost all windows were now covered in the building. All the street lights were dead. It was black. No planes above and no life below. Was it all a test? I was filled with a sadness I couldn't explain.

I felt Miriam quivering in my arms and then she moved away. I felt empty. The silence of the whole black world was like a funeral shroud. It was all closing in on me. I would have run outside, but the Germans or the Order Service might be out there. There had been so many shootings of late, all unprosecuted...most by the barbed wire, the hated barbed wire...the increasingly alluring barbed wire. I remembered the woman dancing for the guard, pointing to her breasts. Would I be begging a guard to shoot me? Not as long as I had Miriam and Regina. I had to stay entrapped here.

I wanted to hold Miriam again, to tell her the truth, how frightened I was during this first air raid, but she was rocking our baby. In the heart of all the darkness, only the tiny thing in her lap was giving us a reason to keep living.

The next morning, I walked to the Jewish Ghetto Administration, eagerly seeking evidence of an allied bombing anywhere. There was none.

People were pausing, looking up at the sky as they walked. There were more zombies than ever, gaunt, hungry, dead facial expressions. My coat, threadbare, my shoes, dusty and worn, gave no sign that I worked within the administration. To the zombies, I appeared deliberately to be one of them and not a target to prey on.

The conversation by the posting boards centered on the first ever air raid in the ghetto. Some cast furtive, perhaps hopeful glances at the sky, nervous glances around, to see if the Chairman's spies were listening. Several uttered cautious blurts about the airplanes that had by-passed us. Some had the temerity to grab onto a friend's arm and whisper, "They're coming. The war will be over soon."

When I got to our room, Singer was already there. "Is the baby okay? How is Miriam?"

"My friend, did you hear the air raid sirens last night? It is almost over."

Singer studied me for a long moment and said, "Lodz would be a prime target for bombing, our factories." He sighed. "They should have bombed the hell out of us but did not."

He was right. Nothing had changed. It had been an air raid but meant nothing. I settled down at my station and sorted through the departmental notes. I stared in silence at the announcement that the Chairperson had ordered a series of concerts to be held at the House of Culture and that all newcomers who were musicians, actors, singers, and artists were to be registered so they could perform at these extravaganzas. I handed the note to Singer.

Singer read the announcement silently and burst into laughter. "And a grand time was had by all," he said.

I typed it up just that way.

CHAPTER 64

DECEMBER 1, 1941: GHETTO POPULATION 163,623

"I need you to do something for me," Cukier said, handing me several reports. "I can't figure out these population figures. Would you please go over them and write an entry?"

"Anything not to have to write about suicides," I said, spreading out the various reports and trying to make sense of the numbers. "In May of last year—is it a year already? —when the ghetto was sealed off, our population came to 160,000."

"That is what we have now," Cukier said.

"Close," I replied. "Up to September of this year, our numbers were dropping, mostly because of the high mortality rate. With the newcomers from the transports, approximately 7,000, and 29 births, our population increased. Then in November, we had 914 dead, and another 1,130 sent to perform manual labor in Germany."

"You're as confusing as these figures. Can you just give me the bottom line?" Cukier's pen was poised to write on his pad.

"From what I can see, and this is very difficult, given all these figures, the ghetto declined by 2,045 people in November."

"Good. We went down."

"No. We went up by 4,118 people. That is our net gain."

"Because so many died?" Rosenfeld asked, rubbing his hands together. "So, dying Jews helped keep our figures manageable?" He shook his head. "There's a reason for everything."

"You never found your gloves?" I asked.

Rosenfeld stared at his hands. "I hope whoever stole them is enjoying them."

I wasn't sure if he was sincere or sarcastic. I made up my mind I would ask Singer if he could conjure up another pair of gloves for our old friend.

Rosenfeld sighed. "Here's one for the books. They found another old man frozen stiff. So, guess where they found him?"

I had no idea, but knowing Rosenfeld I knew it had to be someplace unique, or he would have continued his cataloging of the dead in respectful silence. "Okay, where did they find him?"

Cukier was listening too.

"The poor soul died in the cemetery."

I would have accused him of making that up, but no more. People were finding all kinds of unique places to terminate their lives: lavatories were a favorite, streets were another. I laughed, but felt teary as I said, "Why not save the cost of a hearse trip and end it all in a cemetery?"

Singer entered the room. "What's going on?"

Rosenfeld just waved his hand and handed him the notice.

"Where have you been?" Cukier asked, barely looking up from his work.

"There was a shooting on Zgierska Street," Singer replied.

"By the barbed wire as usual?" Cukier asked, sounding indifferent.

I wondered how many shootings we'd already mentioned by the barbed wire at the end of Zgierska.

"This one's a little different," Singer said, looking upset.

"How so?" Cukier asked.

Singer shook his coat free of snow. "I saw the whole thing happen."

"You were there? What were you doing by the barbed wire?"

"It's not important."

I stared at Singer wondering why he was always looking for trouble. I felt like shouting at him that he was the godfather of my child and should not be taking undue risks, but Cukier had his eyes aimed

331

at Singer and was chastising him, "I've told you a thousand times that you mustn't take risks," Cukier shouted and burst into a fit of coughing.

"There, you've done it again," I said to Singer.

Singer backed away, concerned at Cukier's condition. "I'm sorry."

"Why do you insist on going near the fence?"

Singer barked, "Forget that now. A man and woman were pushing a handcart near the end of the street. the cart struck a post supporting the barbed wire."

"Oh, God! There's a sentry booth down there."

Singer nodded. "The guard jumped out of his booth and shot the woman dead with his rifle. There was no word of warning. Then he aimed his rifle again, and the bullet struck the man in the stomach."

"The sentry killed them both?" Rosenfeld asked. "Were there witnesses?"

"The shooting sent everyone running, but yes, a few furnished details to the Order Service men who soon arrived."

"That sentry should be put on trial," Rosenfeld said.

Singer shook his head. "Fat chance! While I was there, the Gestapo and Kripo appeared, as well as the chief of the Order Service and the head of the Bureau of Investigation, but nothing happened to the sentry."

Cukier sighed. "Nothing ever does. I'm sick of it. Write it up as you see fit." He rose from his chair. "I'm going for a walk." He left the room.

"Be sure to mention the victims' names," Rosenfeld said. "Someday, hopefully soon, our chronicles may help bring these bastards to justice."

Singer replied, "The man's name was Wolf Weder. He was 28 and a bachelor."

"Isn't that about your age?" I asked, sensing Singer was concealing something. "Did you know him?"

Singer ignored me. "The woman can't be identified. Her face was too badly damaged."

My hands formed into fists, useless fists, angry fists. I sat down at the typewriter. At least here my fingers might do some good.

We never learned if any punishment was given to the sentry. Singer didn't bring up the subject again.

I no longer walked anywhere near the barbed wire. Only those who wished to end their suffering dared approach the sentry booths. In the night, and in the day, the zombies jumped when the shots were heard in the ghetto. Then they resumed their mindless digging into the trash, rummaging about in the pockets of the dead, until they too fell from hunger, exhaustion, or the frigid cold, onto the snow.

CHAPTER 65

WEDNESDAY, DECEMBER 3, 1941: *REGISTRATION OF RESIDENTS OF COLLECTIVES*
There are six residential collectives for the newcomers with about 1,000 people in each house. All such residents had to be home tonight to be registered. It is worth noting that the work was done efficiently in all the collectives by 3 A.M.

"So, all went well last night with the newcomer registrations?" I asked Doctor Rosenfeld who had the report from the Registration Department in front of him.

"If you call waking people up at all hours of the night well," he replied. "Have you been to one of the collectives?" He asked, rubbing his hands together, which had become a habit, now that his gloves had been stolen.

"I can't imagine being housed with 1000 people, mostly women and children. I guess we're pretty fortunate, compared to these refugees."

Cukier interrupted. "Someone else has been shot by a sentry. There's more and more of that happening."

"The Germans are all trigger-happy now that they know they aren't going to be held to account," I remarked, wishing Miriam would give up her constant nagging about me finding a way to get us out of the ghetto. I told her things were looking up a bit, but she can only see the dark side. "How did it happen? Was it near the barbed wire?"

"Of course," Cukier said. "The Chairman has warned repeatedly for all to stay away from the guard booths and the wire, but we are like children who don't obey our father."

"I don't know," Rosenfeld interjected. "This man was only 21 years old and from Prague. He was waiting for a job in the saddlery located on the outskirts of the ghetto, merely walking around, unfamiliar with the territory. He wandered too close to the fence, and that was that. Poor boy."

"Just write it up. You can include how it happened if you wish." Cukier looked disgusted. "I'm sure the Kripo investigated?"

"So, it says, but there were no witnesses, so they merely ordered the body taken to the mortuary." Rosenfeld sighed. "Oh, God! This is sad. He had a girlfriend here. She was sixteen years old and on the second transport from Prague. He followed her…to be with her…and gets shot for doing nothing but waiting for a job interview."

I was glad Rosenfeld was still able to feel something for this victim. The more I wrote about the suicides and murders, the more immune I became to the feelings of pain and anger that should have accompanied each incident of violence. Perhaps I was not walking in the streets like the zombies, but my heart and soul was losing the ability to feel empathy for the dead, the dying, the starving, the cold, except in such rare cases where some aspect gave the death a unique twist. Only memorable deaths caught our attention.

After I typed Rosenfeld's entry, I thought of Miriam. I'd hoped a child would bring us closer together, but there was still some unknown barrier between us that I was finding insurmountable. What caused it? When did it start? Was it merely that I refused to consider escaping the ghetto? She had cornered me last night again, holding Regina in front of me, a leveraging tool, as she pressed her case.

"There must be a way to leave here," Miriam said. "How can you look on your daughter and do nothing?"

"Miriam, please? We have been over this so many times. Don't you hear how anyone who attempts to go near the barbed wire is shot on sight? It is a German shooting gallery, and we are the clay targets."

"In here it is better?" Miriam pointed to her breast. "I do not even have milk for my child to nurse. When winter comes, we'll be starving again." She covered herself up. "There will be no fuel for heat. How will we survive? How can you bear to see Regina, our beautiful baby, starving and shivering with cold?"

"The thought of Regina being shot by a guard...we are safe here. Yes, we are suffering, but at least, we are alive." I didn't dare argue that the Chairman was protecting us. This had always been a bone of contention that had grown worse with Miriam arguing, "He lives like a king, but everyone else is suffering and dying like dogs."

"Enough! Miriam, please stop? Enjoy your beautiful daughter and be grateful we are not housed with a thousand other poor souls in the immigrant collectives. The war will be over soon. Remember the air raid?"

"You keep saying the war will end, but will we be here to see it? You should ask your friend, Singer—"

"That's enough! Dammit! Do you want us all to be killed? Even your child?" It was as if Singer's name was a trigger for my outbursts. Whenever she mentioned his name, I blew up, my calm demeanor becoming volcanic. "Singer is a little bragging shit who can do no more than I can. If he could escape this hell hole why would he still be here? He'd be a horse thief in America! He'd be one of their rich capitalist swindlers who care nothing about a bunch of Jews in a goddamn ghetto!" I pounded the table with my fist.

Her face, frightened, the baby crying, my head splitting with a headache, all brought me back to where I was and what I was doing. I was hurting Regina. I gripped the chair, panting for breath, trying to regain my calm. "Miriam, I shouldn't shout at you. I shouldn't belittle my friend, Oscar." I took another breath. "But, sweetheart, you keep hammering me about getting us out of here, and this terrifies me. Every day, I hear of other poor souls trying to escape and ending up in a puddle of their own blood." Another deep breath, my eyes imploring her to grant me a moment of peace. "I can't bear the thought of seeing you, or Regina, with bullets in your beautiful faces. So please, for God's sake, please don't ask me again? Believe me, if I thought there was one chance in a billion Singer could get you and Regina to safety, I would not ask him, I would beg him, beg him, pay him—he does nothing without pay—whatever he wants. My dearest wife, it is hopeless. I wish it weren't. It is hopeless."

Just thinking of our argument, bile rose in my stomach. I glanced over at Singer. He looked thinner, and his hair was showing gray streaks. His suit was showing wear, and he rarely ever spoke of his female conquests and his wild nights anymore. Yet, he still came to work later than the rest of us, making up for it by his eyewitness accounts of some of the incidents he came across in his walks around the ghetto. He looked up. Our eyes met. "Is it dangerous what you do?" I asked.

He smiled, looking boyish again. "Yes. I guess it is dangerous."

"But you do it anyway?"

"Sometimes we can't help ourselves. Sometimes God puts something in our path that like a magnet holds us in its grip."

I didn't understand. "Are you drawn to danger? Is that it?"

Singer laughed. "No. I'm no braver than you."

"Do you know what will happen if you are caught?"

"Yes."

"And you do it anyway?"

"As I said, sometimes there is no choice."

"There is always a choice."

"I used to think so too."

"Be careful then." Frustrated, I turned back to my typing.

Rosenfeld read a memo aloud: "The Chairman rewarded a tailor who wrote a song about him entitled, "Rumkowski, Chaim." The Chairman commissioned him to write more songs. His latest is called, "Leben zol prezes Khaim" ("Long Live Chairman Chaim.")

Cukier sighed. "Write it up. Without comment."

"Long live the Devil," Singer muttered and grabbing his coat, left the room.

"I fear our friend is self-destructive," I said to Rosenfeld.

"I think it's worse than that. I suspect he's in love," Rosenfeld replied.

CHAPTER 66

TUESDAY, DECEMBER 16, 1941: *ROAD TO THE CEME-
TERY UNDER CONSTRUCTION*
    *The construction of an excellent road to the cemetery has been
in progress in Marysin for three weeks now.*

"It's odd," Rosenfeld said, perusing his notes, "how the construction
of a road to our cemetery has aroused such interest."

"It's quite an accomplishment," I replied. "It will run approximately
600 meters along the cemetery walls. Considering our imposed
limitations, it's quite the feather in the Chairman's cap."

"Did they uproot the old graves?" Rosenfeld asked. "It would be
a sin to disturb the dead for a road to the cemetery. I would not
welcome such a disturbance if I were buried there."

Singer looked upset. "You have a long way to go before that becomes
a factor."

"Sometimes I wonder," Rosenfeld replied.

"Seriously though," Cukier said, "How did they avoid moving the
graves?"

"There was a plan to build an overpass supported by thick columns.
The columns would have been where graves are situated." I said.
"Instead, they moved the cemetery walls, many of which were about
to collapse. I understand they brought in 250,000 bricks from other
demolition sites for the road."

"Two hundred and fifty thousand bricks?" Cukier exclaimed. "That
really is a massive job."

"Enormous," I replied.

Cukier said. "Engineer, this is your forte. Write it up. The building of exemplary roads under present conditions is a monument to the ghetto's vitality."

Singer's voice was shrill. "Are you kidding? Are we really calling a road to the cemetery a "monument to the ghetto's vitality"? Am I the only one still sane around here? Yesterday, there was a concert. Today we're lauding a road to the cemetery; and tomorrow we'll extol the birth of a rat as a tribute to the wonderful organizational skills of every shithead that runs this damn ghetto!"

"Calm down, boy," Rosenfeld said, reaching for Singer's shoulder. "We all get the irony."

"Do you? Do you really? It sure doesn't sound like it to me when you call this road to a bursting-at-the-seams cemetery, a 'monument to the vitality' of this shithole we're locked in by the damn Germans."

Cukier stood, handkerchief in his hand. "Singer, that's enough."

"You're putting yourself and us in danger," I hissed, grateful nobody had burst through our door.

"We are in danger," Singer shouted. "We're the walking dead, but we don't know it because our Chairman has us building damn roads to the cemetery, listening to boring concerts, if we're lucky enough to be invited, while everyone else is waiting on endless lines for the bones our German masters throw us in the dirt."

"We have to make the best of our situation," Cukier said. "That is what our Elders are doing for us."

Singer approached me. "You're a man of logic. Do you really believe this road is a masterpiece of organizational skill? Why aren't we using our great, superior organizational skills to fight? Instead, we are obeying an egotist who believes—yes, I think he truly believes—that the wolves will leave us alone if we just build a road to our cemetery for them, so they can stock it with more shooting victims. I don't believe it! Since when are Jews, the descendants of the Maccabees, afraid to fight? If we all storm the wire—"

"That's suicide! We wouldn't stand a chance!" I said.

"Do we stand a chance here?" He looked at me with imploring eyes. "My friend, things are not getting better here. Your wife and daughter deserve better—"

"We all do, but this war will soon be over." What was wrong with him? Why was he snapping now?

"You keep saying this. I just don't know." Singer sagged in his seat.

Rosenfeld put his hands squarely on top of Singer's shoulders. "I'm an old man. I've seen pogroms and hunger. I've seen enemy rise against us and then collapse into dust. I believe the Engineer is correct. Hitler has bitten off more than he can chew. Napoleon attacked Russia and learned the hard way. Hitler's lack of historical knowledge may well result in a major setback on the icy steppes of the Soviet empire. We must just be patient until the madman falls on his ass."

"I've no patience left," Singer said. "I'd rather die fighting than keep singing the praises for new roads that inevitably lead to the cold, hard, ground of the cemetery. Wouldn't you?"

I thought of Miriam and our frequent arguments about escaping the ghetto. I saw her pleading eyes. "No, Singer, my impatient friend, I would not. So long as I can hold a pen in hand, as long as the Eldest of the Jews employs me, I will do the work I must. You have no responsibilities. I don't condemn you for that. But how can you know what it feels like to be a husband or a father? No, I must do what I can to protect them, and even if we did find some miraculous way to escape, where would we go? Is there any safe passage for a Jew in Poland, Germany, anywhere in Europe?"

"You're depressing me," Rosenfeld said, again rubbing his cold hands together. "Did we get any paper yet?"

"You see, even paper is unavailable now," Singer said. "Engineer, what will you do when the Germans stop the paper supply completely? There will be no job writing these laudatory reports that only the Chairman and a few of his chosen elite get to see. Without your cushy job, what will you do to support your Miriam and sweet Regina? We're living the fools' dream."

"I'll find a way," I said, and turned back to my work, fuming at his insolence. I did not hear him reply, "I'll find a way too."

CHAPTER 67

SUNDAY, DECEMBER 21, 1941: CHANUKAH CELEBRATIONS

It was Regina's first Chanukah. Nearly five months old, but hardly larger than a peanut, she continued to hold me in her trance. This miniature portrait of my Miriam, hazel eyes constantly probing my face, seemed much too unsmiling for her age. I attributed it to lacking food, blistering cold weather, and perhaps a reflection of her mother's moodiness. Even when I gave her a small doll Singer had managed to get, she barely smiled. "Why don't we take her to the kitchen 2 Chanukah party?" I suggested to Miriam.

"You can go if you like, but Regina and I will remain here." She examined the raggedy doll and then returned it to our daughter who was reaching for it.

"It would do her good to be with other children."

"There is dysentery in the ghetto. There are too many sicknesses. Why don't you go and enjoy yourself for a change?"

"No. I'll stay here."

"You don't have to. We're fine. I'm not in a celebratory mood."

"It's Chanukah. Isn't there anything you would like?" I realized after I asked that it was a mistake.

"You know what I want." Miriam sighed. "And what do you want, dear husband?"

"I don't know." I rose from my chair. "I think I will go for a short walk."

I grabbed my coat and hat, tied a scarf around my neck, the coat's collar button needed sewing again, and headed down the stairs. "What are you doing here?" I asked almost knocking Singer off the landing where he seemed to be juggling something in his hands.

"I have a few little gifts for Chanukah," he said, quickly proffering the small packages. "I have no family here, so I needed someone to give them to." He smiled anxiously. "Is it alright?"

I looked up the stairs, frustrated again with Miriam. "I'm going for a short walk. You may go up if you like? I'll be back momentarily."

"Are you going to the party at the House of Culture? I understand it is going to be very special, in honor of the Chairman, as always."

"Please don't start? I'm exhausted from arguing with Miriam. She sounds like you sometimes."

"Perhaps, someday, you will too, my all-too-logical Engineer."

"Please, just go upstairs, and maybe you can make my wife happy." I was about to walk out the door when Singer stopped me. "Ostrowski, did you hear the latest news?"

I shook my head. "The way you look I'm guessing it's bad as usual?"

Singer took a few steps down the dark staircase. "Do you remember on the 16th when Rumkowski was summoned to the German authorities? Well, it turns out they demanded that 20,000 people vacate the ghetto."

I stopped moving. "Twenty thousand?"

"From what I've heard the Chairman persuaded them to cut that number in half."

"Half? Ten thousand are leaving the ghetto?" The number seemed so large. Where would they go? Who would go? "I imagine the ones leaving will be the latest arrivals?"

"The Eldest of the Jews persuaded the authorities to let him decide, presumably by who was most needed to complete work in the ghetto for the German orders."

"I suppose that is better than the Germans deciding."

"Yes. I suppose so."

"Do you know where they are going?"

"The Chairman said they are going to be resettled in smaller towns up north, where food is not as big a problem."

"That makes sense. At any rate, we'll have fewer mouths to feed here. That would be a blessing."

Singer gave me a peculiar look. "Do you really believe the Germans are doing this to help the ghetto?"

"No. I suppose not."

Singer glanced up the stairwell. "We are safe...for now. But imagine the Germans wanted 20,000. This means they have the ability to move thousands more at any time."

"They won't do that. They need our factories, just as the Chairman predicted. Even you must see that he has managed to make our factories and workshops a valuable part of the German war effort."

"I hope that is enough."

"Why are you always so full of doubt?"

"It's my nature, I guess. But there is one more thing that bothers me about all this. The Chairman has created a commission of five of his closest officials: Henryk Neftalin; Leon Rozenblat, chief of the Order Service; Szaja Jakobson, chairman of the court; Salmon Hercberg, commandant of the Central Prison, and Zygmund Blemer, head of the Bureau of Investigation. He met with them at a secret meeting and assigned them the role of selecting the candidates, most mainly from the undesirables, criminals and their families." He picked up a package that had fallen to the floor. "Why a high-level commission? Something here isn't kosher."

"What do you mean?" I asked, seeing the worried look on my young friend's face.

Singer leaned closer. "You're always so logical. Don't you wonder why the Chairman would include these criminals and malcontents if they are being sent to a better place?"

"To get rid of them," I said. "These lawless immigrants have been a constant pain in his side and a threat to us forever. He probably just wants to be free of them."

"Perhaps. But to a better place?" Singer sucked in his cheeks. "I'm sorry, it just doesn't sound like our great leader. If he could, he'd send all his enemies to hell."

I let out a frustrated sigh. "I'm in a stairway and in no mood to argue. It's Chanukah. This news will terrify our people as it is." I hadn't thought of how fast the news of the mass expulsion from the ghetto would spread. People were frightened they'd be included, but the Chairman had made it clear that the deportees were being sent to rural areas where there was more food. What was Singer questioning? What was he afraid of? "Please, go upstairs? You've given me one more headache to think about. Please spare Miriam from all this? It's a holiday."

"Of course. I would never want to hurt her or you." Singer hurried up the stairway.

Singer was gone by the time I returned from my short walk. He'd ruined any joy I might have had by his cynical questions. I was glad to be watching Regina playing on the carpet with a wooden car he'd given her. Miriam was sitting in her chair, staring at the far wall as Regina rolled the car back and forth on the floor.

I sat on our other chair, silent as a rock. The car rolling back and forth, back and forth, under Regina's hand was hypnotizing me, lulling me to sleep. But in the back of my mind, Singer's questions lingered.

When I awoke, Miriam was already in our bed. I decided not to risk waking her. Sleep would do her good.

In the morning, I left for work before Miriam or Regina awoke. It was cold in the flat, so I was glad they were both asleep. The frigid air kept most of the zombies indoors.

At work, I was busy catching up on my typing when Neftalin came to see us. "You've heard the news of the resettlement?"

We all nodded.

Neftalin smiled. "It is good that our load is being lightened by the loss of some of these parasites that were dumped in here by the authorities. I do not understand why there are so many negative rumors."

As he spoke, I typed his words: "As usually occurs when a new blow befalls the ghetto, the news has been maliciously and irresponsibly exaggerated and blown out of proportion."

When Singer read my entry, he shook his head and said. "You really are one of them now."

"Nobody reads it anyway," I shot back at him.

"Someday they will. What will they think of us then?" Singer was eyeing Neftalin with angry eyes. "Someday we will be judged by what we write here. You and the Chairman know that."

Neftalin shook his head. "You scholars and idealists know nothing of the real world. Thank God for Rumkowski. Without his practical sense, Engineer, you know, we all would have been at the mercy of the Germans. You must continue to support his efforts to save the majority by acceding to the German request to resettle a small number, mostly miscreants, self-seeking trouble-makers, who seek only to undermine our efficient government."

We all nodded.

"I don't understand," Singer said. "Why is the Chairman rewarding trouble-makers?"

Cukier rolled his eyes.

Rosenfeld shook his head.

I sat up.

Neftalin stared at Singer. "What do you mean?"

Singer looked at me. "The Chairman says they are being resettled to better lodgings and food, so why is he sending our worst citizens for such a reward?"

Neftalin looked as if he was thinking then said, "It is not the Chairman who decides who and where these laborers are going." He shot a look at Cukier. "I would not think being sent to the cold northern frontiers to farm should be considered a reward. Would you if you were selected for this honor?"

I gasped silently. Neftalin threatened Singer. I sensed it in his words and his tone. I couldn't wait for the Deputy to leave. Singer had to tread lightly. He was family now.

"I assume I've answered your questions," Neftalin said and gave Cukier a curt nod of his head and left the room.

Singer waited until the door closed. "You're all fools! Do you really think this is where it will end?" He rose from his chair and stormed out the door before any of us could stop him.

I ran after him but saw German police glaring at me. I quickly returned and closed the door.

Cukier coughed hard into his handkerchief. "The good news is that soon there will be more food for everyone," he said.

Rosenfeld pulled himself painfully from his chair and nearly fell to the floor. He saved himself by grabbing the back of my seat. "And so, it begins," he muttered, straightening up and pacing around our table.

I stared at the professor. He had aged in the year I'd known him. He looked bony and fragile. A chill shot through me. The Nazis had no use for old people who could not pull their weight and justify their rations by their productivity. I wondered if the day would come when men like Rosenfeld, men of experience and well-honed skills, would be included on the list of expulsions. I could not visualize my friend, with the perennially frozen hands, ever working as a farmer somewhere in rural Northern Poland. "I'm going home early today," I said. "I want to give Regina her Chanukah present."

Cukier said, "Be careful if you walk by the Gypsy Camp. Typhus."

"Oh God, why are you doing all this to us?" I asked the smug God who I hadn't believed in for years, but whose name was now constantly on my lips. "Do we really need Typhus added to our woes?"

Cukier coughed and then examined his handkerchief. He shoved it in his pocket.

CHAPTER 68

DECEMBER 25, 1941: SHOOTINGS
Two shooting incidents in a single day have caused a mood of genuine panic in the ghetto, a mood which was heightened by the spread of stories claiming five persons had been killed, a number which by evening had increased to seven. The smallest details of these imaginary incidents were passed by word of mouth, and included exact times, the victim's personal date, the places involved, and so forth.

"So, what is the truth?" I asked Cukier when he returned from what had become a daily morning briefing by Deputy Neftalin. "Is it two, five, seven that were killed?"

"I don't know, and it doesn't matter. We'll wait for the official reports." Cukier handed me a flyer. "The Chairman is having these posted on the notice walls.

I read it aloud: "Sisters and brothers! In connection with the recent incidents, I have chosen this way of informing you that as a result of my intervention, I have been given assurances that there will be no repetition of such incidents. This obviously does not apply to cases where smuggling or attempts to escape from the ghetto are involved." I paused. "Reading between the lines, he's saying the shootings will continue."

Cukier shrugged. "Yes, but only for smuggling and escape attempts. In one case, a man was shot on his way to work at the tailor shop, and in the other, a man was killed when he was attempting to escape from a police escort."

"So those won't happen anymore?" I was skeptical but read on: "I appeal to you to remain calm and to report to work punctually as you have been doing so far. My slogan, 'Work, work, work,' is still in complete effect." I put the flyer on my pile. "Verbatim?" I asked.

Cukier nodded.

Rosenfeld rubbed his hands and muttered, "Nothing has changed."

I had to agree. The Eldest of the Jews still believed demonstrating to the Germans our ability to keep the machine functioning smoothly was our best course of action against their increasingly intrusive occupation.

Cukier jumped from his seat. "The Chairman is getting married! God bless him!"

"What?" Rosenfeld and I blurted at the same time.

"It's true. On December 25th, the Department of Vital Statistics received marriage banns from the Eldest of the Jews, which were registered as Number 1,405."

"I don't believe it."

"When will the happy occasion take place? It is good for him to marry after so long," Rosenfeld said. "I miss my Rosa still."

Cukier gave our friend a sympathetic look. "The Chairman's plenipotentiary paid the normal charge of 6 Marks, 50 Pfennigs. Because the wedding is to take place soon, the marriage was exempted from the necessary waiting period."

"He's an old man, so of course he does not want to wait," Rosenfeld said. "I would not either."

"How old is he?" I asked.

"He was born, Mordecai Chaim Rumkowski, February 1877, in the town of Ilno, Russia," Cukier said.

"Is he marrying his secretary?" There had been rumors about him and his ever-present secretary, Dora Fuchs, for years.

"I would not throw her out of bed," Rosenfeld said, and gave an embarrassed laugh.

"Doctor!" I was surprised but laughed with him.

"Hey, we old farts need a good shtup sometimes too, you know."

Cukier frowned. "Actually no. His fiancée's data is here. Her name is Regina—"

"Regina? That's my daughter's name." I mulled over the coincidence.

Cukier smiled. "That is good luck for her. Mazel tov! His fiancée is Regina Weinberger, born in Lodz in 1907."

"He's a cradle-robber. Good for him!" Rosenfeld gave me another lewd smile.

I'd never seen him like this. It made him more human. "He's a widower. What about her?" I was eager to give Miriam the news if she hadn't gotten it already from the yentas.

"Never married. Oh, oh! She's a lawyer!" Cukier cracked a smile. "Oy! He's in for it now."

"Never mind that," Rosenfeld said, an evil twinkle in his eyes. "She's young and never married. I wish it were me."

I couldn't believe how Rosenfeld's comments, and looks, so uncharacteristic of the usually reserved doctor, fired my imagination. It had been months since Miriam, and I had made love. Her mind had been preoccupied with providing for our child, and with the depressing condition of our lives, and I had no real appetite for 'shtupping,' as the Doctor had called love-making. But all this talk about the Chairman made me wonder if perhaps that was what was wrong between us.

By the end of the day, I was eager to get home, and as soon as possible, settle Regina in her crib. I imagined Miriam's face when I gave her the exciting news about Rumkowski. Even she, so critical of the Chairman, must feel joy that the Eldest of the Jews was finding the precious gift of love, reward for being the savior of our community. I warmed at the thought of turning her to me with a passionate embrace and then leading her to our bed.

I kept myself from running, passing Order Service men, some of whom I now knew. I barely glanced at the barbed wire behind the buildings, the sentry posts at strategic points along the forbidden perimeter.

There were fewer zombies aimlessly roaming the streets. The Chairman had most people working in the factories or on public works. The newcomers were locked behind separate barbed wire enclosed sections, in community houses, old buildings, most without heat or running water, a thousand beds without walls between them. He was doing what he could for them, and for all of us, and now was finally giving himself some pleasure. Marriage is supposed to provide that, comradeship, and love. I would regain those tonight. Whatever was the wedge between us, I would remove. My body was ready. My mind was fixed on one purpose.

No sooner did I open the door, then Miriam, Regina in her arms, exclaimed, "Did you hear the news? The old bastard is getting married."

CHAPTER 69

DECEMBER 28, 1941: FIFTY-SIX THOUSAND WHITE SUITS
The tailor shops are filling large rush orders for the army. Fifty-six thousand pairs of pants and shirts with hoods made of thin white cloth, a camouflage for snow-covered terrain, have been ordered.

"I've been waiting for you," Singer said, rising and cornering me against the wall..

I felt threatened. "What is it? Has something happened?"

Singer peered into my eyes. "I was out Christmas eve. I was walking near the sentry posts." He leaned toward me. "It can be done."

"Have you been drinking?" I sniffed at his breath and detected alcohol.

He shook his head. "Listen to me. There were no shootings on Christmas Eve or Christmas day." He frightened me by his intensity. "The sentries did not shoot anyone."

"You're drunk," I said, trying to push away from the wall, but stopped by his arms blocking me in.

His eyes were inches from my face. "I'm completely sober. But they were drunk. If you want to get Miriam and Regina out of the ghetto, it can be done."

I threw his arm away from me. "No. It can't. Don't even say that."

He gripped my shoulders, his fingers biting into my flesh. "Listen, Engineer, the sentries are all young recruits. They do not want to be here any more than we do, especially on their holidays. I tell you, with your skills, and my connections, we can do it."

"No. Damn you! Don't even think it!" I was shouting, terrified at the vision of my precious Regina bleeding to death in a bed of icy snow. "It is impossible. I don't want to hear it."

The door opened. I froze as always. Thankfully, Cukier entered.

Singer returned to his seat, acting as if nothing happened.

"What's going on?" Cukier asked. "Hey, Singer, you're here early? No girlfriend last night?"

Singer gave him a tight smile. "I was eager to hear of the big wedding."

"Ah, the wedding? It was a wonderful affair. I have not seen such food and celebration in years. But of course, we must downplay that. You understand."

Singer sneered. "Of course." He shot me a glance.

I glared back, still shaken from our conversation.

Cukier belched. "Such food. I will write up the wedding. What else do we have today?"

"I didn't know we had so many Christians among us," I said, noting the Chairman had given permission for Christian religious services to be held at a two-room apartment at Jakuba Street. "There was a Catholic service and a Protestant."

Cukier sat down. "We have quite a number of Christians married to Jews who have chosen to remain with their spouses. Good for them!"

I wondered if it was.

"We also have about 250 registered Christians among the newcomers."

"The sentries are all Christians," Singer said. "They all celebrate Christmas and New Year's. They eat and drink and miss their homes." He shot me a glance.

I shot him back a warning.

Cukier held up his report about the wedding and read it in a dramatic voice. "The Wedding of the Eldest of the Jews, M.C.

Rumkowski, and Regina Weinberger, Master of Law, took place on Saturday, December 27, in the Chairman's apartment. A small group of family and the ghetto leader's closest associates took part in the wedding festivities." He looked at us. "Do you think that is too much?"

"Go on," I said, aware Singer was still staring at me.

"600 telegrams of congratulations attest to ghetto society's unusually great interest in the Chairman's wedding." He looked at Singer. "There really were a great many telegrams."

"You counted them?" Singer asked.

Cukier ignored him. "Despite the most varied stories about the grandiose and sumptuous festivities, the wedding was, in fact, extremely modest." He looked at us. "It only lasted from 6:00 P.M. to 8:00 P.M."

Singer held a paper and read, "One thousand pairs of clogs were distributed to the neediest, free of charge, by the Department of clothing on the occasion of the Chairman's wedding." He stood up and put on his coat. "In honor of the Chairman's wedding, I am quitting work early today." Without waiting for permission, he was out the door.

I was glad to see him leave. From the first minute, when he cornered me against the wall, to the final ironic reading of his short entry about the generous gift of the clogs, he'd been a royal pain in the ass.

Rosenfeld was smiling. There was something in his hands. He undid the small bundle. He looked up at me. "Can you imagine?" He had tears in his eyes as he tried on the new furry gloves.

"Singer gave them to him," Cukier said. "That young man never ceases to surprise me."

Hebrew prayers, muted, banned prayers, came from Rosenfeld's mouth as he held up his gloved hands for God to see his gratitude. "Baruch atah adonei…" He was thanking God for gloves. It was Singer, the playboy, who had gotten him this gift, not God who didn't care about an old man's frozen hands.

As I saw the pleasure Rosenfeld was taking in his new treasure, I vowed to apologize to Singer, and invite him to our home, not as a fellow worker, but as the godfather of my child, a member of our small family. The New Year was a good time to make a positive change in all our relationships.

CHAPTER 70

DECEMBER 31, 1941
In the last few days of December there were persistent rumors that the resettlement was to be suspended. These stories do not correspond to the truth. The special commission's office continues its operations and is compiling lists of candidates for expulsion; the only thing not known is the prospective date for the expulsions...

The ghetto was abuzz with talk about the Chairman's wedding. There was much speculation about the bride, a lawyer who had worked with Rumkowski for many years. Some ridiculed the idea of an older man marrying again. Others felt it would add a more human touch to their leader. I was indifferent, having sufficient marital difficulties of my own.

My resolve to make love to Miriam on Christmas Eve had evaporated with her continued attacks and cynical reviews of anything the Chairman did. "What alternatives do you offer?" I asked over and over. Of course, like all the other critics, she had none. "I'm an engineer. I'm able to design buildings, but I could never have strategized what Rumkowski has managed to do. Don't you understand; he saved us."

"Saved us? Ten thousand of us will soon be shipped out. More are suffering typhus. Yet the Emperor and his friends are partying. Do you know they've just held their 100th concert since the ghetto was sealed?"

"I could get us tickets," I said.

Miriam shook her head. "You know what I want."

I knew, but it was impossible. "I put in for a new apartment, but so far nothing has materialized. I'll keep trying," I said, convinced that more rooms, a cleaner place, would help calm Miriam's nerves and help us rekindle our relationship.

Miriam shook her head violently. "No! You don't understand!" She stormed to the crib and gazed down at Regina. "She is all that keeps me sane," she muttered.

"His new wife is Regina also," I said, wishing I could join her in gazing down at our little girl, but afraid to get too close and set her off again. "Isn't that a strange coincidence?"

When I saw she was ignoring me, I sat down in my chair and tried to calm myself. New Year's Eve and we were still stuck in this claustrophobic apartment, but at least it was only the three of us. Rosenfeld now had seven strangers crowded into his two-room flat. He complained constantly, but nothing changed. I reached into my coat pocket and found a folded sheet of paper. I guessed I'd absent-mindedly placed it there sometime during the day. I unfolded it. It was typed. I didn't give it much thought. It was most likely details about the Chairman's wedding. I'd wanted to share more of the gossip with Miriam, but she wasn't in the mood, and now, neither was I. I folded it and stuck it back in my pocket.

I was on my chair watching Regina playing in her crib when I reached into my pocket again and discovered the paper. Am I becoming forgetful, I asked, unfolding the sheet. It was difficult to read since we were blacked out after dark each night, adding to the claustrophobia that was making me antsy. I shifted the page slightly and peered through my glasses. It was only then I realized I had not typed the letter at all.

Dearest Miriam, beautiful Regina, and my friend, Engineer,

First, I wish you all a better New Year than we have had.

I skipped to the bottom of the letter. It was signed, "Love, Oscar." How strange that he placed a note into my jacket pocket. I read further.

Miriam, you have been my only light in the darkness of my life. I have never loved another woman as I love you.

My hands shook. What is this? Singer, what is this? I read the next sentences:

Our meetings, our discourses, even heated debates, have been the only things that have held me here. I treasure our times together. I want you to know that it is because of you I am leaving. I will come back for you. This I promise with my heart, soul, and body.

I stared at Miriam, unsure of what I should feel. My God! What did it mean? I glanced at her again. She was staring down with such sadness at our child. My God! It can't be. I can't stand one more blow! He loves her? What does he mean? I read it again and then again. It struck at last that he said he was leaving. Good! Let him go! I glared at Miriam. How could she do something like this to me? Was she unfaithful? Did that explain it all?

Miriam looked up. Her eyes met mine.

Did she see the suspicion, anger, hate in my eyes? All this time I assumed it was the pregnancy, or the depression, so common in this hell hole. I lowered my eyes. I couldn't look at her. I felt chills running through my body. I wanted to crush the letter, pretend I didn't see it…pretend it didn't exist. I couldn't. I had to read further. But I could barely contain my anger, my fear. Please, God, tell me I'm wrong? How much more can I take?

My beloved, Regina, you are the image of your mother. I loved you from the first time she put you in my arms.

No. Not this too? I saw Singer's ugly, narrow, lustful, eyes staring down at my daughter, his hands cupping her, her precious body in his arms. Her eyes gazing up at him with innocent love. I felt sick, sour bile rising into my mouth. I couldn't move. My legs were rubber. I wanted to call Miriam, my bitch of a wife, to me, to strike her to the floor… to see the shocked look on her damn face…that beautiful, lying, deceitful face! Oh God, no more? But how could I not read on?

I loved you from the first time she put you in my arms. I pray that you have a chance to enjoy life, but fear you are too beautiful to survive, a flower that is too fragile for this world. I feel blessed to have seen your smile. Having no children of my own, you will forever be my child. I never thought I was capable of such love...

More than anything I'd read so far, these last sentences incensed me beyond reason. I had nothing left. My wife had violated my trust, our wedding vows. She had become cold to me because she loved another...a man more her age, more her personality. I had to admit the truth: Miriam had never truly loved me. How could she? We were matched during a terrible time in history. Who was I compared to a young adventurous lover like Singer? It calmed me a little to settle on the truth. I could read more, though I hated what I was thinking.

Dearest friend, my ever-logical Engineer.

You bastard! You two-faced bastard! You dare call me friend and sleep with my wife? Steal the love of my child? I didn't feel logical. I felt furious, enraged. I had no place to aim my eyes, no place to run. The letter. Finish the damn letter. My hands were trembling. I could barely hold the offensive sheet of paper, but I was driven to finish it, even if it was sharper than a dagger. How could he do this to me?

Dearest friend, my ever-logical Engineer. Knowing you, as I have, I am guessing by now you are furious at what you are reading. But dear friend, two and two, despite your faith, does not always add up to four.

What the hell does he mean by that? Every school child knows that two and two always equal four. Does he think I'm a fool?

I love your wife and daughter more than I thought possible, but I also love you. I can never hurt any of you. I cannot stand the torture of such love and am leaving the ghetto. My friends were killed trying to use a push cart to bust through the barbed wire. Remember the day I read that report to you?

I remembered Singer's face when we got the notice about that attempt to escape. I had asked him if he knew the man and woman who had been shot by the sentry. My God, he never answered. He never said a word. He knew them. He knew them. Had he been in on it? Did he plan it with them?

It was New Year's Eve. What had Singer said about the guards and Christmas? What did he say about New Year's Eve? "Oh, God! No!" I grabbed my coat, hat, and scarf.

"What are you doing? You can't go out. The curfew." Miriam rose from her chair.

I didn't answer. I shoved the letter into my battered briefcase. Miriam must never see it. She must never suspect that I know.

Miriam seemed unsure of what to do. "It's late. Stay here. Please?"

I hurried to the crib. I gazed down at Regina and understood what Singer meant about loving this child. Even if I had lost Miriam's love, I had the love of my daughter. I could not lose that, and I could not let Singer, her godfather, sacrifice himself with such a reckless scheme. I'd never forgive myself if was killed, even if I now hated him. "I'll be back, little one," I whispered, and placed a kiss on Regina's forehead.

"Where are you going?" Miriam repeated. She sounded tired. Or was that fear? Did she know what Singer was up to? Had she pushed him to it? "Please, Benny, what are you doing?"

I didn't answer. And I didn't kiss Miriam on her lips as I should have, as I wanted to. I forced myself to lower my lips to her forehead.

Miriam looked up. I saw questions in her face I could not answer as I raced into the night.

THE END OF BOOK 1

Thank you for sharing this experience with me. I hope you will want to learn more about the fate of Lodz Ghetto in Book 2.

Ostrowski and his young wife, Miriam, have received the blessing of a child. They regard Regina as a ray of hope in the darkness of the ghetto. To provide for his loved ones, Ostrowski will fight his doubts about the controversial leader of the ghetto, and with his fellow chroniclers, continue to support the Chairman's efforts to forge the ghetto into a manufacturing powerhouse for the Nazis. Locked in a stifling conference room with an ailing Cukier, elderly Rosenfeld, and the combative young Singer, Ostrowski witnesses the ominous events as the Nazi noose tightens around them. Can Singer help them escape? What terrible sacrifice will Ostrowski face to save his loved ones? As the Nazis tighten their grip, will anything save them?

People disappear and are never heard from again.

A PERSONAL NOTE:

Several years ago, my mother, a Holocaust survivor from Lodz, gave me a monster of a book. After Mom passed away, I relegated this unread massive book into my thrift store pile. When the cover opened, I saw it was personalized to my mother and my step-father, another survivor. I sat on the carpet and read this treasure I was about to trash, *The Chronicle of the Lodz Ghetto*, translated and edited by Lucjan Dobroszycki, (Yale University Press, 1984). For the first time in my life, I got a sense of what my parents suffered as the Nazis inched the Lodz ghetto toward annihilation. There were nearly 250,000 Jews who lived there from 1941 to 1944. My parents were two of the less than 5,000 who survived.

The *Chronicle* entries are nearly all anonymous records of the daily events these writers witnessed under Nazi rule. Reading them, I felt what the authors might have experienced with each harbinger of their fate. I wanted to learn more about the writers of this amazing book.

The more I searched for the authors, I became convinced they are nearly 'invisible'. Something compelled me to tell a story to make their accounts come to life. Even if the book was never published, it would be a legacy to my family, to help the understand what had been largely unknown to me. I wrote the first draft, more than 700 pages, in one month. It was as if the ghosts of my grandparents and my relatives, killed in Hitler's nightmare, were driving me. When I finished it, I was drained, but felt I'd given the entries the human context, emotions, that could drive readers to seek out the original. My early readers confirmed the power of the book, encouraging me with such comments as "an amazing achievement," "It left me numb," "It made me mad…but in a good way." Most encouraging was, "I couldn't get to sleep."

My objective in writing this novel was to follow the chronology of events, many seemingly insignificant out of context, to capture the steps toward the ghetto's annihilation as the Chroniclers and their loved ones experienced them. I love the movie, Twelve Angry Men", about a jury locked in a room deliberating a case that reveals so much about the character of the jurors. I wanted to recreate the emotional reactions of the writers to the disturbing items of news that prompted their entries. What arguments would be provoked by the Chairman's controversial decrees and actions? Viewed from the eyes of the main character, how would he deal with the torturous uncertainty and the unanswered questions that plagued their lives? People disappeared and were never heard from again. The Lodz ghetto, sealed off from the rest of the world, received few clues to what was happening to Jews in other places. They believed the Germans when they said deportees from Lodz were being sent to farmlands in the North where they would be given housing, food, and work. They could not imagine that while they worked and lived in the ghetto's deteriorating conditions, the Nazis were executing their Final Solution.

In telling this story, I made a conscientious effort to adhere to the timeline of events but had to select items that furthered the plot. Omitting entries was difficult since what some might consider minor incidents became important steps to the tragic climax. People fighting over potato peels may seem hardly worth mentioning until you realize the starvation this portends.

I chose to use the real names for my fictitious main characters to honor them. Other characters, the relationships and personal attributes were invented for dramatic effect, as are the settings and dialogue. I wish there were recordings of what went on as these events unfolded. As it is, we must feel blessed to have most of the *Chronicle*. The Germans believed they had found all the copies, but some were concealed and retrieved by the only surviving writer after the war. As Rumkowski stated, they are a "message in a bottle" for the future.

I thank Yale University Press for permission to extract from the original Chronicle. I chose to include errors and typographical idiosyncrasies as presented in the Yale University edition. My editing programs urged me to correct these errors, but I felt they should be presented as close to the originals as possible. Reading the entries alone offers a chilling glimpse of what so many suffered.

A recurrent question is when did the Chroniclers know the fate of the deportees. Book 2 will present clues about the fate of the deportees and examine the growing uncertainty of ghetto life. When people disappeared, there weren't answers, only hollows in the hearts of their friends and loved ones. Ostrowski's torment is magnified by his impotence to know what is happening to those he cares about. While the reader may want answers and happy endings, the battered souls in the ghetto had the additional torture of not knowing what happened to those they lost. Uncertainty permeated every day of their tenuous existence. To this date, I don't know how my mother's and father's families were killed. People disappeared…

This is a work of fiction that is historic in that it presents the events that occurred as described in the *Chronicle of the Lodz Ghetto* from 1941 to 1944. Any resemblance to the real people is strictly coincidental and not a historical record, but a novel. I hope this novel stimulates you to read the original *Chronicle.* It is well worth the effort. I hope it triggers research into these amazing men and women who created this 'message in a bottle'. There are many books that provide personal views of the Holocaust, but this one reveals the steps to annihilation as few others do. Its purpose was to support the work of the Chairman and serve as evidence for the future. Rumkowski knew he would be judged, and the *Chronicle* might be the only evidence that might survive. In Book 2 and 3, we will learn how far this still controversial leader was willing to go to achieve his goals. Was he the ghetto's savior or the devil? I will leave that for you to decide. Who can say what we might have done in his shoes?

Most importantly, let us pray it never happens again to anyone anywhere.

BIBLIOGRAPHY

Dobroszycki, Lucjan, *The Chronicle of the Lodz Ghetto 1941-1944*, (Yale University Press, 1984), 550 pp. Incredible, mostly anonymous entries documenting the daily ordeal suffered by the residents of the second largest ghetto in Poland, under the leadership of its controversial leader, Chaim Rumkowski. A must read. You experience the noose tightening.

Adelson, Alan, Lapides, Robert, *Lodz Ghetto: Inside a Community Under Siege*, (Viking Penguin, 1989) The source book for the award-winning documentary film of the same title. An eye-opening view of the ghetto: "Listen and believe this. Even thought it happened here. Even though it seems so old, so distant, and so strange." Jozef Zelkowicz

Grossman, Mendel, Smith, Frank Dabba, *My Secret Camera: Life in the Lodz Ghetto*, (Gulliver Books, 2000) A picture book with photographs taken by a concealed camera at the risk of his life.

Sierakowiak, Dawid, *The Diary of Dawid Sierakowiak*, Daily diary of young man who died at age 19. The Anne Frank of Lodz.

Trunk, Isaiah, *Lodz Ghetto: A History*, translated by Robert Moses Shapiro (Published in Association with the United States Holocaust Memorial Museum, Indiana University Press, 2006) Most complete sourcebook for researching the Lodz ghetto.

Photographs of the Lodz Ghetto by Mendel Grossman and other clandestine photographers helped provide background information and may be found on the internet. Google Lodz ghetto photographs.

Visits to the United States Holocaust Museum were also most helpful in providing glimpses into the physical elements needed for making my settings authentic. I'm proud to be a supporter and invite you to join in their effort to combat hate and genocide.

More from NCG Key and Newhouse Creative Group

Visit NewhouseCreativeGroup.com for more from NCG Key and the rest of the Newhouse Creative Group family of authors.

About the Author

Born in Germany to Holocaust survivors, Mark loved teaching in Central Islip, Long Island, and was named Elementary/Secondary Teacher of the Year by the New York State Reading Association, among other honors. His mysteries for children, Welcome to Monstrovia; *The Case of the Disastrous Dragon*; and *The Case of the Crazy Chickenscratches* have won awards from Readers Favorite, The Benjamin Franklin Book Awards, The Florida Writers Association and others. *The Rockhound Science Mysteries* received Learning Magazines' Teachers' Choice Award. A former adjunct professor, Department of Education, SUNY, Old Westbury, he enjoys helping other writers and children, leading critique clubs and serving as the state Chairman of the Florida Writers Association Youth Program (FWAY). You may learn more about him and his books at www.newhousecreativegroup.com. He welcomes your comments, kind support, and reviews.